POOR BLOODY MURDER

POOR BLOODY MURDER

GORDON REID

Personal Memoirs of the
First World War

MOSAIC PRESS
'Publishers for Canadian Communities'

Canadian Cataloguing in Publication Data

Main entry under title:
Poor bloody murder

ISBN 0-88962-123-3 (bound). — ISBN 0-88962-122-5 (pbk.)

1. World War, 1914-1918 — Personal narratives.*
I. Reid, Gordon, 1954-

D640.A2P66   940.4'8   C81-094027-2

All the photographs in this book are from the Public Archives of
Canada and from the private collections of the veterans.

Published by:
Mosaic Press
Box 1032,
Oakville, Ontario L6J 5E9
Canada

Published with the assistance of the Canada Council and the
Ontario Arts Council.

ISBN 0-88962-123-3 cloth
     0-88962-122-5 paper

Typeset by Erin Graphics Inc.
Printed and bound in Canada by Webcom
Designed by Doug Frank

Dedicated to Gordon W. Reid (50th Battalion)
and to those of The Great War
who never lived to tell their story.

TABLE OF CONTENTS

ACKNOWLEDGEMENTS

I have many people to thank for their assistance, kind thoughts, and words of general encouragement over the last two and a half years. Thanks very much to: Jim Cox; Mike Walsh; Howard Aster, Mrs. Mary Haaland and Mrs. Gladys Elliot (of Royal Canadian Legion Branch 4, Lethbridge, Alta., and their W.W.I. Veteran's Association); the Canadian War Museum, Ottawa, Ont.; Mrs. Ella Stewart; Mrs. Moorhouse; Mrs. Alfred O. Wolter; Harry Wilson (for his photographic help); Mrs. Castle (c/o Oakville Historical Society); The Black Watch Association, Toronto; Major F.G. Holyoak, author of the unpublished manuscript, "The 39th Battery" (1948); Mr. R.E. Norman, Royal Canadian Legion Branch 114, Oakville; Mr. Andris Kesteris (Public Archives of Canada); Ontario Public Archives, Toronto; The Sappers Club, Toronto; Captain Charles Rutherford, V.C.; Mr. Phil Shaw (son of William Shaw); James Johnson (grandson of James F. Johnson); James F. Johnson for his unpublished manuscript, "The Story of a Maverick" (1969); Karin Savage (great grandaughter of James A. Doak); Mr. and Mrs. Sandy Saunderson; Mrs. Victoria Branden; Imperial War Museum, London, England; Keith Dunnet; John Hampton; Peter Languas; Richard Zahn; Mr. and Mrs. Neil Leadbeater; Mr. and Mrs. Doug Cameron; Doug Bailey; Bill Herod; Carol Williams; Cheryl Campbell; Steve Dashney; Terry Fillion; Tom Koperwas; Peter Johnston; Ron Brown; Rod Crocker; John Smith; Mr. and Mrs. Johnny Walker; Mr. Al Candy and Grandma Reid.

My sincere apologies to anyone I may have not credited. Everyone helped in some small way or another.

Gordon Reid
August 1979
Oakville, Ontario

PREFACE

My fascination with World War One stories began at an early age. My Grandfather, the late Gordon W. Reid, used to tell me about his war experiences in the kitchen over some toast and jam. Once, at age ten, I innocently asked him how many Germans he had killed. He solemnly replied, "I just sat in the trenches and fired into the fog." He was only in action during the final two weeks of the conflict, but that was enough for anyone who had been over in France and Belgium. Unfortunately, he passed away, in September, 1975, before I could record any of his stories. I never dreamed at that time that I would be writing a book on this subject. However, I did manage to remember a few things he told me. I had the foresight to write them down. His diary notes helped as well.

One winter evening in December of 1976 I started thinking about my Grandfather's stories again. I decided it was time to capture the personal anecdotes of these First World War veterans on my own. My Grandfather, who died at age eighty-one, had a very clear memory when it came to recalling the old days. He remembered various people's names from the early 1900's as if it were yesterday. I was sure he was not the only "old timer" with intact memories. Old soldiers, even those who only spent one to four years in the forces during the 1914-1918 war, were always proud of their services rendered to King and Country. Their medals are proudly displayed across their chests every November 11th. Unfortunately, most people do not have time to listen. Times have changed. The youth of today cannot identify with the youth of the past in terms of war. We see evidence of distant wars on our television sets. These "old sweats" were there. They can never forget. Their stories may have become a little coloured or tarnished with time, but the general, over all vivid picture of it is still very real to them. Some veterans even have nightmares to this day as a result of what they witnessed "over there".

Many books of a scholarly or autobiographical nature on World War One have been and are still being published, but I believe this is one of the first to deal with the personal narratives of the lower ranks such as Privates and Corporals, right up to the Colonels and Brigadier Generals. Many Great War books were released shortly after the closing months of W.W.I, but these have long since passed into oblivion. Lieutenant Colonel I.M.R. Sinclair could not have said it any better when he told me, "Anybody who reads a regimental history (e.g. Black Watch) must think that we were the dullest, stupidest gang that ever lived! They quote all the facts and the casualties and the deeds of gallantry and everything like that meticulously, but it doesn't sound as if we had ever been human beings at all! I can see that in every history book I have ever read." I have researched all the dates and names of persons and places that can be found in the text. For the most part the facts quoted by the veterans were very accurate. In some cases I had to correct their obvious mistakes. Footnotes and additional material from unpublished manuscripts and diaries have been added where necessary. Sketches and photographs were procured through private collections and museum archives. I can only add that if you were shot up in a field and left for dead for many consecutive hours or days, you would probably never forget the dates either!

Most veterans were anxious to prove that their service records were truthful. I learned as I met more and more of them who hailed from all walks of life, ranging from ages seventy-nine to ninety-two, that they were not as senile as one might expect. Their physical bodies may have slowed them down to a certain degree, but their minds are still very sharp. I never met one veteran who did not have at least five good stories to tell. Some talked more than others. In most cases I found that the Scottish Highlander veterans had the best stories, though other units had many unique and equally interesting tales. The Scottish were always known as gutsy fighting men. This book contains interviews with over fifty veterans of which about sixty per cent are Canadians. The rest are mainly British, with a couple of Germans, a Frenchman and even a Canadian who served with the American Army. The Australians were generally looked down upon by most of the allies as tough and undisciplined, though hailed as great combatants, whereas the Ghurkas were highly praised. The Americans are sporadically mentioned as the "new arrivals about to find out what war is all about", and other nations like the Portuguese and Chinese are seen as tragically funny types.

I began my first interviews in Oakville, Ontario, using a cassette tape recorder and a camera. Mr. Albert E. Winn and Mr. Thomas Chambers were my first subjects. I had read and researched a great deal about the First World War outside of the history classes and with four years of Militia training (with the Calgary Highlanders and Lorne Scots), and I felt that I was prepared enough to tackle this book. I did not have a publisher when I started. I had faith in my subject material and I believed in what I was doing was worthwhile.

A few people I met did not want to talk of war or else they thought the retelling of war stories was just plain bad news. "It should be buried in the past. We should forget that stuff!" As they say on Remembrance Day, "Lest We Forget". After all, I look at this book as an anti-war volume. I am sure that anyone, who after reading all these stories, will agree that war is hell and not glorious by any stretch of the imagination. There are some humorous stories to be found here, but they are only the grays, meshed and blended in to contrast with the darkness of the trenches, vermin and lurking, ever present death.

I worked on the interviews and transcriptions in my spare time while attending a Media Arts course at college. By June, 1978, I had a bit of luck in contacting Mr. Jim Cox and Mr. Mike Walsh, who led me in turn to my publisher, Mr. Howard Aster. College was over, so the interest of Mosaic Press in my project spurred me on to complete more interviews, which led me to Toronto, Hamilton, Milton, Lethbridge, Calgary and Drumheller. I had over thirty-five veterans anxiously awaiting to see themselves in print at that time. Infantry veterans were most common, followed by a sparse amount of flyers. Navy veterans were almost not to be found!

Newspapers, word of mouth or one veteran who knew another, provided me with an abundance of interview subjects. By early 1979 I had interviewed approximately fifty veterans. Some stories told were shared by other veterans, so in lieu of that fact I have chosen only the best stories or the most unique. The editing task was enormous to say the least. Some veterans were P.O.W.'s, some were in hand to hand combat, some never got overseas into action, some were shot down in planes or shot others down, and some were more heroic or well known than others. However, every veteran had something unique to say. Some of them took two or three repeat visits before I was able to unscramble their disjointed stories. I knew that the book had to represent their stories in chronological order. To the best of my knowledge there are very few mistakes, but, as in any work of this nature, I'm sure that some errors may crop up. These "old soldiers" gave me their time and were patient enough to put up with my sometimes prying and numerous questions. For that I am thankful. I was only sorry that I could not interview more veterans, as each one was very interesting and most hospitable when I held out my microphone. At least eight of them have passed away at this writing and I only hope their relatives and friends will enjoy reading about their exploits and cherish their memories of W.W.I. for years to come.

Mobilization for War
1914-1918

THE EASTERN PROVINCES

Private James Foster Johnson (1893-)
6TH CANADIAN MOUNTED RIFLES

In the summer of 1914 war clouds started to gather in Europe. On August 4th, World War One started and Canada declared war right away along with the Mother Country.

On December 8th (my birthday), I went into Truro and enlisted with a unit of about forty men who were training but had not as yet been attached to any battalion or regiment.

Early in 1915 a request came from the officer commanding the Sixth Canadian Mounted Rifles for some men to bring the regiment up to full strength so they could proceed overseas. Anxious to get going, I, along with four others, volunteered. Soon after we left Truro for Amherst where the Sixth Canadian Mounted Rifles were in training. We were quartered along with the 22nd Battalion, known in both wars as the Van Doos. Eighteen hundred of us slept and ate in one building.

While in Amherst, I nearly received my first mark on my crime sheet. At that time, Mary Logan, who after the war became my wife, was teaching in Manganese Mines a few miles from Truro. On a Saturday aftenoon I was standing on the platform of the railway station when a Truro bound passenger train came in. On the spur of the moment I climbed aboard, knowing it was my last chance to visit Truro before I left for overseas. Of course, I had no pass! I spent the weekend in the Truro vicinity and Manganese Mines and arrived back at the barracks around two in the morning Monday. I hid in the brush while the sentry walked to the end of his beat. I passed through the gate, and crawled into my blankets. I went on parade Monday morning as usual. When I was waiting to fall in, the Sergeant said to me, "Did you have a nice weekend?" I said, "Yes, I did." On Thursday the same Sergeant came to me in my quarters and said, "You did not have a pass last weekend did you?" I said, "No." "Oh well, lucky for you it's too late to have you up as I would be in as much trouble as you for not reporting your absence."

A BRITISH RESERVIST

Private David Shand (1887-)
2nd GORDON HIGHLANDERS

When the First Great War was declared in 1914, I was working away peacefully on a farm at Sheridan, Ontario. Being a British army reservist (I had joined in 1906 and 'Stand Fast' was the translation of our Latin motto), I knew it would only be a matter of days or weeks till I was called up. My employer and his brother in law were in Toronto with two team loads of apples, when I got the papers calling me up. I had to report to Point Levis Quebec in so many hours. I proceeded along the road on horseback and met a farmer and his friend. When I told them the news, they were surprised I had received such short notice. On visiting Oakville, to inform my sister, I heard there were four reservists leaving Oakville that night. I decided to join them. After packing a few things I would need, the farmer's brother in law drove me down to the station on his horse and buggy. There were hundreds of people gathered around the station, with the Mayor of the town on a raised platform. The main street was lined with people and a brass band was coming up the centre. About this time, the train arrived in the station. When I bid my friend goodbye, his last words to me were, "Be sure and write and when you stop writing, I'll know you're dead."

When we landed at Point Levis, we discovered men from every walk of life: there were teamsters, policemen, newspaper reporters, Salvation Army men, men of the N.W.M.P. (North West Mounted Police), farmers, etc. I met sixteen men of my own regiment (the Gordon Highlanders) there.

Six hundred British and several hundred French reservists boarded a large American freight ship called the Minneapolis. We docked at Bristol. Our French comrades immediately went ashore amid bands playing, cheering people and the singing of the Marseillaise. They boaded a huge French boat on our right which departed an hour later. Their destination was France.

We were not allowed off our boat until the following day. Next morning we disembarked and entrained for our different depots. We stopped at very few places on the way and we couldn't purchase anything with Canadian money. One stop at Cardiff, Wales had us locked in our cars for the day.

After visiting with friends and relatives first, the seventeen of us reported to our depot in Aberdeen which is on the northeast coast of Scotland. We entered the depot gate dressed in civilian clothes. Our old Sergeant Major stood there. He asked us, "Where are you guys from?" "Canada", we answered. "You're a day late." "We know, but the war's still going on." He said, "You don't have to be passed by a doctor do you? You're all healthy enough!" "Sure," we said. "All right. Go over to that building and get your uniforms, rifles, and ammunition."

We went inside and were issued with new webbing equipment. We had no idea how to put it on as it was different from the webbing used in India prior to the war. So the drummer boys layed it out on the floor fo us. In less than half an hour we were in full marching order.

A few days later we were paraded in a draft of about sixty strong. Word came down that we were to go to England to join our 2nd Battalion who had just arrived from Egypt. Our Battalion was part of the 7th Division.

In due time we arrived at Lyndhurst where we joined our battalion. That was the battalion I left in Cawnpore (now Kanpur), India, about eighteen months earlier. I knew many of the officers and men. They had just arrived from Egypt the day before.

The Division started training immediately. On Sunday, the 4th of October, embarkation orders came through for us. Within a few hours we were on the march to Southampton. We boarded the boats in half battalions. Next morning we proceeded up the English Channel halting for a few hours off Dover, sometime in the afternoon. As the boat moved off again, some torpedo boat destroyers accompanied us sailing parallel to us. We were all curious about our destination.

A typical recruiting station in Halton County (1917).

BRITISH REGIMENTS PREPARE

Private Craigie Mackie (1898-1977)
GORDON HIGHLANDERS
When I joined the army in 1914 I was only sixteen. I lied about
my age. When I went to join the first time in the morning the
doctor examined us, knew me, so I couldn't fool him about my age.
I waited until later in the day and then I tried again. By that time
another doctor had taken his place, so I told him I was eighteen
and he enlisted me.

Private Alfred Eastwood (1894-)
5TH KING'S OWN YORKSHIRE LIGHT INF.

On the 3rd of June, 1913 I joined the 'Old Territorials' (the 5th
Koylies or K.O.Y.L.I.). Meanwhile transports were being formed.
My Colour Sergeant, George Nigh (God he was a smart fellow)
called me into the orderly room and said, "You're used to horses
aren't you Eastwood?" I said, "Oh yes," so my Company Officer,
Lieutenant Clayton Smith (also my Platoon Officer) said, "Oh yeah.
I know. I've seen him handling horses where I worked." He took
me in front of the adjudant, who asked me, "How would you like
to be officer's groom?" "That will be swell," I answered. "I'll be
following in my Father's footsteps. My Dad was officer's groom," I
continued. The adjutant asked, "What was he with?" "The York
and Lancs." "What was his name?" "Eastwood." "Who was he
groom to?" "A Captain Mooney." "Oh. I remember him! How
would you like the officer's groom job?" I got the job of 'officer's
groom'. It was a lovely, soft job.
   The ship we were to take to France was an old cattleboat
named, 'The City of Lucknow'. God! There were more bloody rats
on it than there was men!

EASTERN RECRUITS

Lieutenant Walter Moorhouse (1884-1977)
4TH CANADIAN MOUNTED RIFLES/CDN. MACHINE GUN
When World War I started we all were afraid it would be over
before we got to the front. Our Hon. Col. H.C. Cox subsidised an
army of approximately 150 all ranks at Long Branch camp in
September & October. When the 4th C.M.R. was established, we
moved to the Exhibition Grounds and were billeted in the old
Horse Palace, from which we paraded without saddles, and trained
remounts which were promptly sent overseas in batches. We must

have handled about a thousand remounts. Lt. Col. LeGrand Reed of the 9th M.H. presented the regiment with a battery of four Colt machine guns complete with pack-saddles which the latter we never used. Maj. Butcher, a musketry officer in the Permanent Force, coached us from a field-service training manual of the Boer War, — only a few measly paragraphs and those about the Maxim gun. I was appointed M.G. officer with a section of about 50 gunners and drivers selected from the squadrons.

Paper work expanded and I applied for an Asst. Officer, obtaining Billy Bishop, to whom I gave his first M.G. training in assembly, operation, stoppages, etc. We were billeted together in grooms' quarters in the old Horse Palace. Billy left us shortly to join the Air Force, where he became famous.

Early in 1915 we were much disgruntled when the 19th and 20th Battalions who were also at the Exhibition Grounds received orders to proceed overseas with the 2nd Cdn. Infantry Division. They were naturally much elated, and organized a procession round the cantonments, led by a fife & drum band. The 4th C.M.R. officers were billetted on the 2nd floor of the Women's Building, while the first floor was occupied by Artillery officers. Late at night the noise approached, and the Field officer of the day, a stout artillery Major, jumped out of bed, donned a dressing-gown, buckled on his sword & Sam Browne, and in strident tones denied them entrance. However, pressure from the rear forced the head of the line, the band, into the vestibule. The doughty Major drew his sword, shouting "Get t'hell out o' here", pierced the bass drum, and waving his trusty weapon, forced the band out on the entrance platform. One bandsman was holding up two pieces of his instrument and telling all and sundry, "The sonofabitch, he cut my piccolo in two!"

An early C.M.R. band in Ontario (1915).

Sergeant Len Davidson (1893-)
123rd BATTALION/CDN. ENGINEERS

I joined up in October, 1914. I was a policeman in Toronto, so
I called the Chief of Police, Colonel Carl Brazett. He was an old
Colonel of the Grenadiers from the Northwest Territories who saw
service during the Riel Rebellion. He told me, "There's a new unit
being formed with the Grenadiers." Through him I got into the 10th
Royals who were recruiting at the time. They sent me on a course
back at the old police headquarters - M.D. Two Headquarters on
149 College Street. I received three stripes and became a full fledged
Sergeant. My promotion meant another course which I took at the
exhibition grounds. As senior N.C.O. of the unit I trained the men
in physical training, bayonet fighting and so on. Everything was
rushed through, so we had to assimilate a six month course into
about six weeks. Then I went back to my unit as physical training
instructor for the Company.

Major Conn Smythe (1894-)
40TH BATTERY/CDN. FIELD ARTILLERY

Squib Walker was our scout with the Maple Leafs for many
years, and there never was a better one. He tried to enlist in the
First War in the 25th Battery with his friends from the University.
When the eye examinations were held in the old mining building on
College Street in the basement, Squib, who could not see five feet
without his glasses, had us drill a hole in the door and he backed
up there, and when they called out the initials in the lineup, the best
visual man we had whispered in his ear from behind the door, and
he passed with flying colours.

Private William (Bill) Hemmings (1897-)
74TH BN./C.M.G.C.

I joined in 1914, but I joined the wrong unit. I was under age
and under weight. The Medical Corp unit at University Armouries
in downtown Toronto was not sending men overseas, so I walked
around the armouries and joined the Mississauga Horse Regiment.
After signing with them I went down to drill. The Sergeant said to
some other fellows and myself, "Here's a uniform for you! Put it on
and we will go on a recruiting parade up Yonge Street." So this
young kid and I looked at each other and said, "Well I guess we
better get dressed." All we had were our civilian shoes. We picked
up a pair of riding britches, and took our own trousers off right on
the floor of the armouries. The tunics we tried on were made for a

man ten times our size! I only weighed about 128 pounds then. The kid with me said, "Look at mine." His were dirty. I said, "I'm not going to wear this." He said, "You've got to. They're going to march us up Yonge Street." I said, "Well I'm not going to wear it." He said, "I don't want to wear this either. What are you going to do about it?" I took him to a corner and said, "Go out tha door." We dropped the uniforms in the corner and went out the door.

I went to the other corner the next day to join the Grenadier Guards. They were in the north-west corner of the old University Armouries. The Misissauga Horse were in the south-east corner. I just crossed the floor.

Private Charles Haddlesey (1888-)
248TH CANADIAN FORESTRY CORP

At that time all the girls were going around with white feathers. They'd stick one of those feathers on you if you were not in uniform. My brother and I went to enlist near the end of August 1916. The army took him, but they wouldn't take me. I went back to the recruiting office and complained to them, "Gosh. You walk down the streets here and somebody sticks a feather on you." The Lieutenant there said to me, "Do you want to go that bad?" I said, "Sure I do. My brother is going and I want to go with him." He said, "You be at the docks, take the boat to St. Catherines, go to a certain hotel in St. Catherines and I'll be there. I'll take you to a doctor that will pass you." That's how I got in. On Friday, the 13th of September, 1916, we pulled out of Halifax harbour.

2nd Lieutenant Geoffrey Marani (1895-)
42ND BATTALION - R.H.C.

I wanted to join the 48th Highlanders. A friend of the family suggested I go and see Colonel Donald. I went to see the Colonel, but was forewarned that I'd come out of his office with my tail between my legs. One of the first things the Colonel asked me was, "What right have you to join us in this battalion?" I said jokingly, "With my name I guess." He just roared with laughter. I continued, "Well, I have relations in Edinburgh." Hearing that he just put his head back and laughed. That probably broke the ice. I left his office feeling I didn't have a chance. I was living at the fraternity house at the university because my Mother was overseas like so many of the families in those days.

About a week later I got a call from Colonel Donald. He told me, "You're going on a course. Report to so and so next week."

That was when I received my commission to the 48th Highlanders.
Our officer's training course ran about six to eight weeks. Our
battalion recruited well over its limit within a week and a half. Two
or three other battalions were registering men at the same time.
There was a terrific rush to get recruits because they must have
realized the war might drag on. I must have had ten light machine
gun courses mixed with heavy machine guns. I was a specialist in
using machine guns. The Lewis gun became my specialty.
In 1916, ten thousand of us were sent to Camp Borden.
Colonel Sam Hughes was there at Headquarters. The facilities were
not ready to accommodate all those men. There was no running
water or any other basic essentials. The men were in an uproar. As
a result they rioted. The men gathered and stoned the Headquarters
building. Someone ordered the men to parade on a common area.
The sandy ground provided for the commons had previously been
covered with thick brush. It was burned clear just a few days before
use as a parade ground. Soot and ashes were left all over it. When
the men paraded they purposely shifted their feet through the
debris, raising a great black cloud of dusty smoke. It was an
exacting revenge on the C.O. Colonel Sam Hughes left in his
motorcade. Of course, many of the men at Camp Borden were just
undisciplined labourers from every corner of the province.

Sapper Robert Dickson (1898-)
5TH BATTALION/CDN. ENGINEERS
I went to enlist in 1917, but was rejected for having flat feet. In
1918 they weren't so particular. Those flat feet carried me up into
Germany. I can recall two or three returned men that I had spoken
to before joining up. But I read the newspapers and had a general
idea of what the conditions in France would be. I wasn't too
bothered. I managed to cope with things without much difficulty. I
was young and healthy.

Gunner Arthur Charlesworth (1902-)
CDN. GARRISON ARTILLERY
I joined the C.G.A. on the 6th of November, 1916, at Citadel
Hill in Halifax. I was too young to go overseas which resulted in
my placement at McNab's Island. It was just outside Halifax, where
I stayed practically until the war ended.
McNab's Island was quite a size, jutting right into Halifax
harbour. It goes out about seven miles. There were steel gates put
across the harbour as a preventive measure against submarines. We

did see one sub get in though. Whether they left the gates open or what I don't know.

The 'Halifax Explosion' was supposed to be an accident, but how did those boats get there? The boats were generally examined, before entering the harbour, but they got in somehow with ammunition on board. The boats collided and exploded. One thousand, six hundred people were killed.

On the morning of December 6, 1917, I was on leave. We were allowed so many hours leave from the island to go to Halifax. A war picture was on that afternoon. I used to give a married man my pass when I didn't want to go out. We took turns. One man would do the other's duty while he was away. Both of us wanted to see that picture, so I wouldn't let him have my pass. He acquired a special pass. That guy visited his family in the vicinity of the explosion. He died along with his family.

I was just going downtown to the hotel on Barrington Street (the main street in Halifax) to get my breakfast. I stopped to take a look in a jewelry store window. While I was standing there the window fell away from me, before I could hear the report of the explosion. I thought it was something wrong with me! There was no sound or anything at that point. I turned my back on the window to look at the street wondering what was wrong. Then the blast came. The people who were just on their way to work came running. People from the stores ran outside, holding their faces, and yelling. It happened just after the stores opened at nine a.m.

I guess we thought we were being bombed at first. As we browsed around the army picked us up for work details. All available army men were taken to the north side to put dead bodies in trucks. We worked around the stores retrieving oranges and other items that were blown out of cases. Everything was wrecked. The houses were burning. What a mess! We stayed there for seventy-two hours.

The army had dark, heavy blankets. When we wrapped one around a badly burned victim, the person would squeal because of the irritation. If they didn't yell we could tell their nerves were dead. Sometimes we couldn't distinguish the dead from the living. All the casualties were transported to the Y.M.C.A. which was soon filled. Other vacant buildings in the south end of Halifax were also used. The south side wasn't damaged much. The railway station was blown to pieces. The north half of the city was in ruins.

The Navy looked after all the ammunition which was stored underground. The Navy took us down to take the primers out of the cartridges because they thought the magazines might explode. We moved all the ammunition out from below ground. We passed it from hand to hand, a human chain of soldiers and sailors (anyone wearing a uniform), and tossed the ammo into the harbour. We had our sleeves rolled up. The blood caked on our arms. It was a hell of a time trying to clean the blood off, so we could go for a decent meal. It's hard to believe, but it was terrible. When it was all through the navy put us all in white clothes and wooden shoes.

Only two ships were involved, the Imo and the Mont Blanc. Instead of reporting to the navy, some of the survivors from one of the boats took a motorboat to Dartmouth. Dartmouth was on the other side of the harbour, much farther away than the navy base. Those men were still at Dartmouth behind iron bars when I got my discharge in 1919. They still say it was an accident.

THE WESTERN PROVINCES & RECRUITS

Major John Smith Stewart (1877-1970)
25TH INDEPENDENT FIELD BTY./BRIG.-GEN. O.C. 3RD

Having been a Battery Headquarters for a number of years, Lethbridge in 1914 became an Artillery town. When Armistice was signed in November, 1918, three batteries in the Canadian Corps had come from Lethbridge. The 20th was in the 2nd Division as a Unit. The 39th belonged to the 3rd Division and the 61st was a battery in the 5th Divisional Artillery. The 79th was a Depot Battery and did not leave Canada.

Bombardier James Logan (1892-)
25TH BATTERY/39TH BATTERY C.F.A.

The 39th Battery was recruited in Lethbridge, Alberta from the city and surrounding districts on the 11th of October, 1915. The enlistments the first day of recruiting practically brought the Battery up to strength. Though no barracks were available, training was commenced immediately, the men falling in daily outside the Herald office on 6th Street South, and a fatigue party were prepared to start a building at the Exhibition Grounds to serve as a barracks. The Battery moved in there on December 1st.

Some of the 'City gentlemen' not at first fully realizing they were now in the army, changed nightly into garments of many and varied hues. They won themselves the name of "The Pajama Brigade."

We finally received our marching orders, though not before many had said the war would be over before the unit left. We paraded at nine o'clock Sunday morning, the 20th of February, with kits ready. A general clean-up of the camp was made, photos of the battery taken, a presentation made to each man by the Local Independent Order of the Daughters of the Empire, a fatigue party detailed to look after the baggage, and the Battery dismissed with orders to fall in again that night at nine o'clock on 5th Street South between 4th and 5th Avenues. Everyone was present at the appointed hour. Crowds thronged the streets, the Battery were played to the C.P.R. depot by the 113th Highland Battalion and the City Bands. At the station a limited time was given to the men to say good-bye to their wives, families, sweethearts and friends. Shortly before midnight the train pulled out. The 39th Battery commenced its 'unknown' journey.

The 116th Bn. changes sentries at Sarcee Camp, Calgary (1916).

Sergeant Sidney Taylor (1892-)
229TH BATTALION/71ST PUNJAB REG./ &
ROYAL INDIAN ARMY SERVICE CORP

Our battalion contracted some disease. They had to be isolated
in their barracks. They didn't like this, so one day they broke out of
barrcks, avoiding the main guard, so as not to get him into trouble
and the whole battalion marched down to the centre of Moose Jaw,
where they proceeded to tear the place up! We weren't interested in
what the police or civilians thought of us. After all we were a large
body of men. We went into different shops and helped ourselves,
smashing things up. I remember seeing somebody with a big dish of
custard. He ran out of the shop and crowned another soldier with
it. The police and civilians stood agape wondering what was going
to happen next. We had left our rifles behind at the barracks.

   We entered a theatre and sat up on the stage while a play was
in progress. There was considerable damage done in Moose Jaw.
Many windows were smashed. After wrecking the place, we got
ourselves together and marched back, being led by a peanut stand
on wheels. It was pushed back to the armoury where we reported to
Lieutenant Colonel H.D. Pickett. The result was a court martial.
Some men were sent away for a considerable time. It was treated as
a very serious matter.

Private John (Jack) Stacey (1894-)
12TH CDN. FIELD AMBULANCE/61ST BN.

In England as a kid, I had some first aid. I attended first aid
lectures in the village I was raised in. All those things like first aid,
gymnastics and so on were important to life! We were proud of our
school life. After coming to Canada I decided to join up. I wanted
to join with the Lord Strathcona Horse, so I went to the 61st
Battalion (which never got overseas — when mobilized they were
split up into other battalions overseas). After examining me, the
medical officer said, "Have you ever had any experience in first
aid?" So I told him I had. He said, "Well, you're not just infantry
standard physically, but I'd like you to go over to the recruiting
office at 12th Field Ambulance and mention my name." I did what
he told me and the 12th Field took me in. That medical officer
became the O.C. of the 12th Field Ambulance, even though he just
seemed to be a worker at the recruiting station before. I don't know
how he became O.C. but we became good friends. We went
overseas six weeks after I had joined, with the Fourth Division in
1916.

Private Gordon W. Reid (1894-1975)
21ST CDN. RESERVE BN./50TH BN.

On January 29th, 1918, I became a soldier. We drilled in
Calgary, occasionally going to camp Sarcee for other training. The
bell tents we lived in at Sarcee could hold up to twelve men. We
were packed in like sardines. In the middle of the night if you had
to go outside, you had to step over all these groaning bodies in the
dark. It was the same thing going back in again. Then you had a
devil of a time finding your place again, because someone had
shuffled over on to it in your absence.

Once in February I had some leave, so I went to visit my
parents in Lethbridge. Upon returning to the barracks in Calgary I
found out I had stayed away too long. As a result, I was confined
to barracks for two weeks! For entertainment we used to go to
picture shows and dances in Calgary, but on March 1, 1918, the fun
was over. We were called on a draft for overseas duty. The train
ride was like any other. By March 11th we were in Saint John, New
Brunswick. The draft was split up there with the rest of the men
going to Halifax. We went to Campbellton for a few days, before
embarking overseas on March 25, 1918.

Musketry training for "A" & "B" Coy of the 116th Bn. at Camp Sarcee

VALCARTIER CAMP — EMBARKATION

Private James F. Johnson
6TH CANADIAN MOUNTED RIFLES

The regiment moved to Valcartier Camp about twenty miles north of Quebec City. It was the largest camp in Canada. The 1st Division of thirty three thousand men had trained there before going overseas. It was all under canvas on sandy ground with lots of wild bushy country surrounding it. The largest rifle range in the world at that time was situated near the camp. It consisted of twenty-four hundred targets.

We had a character in our unit named Bill Hanlan. He was a big, good natured fellow, a real individual possessing a wonderful sense of humour and wit. One day shortly before going overseas the entire personnel of Valcartier Camp took part in a day's tactical manoeuvre. Our brigade of about twenty-two hundred was just a small part of it. During the morning our regiment was placed in a position out in the bush. No one seemed to know just what our role was but we thought we would get orders from headquarters sooner or later. During the afternoon Bill got into a friendly wrestle with one of the boys. During the tussle the peak of his cap was torn off. The Sergeant Major noticed it and said, "The Brigadier and his staff may come riding through here any time and he mustn't see you dressed like that!" All the high staff rode horses and wore a sword in those days. So Bill was detailed to a lonely spot half way between the two companies. He was told he was to be what they called a 'connecting file'. His duty was to report anything that might happen in that area. Bill stood there, bayonet fixed on his rifle until three o'clock p.m. thoroughly fed up with his lonely job. Then all of a sudden he heard the sound of galloping hooves. Low and behold who should ride up in front of him but Brigadier Smart with all his staff! Bill told me later that he didn't know whether to salute, present arms, stand to attention, or run! However, he stood his ground. The Brigadier waved his sword in front of him and said, "Well my man what is your role in this position?" Poor Bill couldn't remember the term 'connecting file', so he said, "Sir, I am the 'missing link!" The Brigadier said, "I don't doubt it a damn bit!" and barked at him, "Turn your cap around to the front!" Bill reached up and turned his cap but it was just the same with out a peak! The last words Bill heard from the Brigadier as they galloped off were "My God, what an army!"

Time was drawing to the end of our Canadian soil training. Toward the end of June, 1915, a muster parade was held for our brigade. Every man had a physical examination topped off with a kit inspection to see that every man had everything he had been issued. Up to that time, all Canadian soldiers had been issued the Ross rifle which was manufactured in Canada. The rifle did not stand up to service in action. It was abandoned for the Lee Enfield in the early stages of the war.

Early on a Sunday morning our regiment, the 6th, boarded the steamship "Hershel". I think the boat had been captured from the Germans earlier in the war. The Hershel was an old tub. I don't think it had ever been used for passenger service; more likely for cargo and cattle.

To make matters worse we were told after we boarded that we would have to tend over two hundred horses on our way over as the crew that was supposed to look after them had quit the boat at Montreal on account of German submarine action in the Atlantic. My company was detailed every third day for the unpleasant task, whch could have been worse. We had at least two days in between shifts! The horses were quartered away down on the bottom deck. The air was foul and hot. All the cleanings were forked into a large wicker basket, hoisted up and dumped overboard. All the hay was stuffed into nets three times a day and placed in front of the horses. They also had to be watered.

We had no bunks or beds on the boat. On the second deck, which was practically the length of the ship, everything had been cleared out and wooden tables were erected. At night we strung our hammocks up over those tables. In the morning we took them down. I didn't mind the hammocks, but with eight hundred men sleeping in one compartment the air was not good.

A couple of days out I spied a large box at the stern of the ship open at one side. It looked like a cage, so I asked the Sergeant Major if another fellow and I could sleep there. He said, "Sure, go ahead. I don't blame you." That was where we slept for the rest of the voyage. An officer walked by one evening after we had retired. He stopped and said, "Sorry I have no peanuts!"

Corporal Jack Finnimore (1890-)
TORONTO REG. — 3RD BATTALION

In August of 1914, Colonel Sam Hughes who succeeded Sir Robert Borden as Minister of Militia and National Defense promised Great Britain 25,000 men. Such was the response that by the 8th of September, 32,600 officers and men had assembled at Valcartier, Quebec where no camp yet existed. He did not mobilize the units of militia that were in force then across Canada; instead he raised new battalions which were known by number and thus did not perpetuate traditional and honoured names. One new battalion had the name Princess Patricia's Canadian Light Infantry. Battalions had to be formed; clothing and equipment had to be issued. Men had to be examined medically, and formed into Provisional Brigades.

Embarkation of the 1st Division of Canadian troops at Quebec (at Gaspe Bay) was on October 3rd, 1914. We began the Atlantic crossing in thirty liners. Another ship carried the 2nd Lincoln Regiment (British) which the Royal Canadian Regiment had relieved in Bermuda. The thirty-third ship with the Newfoundland Contingent joined the convoy at sea. Thirty-two ocean liners closely escorted by four British Light Cruisers and protected by battleships further out made the crossing safely. We arrived at Plymouth after a twelve day crossing. We were in the last ship of the middle line — the Tunision.

Lieutenant Ian Sinclair (1891-)
13TH BATTALION—BLACK WATCH—R.H.C.

I found, as did a number of others, that the 48th Highlanders had taken on far more officers than they were entitled to. The 48th officers were comprised of two groups: those actually in the battalion strength and the first reserve who were to cover for the first casualties from France. The Black Watch of Montreal had underestimated their recruiting. They needed officers badly. As a result, several of us transferred to the Black Watch. I served throughout the war with them.

In Irish waters, the Tuscania is escorted by Torpedo Boat Destroyers (1916).

Private James A. Doak (1873-1946)
52ND BATTALION

We were just beginning to make lots of friends when on the evening of the 22nd we were ordered to prepare to embark the following morning. Hasty farewells were exchanged during the evening, and we were loaded with gifts of all kinds. We boarded the transport "California" on the morning of the 23rd. At noon we cast off and steamed down the harbor, while thousands and thousands of St. John citizens packed the wharf, warehouse roof and all vantage points. At dusk we were out of sight of land, and thus commenced the second leg of our great journey.

Twenty-four hours out we ran into rough weather and for 11 days we enjoyed all the "comforts" of a winter ocean voyage. On the fourth day out a young sailor who had been on lookout fell while coming down from the "crow's nest" and was instantly killed.

The ship 'layed to' the next morning while the body was consigned to the deep. I shall never forget that ceremony; the silent body covered by the Union Jack rested near an open gangway and as the chaplain pronounced the words, the flag was removed and the canvas covered remains slipped into the sea and vanished.

During the entire voyage food was uneatable, bad eggs and rotten sausage forming a big part of our daily menu. The stewards made small fortunes selling sandwiches and tea to the troops at 25 cents a time.

On the S.S. Hesperian—Sgt. J.C. Hartley on the Colt machine gun.

Major John Smith Stewart
7TH BRIGADE/CDN. FIELD ARTILLERY   *(Diary Notes)*

Tuesday, August 10th: Left Halifax at 3:00 a.m. When we got
up we were out of sight of land. The wet canteen was closed.
Weather very good. Very little sickness on board. We are going
south. Was given sealed orders before leaving which contained
nothing but information - re: submarines.

Wednesday, August 11th: Still going south. We are now in the
Gulf stream. Water is about 72 degrees, still misty at times. Not
much for men to do but a little physical exercise. Have a very fine
cabin. Made a thorough inspection of the boat each day.

August 13th: Sighted three ships early in day. Had a medical
inspection of all troops. Was chairman of a concert in aid of the
Seaman's widows and orphans fund. Had a collection of $122.00 for
same.

August 14th: A lovely morning. The ship is making good time.
Sea is still calm. Learned that we are allowed ten dollars to pay tips
to waiters.

Tuesday, August 17th: By 10:00 a.m. we were in the English
Channel.

Bombardier James Logan
39TH BATTERY/CDN. FIELD ARTILLERY

On March 2nd, 1916, we were joined by the S.S. Scandinavian
carrying other troops. The passage commenced, the Scandinavian
leading. We had a concert in aid of the seaman's house in
Liverpool. A fellow named Cook, played the piano lying on the
floor, standing on his head, sitting backwards to it, and every way
imaginable. Cook was blindfolded, the piano keys were covered
with a tablecloth and he was still able to play it.

The sun was shining one day. The boys were lying around on
deck like a bunch of dogs, not caring if the boat went down or not.
That's how sick they were! I was one of them.

There was lots of grub on board, but the darned guys who had
money were buying roasted chickens for a dollar each. We only got
$1.10 a day, so we couldn't afford them. We complained so much
that we got better grub after that.

26

GREAT BRITAIN — CANADA'S FINAL TRAINING GROUND

Private James F. Johnson
6TH CANADIAN MOUNTED RIFLES

When we sailed into Plymouth Harbour, we received a tremendous welcome from the citizens of that city. Hundreds of people lined the docks. On hills surrounding the harbour, people were waving flags and cheering for Canada. It sure made us feel good. Before we disembarked we saw the horses being led out of the hold of the Hershel and loaded on another boat bound for the Mediterranean. Those horses never made their destination as the boat was torpedoed en route.

Early that evening we boarded a troop train bound for Shorncliffe Camp where the Second Division was stationed. Early next morning we arrived at Shorncliffe Station where we changed trains and marched to our assigned camp which was called Dibgate.

Our training was somewhat similar to what we had previously, but we were getting more shooting practice and bayonet fighting experience. We had some instructors from the British Army. One day while practising bayonet fighting, jabbing dummy men, the instructor came up to me and said, "Put more into it! Just imagine these dummies are German and you hate Germans don't you?" I said, "No, I don't hate anybody." He turned around to the men and said, "Blimey. Some of these Canadians are funny blokes!" One day later he came over and said, "I've been thinking about what you said the other day. I guess none of us really hates anybody!"

On a warm day in July, our brigade went on a long gruelling route march in full marching order. We carried about fifty pounds of equipment. After the march many of the fellows had bad blisters on their feet. Colonel Ryan came around to the tents and examined everyone's feet. The next morning orders from brigade headquarters was parade as usual. Someone saw Colonel Ryan reading those orders. I guess he expressed himself in no uncertain manner. Later we received orders to fall in whith no equipment or rifles. To our surprise we were marched down to a beach near Hythe about a mile from camp and told to take off our shoes and socks and wade in the salt water. We spent most of the forenoon taking it easy. On the way back to camp the regiment headed by Colonel Ryan was reprimanded by Brigadier Smart. Colonel Ryan was severely reprimanded for disobeying orders. The Colonel told the Brigadier a few things but that was not the end of it. Brigadier Smart had Colonel Ryan up for court martial for disobeying an order and insolence to a superior officer.

When Colonel Ryan resigned his commission and was leaving us for good we were quite a downcast outfit. The next day quite a number refused to go on parade till they got a satisfactory explanation. However Colonel Ryan called his last parade with us and told us to carry on under our new Colonel as well as we had done with him. Colonel Ryan returned to Canada, re-enlisted as a Sergeant, and went overseas with another regiment. It was interesting to note that during the court martial, Colonel Ryan received a letter from Lord Kitchener, Commander-in-Chief of the British Army, stating that he would help in any way if need be, but Colonel Ryan was not the kind of a man to take advantage of a great man at a time like that.

Then I received my first seven day leave. One of the highlights was Madame Tussaud's Wax Works where the wax statues were almost a perfect likeness of most of the important people of the world. They even had one of Kaiser Bill of Germany which was not accepted very well by the British. One day a woman who had lost a son in the war saw the statue, became quite agitated, and with her umbrella, knocked his head off.

With September approaching we moved to a new camp called Caesar's Camp just at the foot of Caesar's Hill, about a mile east of Dibgate Camp.

Training at that camp was mostly shooting at the rifle range just on top of the Cliffs of Dover. It was about eight miles from camp. We marched to and fro each day, so we had to get up bright and early each morning. As we sat atop the White Cliffs of Dover, looking over the channel to the shores of France, which we could plainly see on a clear day, we could hardly believe that less than a hundred miles away the greatest conflict in history was under way. Some days we could hear the rumble of the guns on the Western Front. In England everything seemed so beautiful and peaceful.

After a tiresome route march in Kent, England, the 5th C.M.R. take a two hour rest.

Had it not been for so many in uniforms one would never have known that there was a war on.

Lieutenant Walter Moorhouse
4TH CDN. MOUNTED RIFLES

While the troops were entraining for Shorncliffe, the C.M.R. officers were grouped on the dock and close by was a small cluster of officers of a Cdn. Forestry unit from B.C. who had crossed with us. Their colonel was smoking a cigar and had one foot up on a bollard, when an old Imperial W.O. passed, swung his silver-topped cane under his left arm and gave the colonel a snappy salute. The O.C., his foot still on the bollard, waved his cigar at the W.O., and turning to his officers, addressed them thus, — "There ye have the true British army tradition,—'e don't know me, but 'e salutes me!"

I must here describe a hitherto unrecorded event in the life of the 2nd C.M.R. Bde. While camped on Dibgate Hill, word came suddenly to Bde. H.Q. that Sir Sam Hughes was coming to inspect the troops. Our brigadier was away on duty to the War Office and this bomb-shell fell on the Bde. Major. He treated it as just one of those things, — the Bde. formed up in mass, — bayonets fixed, — 'Shun, — "Slope 'ums! Present 'ums! — Slope 'ums! Order 'ums! and then the usual 'Stand at ease!' 'Stand easy', and the inspecting officer walking round the troops, then the 'March Past'. But Col. Sam wasn't having any! Officers were mounted, and the Bde. Major galloped up and saluted Sir Sam. "Stand 'em at ease and easy,— Now I want to see a tactical exercise. The enemy are there and there and there" (pointing to the valley, right, centre and left). "Dispose your Brigade for the attack!" You could almost hear the Major's jaw drop! He saluted and galloped over to the O.C. of the 6th C.M.R., (a much decorated veteran) on the left flank. Pulling up his horse suddenly, he nearly went over its head, but managed to slither down and called out a front rank man (still with fixed bayonet) to hold his horse. Whatever they cooked up, the Bde. got in a terrible mix-up and Sir Sam shouted an informal order to 'un-scramble' and galloped away with his staff in disgust.

We junior officers had a helluva time getting our troops together and back into Mass, and the Bde. Major brought them to attention, sloped arms and marched them in column off the hill with bayonets still fixed. Some officer up forward ordered his squadron to un-fix bayonets on the march by troops, and this was carried right down the column. The whole scene was probably unique in the history of brigade manoeuvres. What would have happened if the Brigadier had been in command is a matter of conjecture.

Corporal Jack Finnimore
3RD BATTALION

We were not fully trained nor equipped for battle. Fitted out, we exercized on Salisbury Plain during the dampest and coldest winter in living memory. Ours was the Canadian 1st Division under Lieutenant General E.A. Alderson, a British officer. Meningitis was going around. We lost two or three men in our brigade from it. Some of the men were moved into huts, but they were in bad shape compared to us. We were deemed ready for France by the end of January 1915.

Private Bertram Ashbourne (1896-1979)
3RD BATTALION

We were stationed at Salisbury Plains, England. We were the only Expeditionary Force under canvas in 1914. Oh, the cold and the flooding. The rain and mud up to our waists! Salisbury Plains was a terrible place! Of course it was just as bad when we got over to France as far as that goes. Nothing but mud and water. We never gave up; despite all we stuck with it. It was pretty difficult at times, but we did all right and more or less got used to it, day after day, for the next three months. Never any sunshine in England during the months of December to January.

Private Frank Ashbourne (1892-)
3RD BATTALION

We plowed through the mud at Salisbury Plains every day. The nurses who visited some of the men who were ill, used to tuck their skirts in their boot tops and wade from tent to tent. We had a lot of sick men around. One night before leaving for France we marched by the nurses' building. We sang "Goodbye Sisters" to the nurses.

Private Albert Smith (1892-)
3RD BATTALION - 2ND DIVISION

Once during our training in England we had to engage in a sham battle on a huge hill near Salisbury Plains. Little did we know that the farmers had just cleared away their sheep to make ready for our mock exercise. When we arrived we were ordered to crawl, sprint, and jump down again. The trouble was that the hill was

covered with sheeps' manure. We were covered with the smelly
stuff. As we diligently cleaned and scrubbed our uniforms that night
we vowed we would never forget what we came to call, "The Battle
of Lamb Shit Hill"!

Lieutenant Ian Sinclair
13TH BATTALION

Salisbury Plains was a huge place. Our 1st Division of about
20,000 troops were scattered all over the plains and adjacent
villages. The mud was beyond belief. It was in our tents, our food
— everything. We never got away from the mud at all during the
winter. You couldn't imagine troops living in conditions like that.
We were eventually moved into huts which had been built while we
were in tents out on the plains. We continued to train. The mud
never slowed us up. It just showed what the human body could
take.

There was a rumour that we were going to be sent to the far
east somewhere. Headquarters sent down a supply of summer
uniforms. It was a hell of a joke in the midst of all that mud!

Private Ernest C. Robins (1895-1979)
LORD STRATHCONA'S HORSE

We lost six hundred men in a very short time from that spinal
meningitis going around. It rained practically every day of the week.
Chalk was underneath the top soil. In years gone by that chalk
came up above the ground until it was affecting our men.
Meningitis is when the fluid in your spine is sent up your back.

During cavalry training we used to form up and charge at
dummies. We practised our thrust and parry. Some men fell from
their horses, but we practised till we got it right.

Private James Doak
52ND BATTALION

From Witley we moved to Bramshott where about 12,000
Canadian troops were stationed. Here the battalions were rigorously
inspected and passed O.K.; was brigaded with the 43rd Camerons of
Winnipeg, the 58th of Toronto and the 60th of Montreal, forming
the 9th Brigade.

Sergeant Len Davidson
123RD BN - CANADIAN ENGINEERS

The main Canadian camp was at Bramshott. We did infantry drill at that time. Then the Major came over to me and said, "I've got sad news for you. They're breaking us up." That's how I got into the Engineers. We had to learn a six month course in about two weeks.

Our first task was to learn how to make a South African apron. It was all supposed to be done out in No Man's Land. Did you ever try to drive a spike in the ground with a huge hammer muffled with sandbags, so it wouldn't make too much noise. it was something different for us to do anyway! A South African apron was made out of barbed wire. We had to wear gloves and string the wire out. One man was detailed to take the wire, one took the spikes and screwed them into the ground. That was all supposed to be done without any noise in No Man's Land, so the Germans wouldn't hear us.

Major John Smith Stewart
7TH BRIGADE/CDN. FIELD ARTILLERY (Diary Notes)

On Wednesday, August 18th, 1915, we arrived in Plymouth Harbour. We boarded the Great Western train for Otterpool Camp.

On Oct. 13, 1915, a zeppelin raid occurred. Seven bombs were dropped, four on Otterpool Camp. Ten men of the 5th Brigade and two of the 8th were killed. Our lights were quickly put out. One of three bombs dropped on us was only seventy-five yards from a direct hit. The next day — October 14th — as a result of the zeppelin raid, we had our lights out at 7:00 p.m. Everyone was on edge. Five rounds per man were issued to each guard. The next day we dug up fragments from zeppelin bombs.

On November 29th, General Sharman gave me a scorching lecture about the men who were absent without leave. At the time there was only one man absent.

On Christmas day we had turkey. I spoke a little to all the men. Many of them got more or less drunk. One man got very drunk and fired off his revolver several times.

On December 27th I had the fellow who shot his revolver up before me on a charge, but I let him off. We had an exercise ride and cleaned the guns. Then a draft of 78 men joined us from a reserve brigade.

On December 30th the brigade took an exercise ride to
Romney Marshes in the morning. A chap from the Canadian
Magazine visited us. Our photos will be in the next issue.

Private Thomas Rattray (1896-)
10TH BATTALION

When I arrived in England I was put in the Ninth Reserve.
Then I was reinforced with other men into the 10th Battalion just
before going into action in France. We had landed at Liverpool and
proceeded to Shoreham. The constant rain was annoying, but I was
amused at seeing those little English farms. Quite a difference from
Alberta farms!

Private William (Bill) Hemmings
CDN. MACHINE GUN CORP

We were broken up into different units in Bramshott. I was a
machine gunner in the battalion's machine gun section. Thirty-five
of us were broken up and put into a brigade. The brigade had a
machine gun company with sixteen guns. We became the Canadian
Machine Gun Corp later on. Those were the formative years.

Corporal James Rourke (1890-)
107TH BN./1ST FIELD CO. ENGINEERS

During our training at Bramshott and Folkestone we all went
through the gas chamber to test our gas masks out. The officers
told us to take our rings and watches off before going in. Then, by
God, we had an awful time cleaning our buttons off. The buttons
turned green. All the respirators were tested that way. That's why
the boys used to volunteer to go back to France after being
wounded and sent home to recuperate. They didn't want to go
through the damn parade ground again.

Mess arrangements in camp were not too good. Some seven
hundred men had to eat together in one hut with only one small
door used as an entrance. Owing to the slowness of entry, it took
the best part of an hour for all the men to gain admission. As it
was often wet, many of us got soaked to the skin waiting for a
meal.

Bombardier James Logan
39TH BATTERY/C.F.A.

There was a hill in Bramshott. Near the bottom of that hill was
a place called Hazelmuir, about two miles from the camp. We used
to go down there. The 22nd Battalion (French Canadian Infantry)
were there before us. The 22nd used to hold up other infantry
fellows, beating them, and stealing their money. One night they held
up one of our fellows. Our man had those long Canadian Artillery
spurs on. A couple of Frenchmen held him, but he chopped them
all to pieces with his God darned spurs. After that if one of those
Frenchmen came along and heard those spurs jingling he'd give way
the whole road. He never approached another artilleryman. It didn't
take long to pass the word along! We never got held up again.

Before we got to Bramshott the huts were held off the ground
by 4x4's a out a foot high. The authorities were searching for a
missing 22nd Battalion officer and Sergeant. Somebody thought to
look underneath those huts. they found the bodies of the two men
laying there.

At Hankley Common, a parade ground, our officers were
preparing to take us out on manoeuvres. They got whiskey, chicken
sandwiches and other stuff, because they were going to have a
regular picnic out there. Some of our fellows got wise. We found
the grub and stole it from the officers. When we got out there all
the officers could find was bully-beef. They were wild! They tried to
find out who did it for months, but never did. General Steele, a
former N.W.M.P. man, must have found out. During a lecture he
said to us, "I was commander of the troops in South Africa. I used
to parade up to Lord Roberts and ask him for horses. Everytime I
went up he told me, "When we get our own men in the saddle, we'll
give you horses." So I got tired of parading one time. I asked him,
"Sir. Will you give us some ropes?" He asked, "Why do you want
ropes?" I said, "I've got the best bunch of horse thieves that ever
left Canada. If you give us ropes, we will get our own horses." In
two weeks there wasn't a Canadian who did not have a horse.
When the men can start stealing from their officers they are getting
to be good soldiers." He grinned at our officer. Everybody was
laughing except our officers.

After obtaining the horses and guns in May, camp life became
a daily routine: reveille at 6 a.m.; stables for all, 6:30 to 7:30;
breakfast and clean up, 7:30 to 9:00; gunners gun laying, drivers
harness cleaning and grooming, 9:00 to 12:00; the afternoon being a
repetition of the morning's work.

During training only thirty seconds to a minute was allowed

for trotting up, unlimbering, and getting the guns into motion and the limbers to the rear. When the Battery eventually got to France it was discovered that the trotting part was out of the question. All movement of guns took place under cover of darkness. Driving up in line, because of the shell holes in the ground, would not permit the guns to go by. It took picks, shovels, and planks to get the guns out of the shell holes. Guns going into action took all night. Later, when open warfare commenced, the Battery trotted into action when possible. It was a poor effort though, because guns and horses would get entangled in the wire. Drivers had to dismount, cut their horses out with wire cutters, while the gunners vainly but valiantly tried to clear the wire from the hubs of wheels of their guns and ammunition wagons.

Private Harold (Pat) Wyld (1900-)
CANADIAN FORESTRY CORP

I was under age like a lot of us were when they formed a boy's battalion in England. All of us were shipped to Shoreham where we were broken up and sent to different units. I went to the Forestry Corp. Our job was preparing lumber for the trenches.

Sergeant Charles Haddlesey
248TH CANADIAN FORESTRY CORP

Our work involved a gang of men cutting the timbers and making the framework to set up for sawmill machinery. The wood was squared up with broad axes. We had a large fireplace. Someone got a stick. After it burned awhile, we got the charcoal off of it, put it on a line; then the men would strike it down the log. They would clean that log almost as good as if they had used a saw. I stood there ready to use my broad axe which was a foot and a half broad. Eventually we had saws and machinery set up.

Once while on leave I sort of got lost. A fellow invited me to his house for some supper. At a corner, we got to his house, shoved open the door, and his wife stood there glaring at him. He was holding our package of fish 'n chips as he tried to explain how he found me. She grabbed the food, hit him in the face with it and knocked him out cold. I found my own way back with the aid of people who guided me.

The Princess was holding a banquet for the soldiers at Sunin Hill. My brother and I wanted to go to town instead, so we left camp and headed up a busy roadway. Many trucks were going into camp. One of the trucks had an appendage which caught my brother in the back of the head when he wasn't looking. He died instantly. All because we missed the Princess's banquet.

Lieutenant John (Jack) Chambres (1887-)
164TH BN/54TH BN - 4TH DIVISION

We had our own mess in Witley. Our beds consisted of three boards, two trestles and a blanket. That was it. Lots of officers took cots overseas. I never had one. I just took the boards and a couple of blankets. Once there were two officers in one hut. One had to go to France, so he offered me his cot. I took it and tried it that night, but I couldn't get to sleep on it. I got off the darn thing and went back to the boards!

Private Gordon W. Reid
50TH BATTALION - 4TH DIVISION

One story circulating around Bramshott Camp in 1918 was in a large area set aside in England for German prisoners of war. The Chinese Labour Corp or 'Coolies' as we called them, hated the Germans because they had seen how the Germans treated our prisoners. One night, the Coolies broke into an ammunition hut. They stole some Mills bombs. The Coolies headed straight to the prison grounds, where the Germans were enclosed by a barbed wire fence. In order to wreak revenge on 'Fritzie' (or 'Heinie'), the Chinese unceremoniously lobbed the bombs at the startled Germans. They hit their targets with defiant accuracy.
Unfortunately, the Coolies knew nothing about using grenades. They forgot to pull the pins! Needless to say the Germans knew what to do.

GREAT BRITAIN MOBILIZES

Private George Black (1898-)
8TH BN.- BLACK WATCH - B.E.F.

When I went to join the Black Watch in the Queen's Barracks at Perth, Scotland, the sentry at the barracks door said, "What do you want?" I said, "I want to join the Black Watch!" He said, "Get the hell out of here! You're too little!" I was as big as him. I would have turned away only an officer came over and said, "What's the trouble here?" The sentry said, "This man wants to join the Black Watch!" The officer said, "What's wrong with that? The sentry told him I was too little. The officer told me to go inside. I had my medical and joined the Black Watch. I never regretted it. That was November 1915.

Private Charles Brice (1899-)
NORTH DEVON HUSSARS
I joined in 1916 in Barnstaple, Devonshire. From there we went to Norfolk. We were supposed to have horses for the North Devon Hussars, but we trained on bicycles.

Our Sergeant was a rough old timer. He said to us, "You might have broken your Mother's heart, but you won't bloody well break mine!"

Canadians trained by British in the event of a gas attack. (England, 1916).

Bombardier William Shaw (1889-1977)
ROYAL GARRISON ARTILLERY - 151ST SIEGE BATTERY

In 1916 I was among the first twenty signallers who were
trained together at the Royal Garrison Artillery School. It was
situated a short distance west of Bexhill-on-sea, Sussex, better
known at that time as Cooden Camp.

Signals came to be looked on as a 'suicide club'. Fearful yarns
of what happened to 'flag-waggers' in that and past wars was
sufficient to deter most men from volunteering for such hazardous
duties.

We trained as signallers and telephonists and passed our tests.
After receiving certificates it was not long before we had to go.

The British Somme offensive of July 1st was soon to start, so
the training of signallers and the formation of siege batteries was
speeded up. Training involved the use of all the signalling and
observing apparatus and working instruments; such as 'D' Mark 3
telephones, transmittor vibrators, telescopes, compasses, telephone
wire reels, insulators, poles, flags, clippers and everything used for
the laying of wires on the ground, in trenches — overhead and
underground.

Sometimes the laying of a line at short notice, to a new
observation post at night, over roads, fields, across and along
water-logged trenches, through shelled villages and at times in view
of enemy flares, was a risky, hazardous adventure. The whole staff
of signallers were often engaged. Sometimes gunners would be
loaned to help in the carrying of reels and large drums of wire.

Lieutenant Ernest J.T. Hayes (1896-)
*SOUTH LANCASHIRE REG./CYCLIST CORP/MACHINE GUN
CORP & 1/50TH KUMAON RIFLES—INDIAN ARMY*

I had just joined the Reeves (paint) Company at age 17. War
broke out in August, 1914. I turned 18 on August 2nd, 1914.

Seeing the boys in uniform had something to do with my
joining up. I thought the war would be over any day. I ended up
being in for five years.

We were sent to Cambridge University for a month of officer's
training.

After a few weeks under canvas a notice came. They wanted
officers in the Cyclist Corp. That appealed to me because it saved
walking.

Private Thomas Chambers (1899-)
15TH BN. - LANCASHIRE FUSILIERS

I did my training in Scarborough. I came from Wales, but joined the Lancashire Fusiliers because they needed more men. It was at the time of the last German offensive in March, 1918. By July, 1918, I went to France and was put in charge of a Lewis gun in the trenches. I didn't even know what a Lewis gun was!

The British Expeditionary Force 1914

BRITISH EXPEDITIONARY FORCE IN FRANCE (1914)

The British Expeditionary Force (B.E.F.) consisted of one hundred thousand troops upon its initial movements into the Mauberge (near Amiens) area of France, on August 16th-20th, 1914. The opposing German forces consisted of The First Army under command of General von Kluck, the Second Army, under General von Bulow, and the Third Army, under General von Hausen. Sir John French commanded the allied forces of Great Britain. Statistics point out that "The Triple Alliance" consisted of Germany with its 4,600,000 land troops, 174 warships, manned by 118,000 sailors and marines — Austria-Hungary with its 2,500,000 land troops, 89 warships and 46,000 sailors and marines — Italy with 1,100,000 troops, 74 warships and 43,000 men and the services of Slavonia, Croatia, Herzegovina, Bulgaria and Albania (The Balkan group) with its 1,200,000 troops and a few warships against "The Triple Entente" of Great Britain with 1,400,000 land troops, 423 warships and 228,000 sailors and marines — Russia with 5,500,000 land troops, 217 warships and 176,000 sailors and marines — France with 4,000,000 land troops, 192 warships and 158,000 sailors and marines. The allies of "The Triple Entente" constituted (the Balkan group) of Servia, Roumania and Montenegro with 1,100,000 land troops and a small naval force; Norway with 800,000 troops, 37 warships and 32,00 men; Sweden with 650,000 troops, 47 warships and 35,000 men; Denmark with 540,000 troops, 39 warships and 30,000 men; Holland with 615,000 troops, 52 warships and 39,000 men; Belgium with 370,000 troops, 47 warships and 32,000 men; Spain with 1,200,000 troops, 84 warships and 43,000 men; Portugal with 400,000 troops, 22 warships and 17,000 men; Greece with 1,100,000 troops, 35 warships and 27,000 men. The countries Switzerland, Heligoland and Monaco were neutral. The allies promised the moral and perhaps physical support of the "Triple Entente" nations. *(quoted, in part, from "THE TRUE STORY OF THE GREAT EUROPEAN WAR", by Professor C.M. Stevens, Ph.D., Pages 237-239, The Hamming Publishing Co.,Chicago, Illinois, U.S.A., 1914)*

Lieutenant Albert Edward Winn (1894-)
ROYAL FIELD ARTILLERY

I went to France with the B.E.F. 1st Division in August, 1914. We marched up to Mons over the Aisne River.

Private Leonard Wood (1891-1980)
1ST EAST LANCASHIRE REGIMENT

In August 1914 I went to France with the Lancashire Regiment and we spent two weeks behind the battle lines. Then we heard rumours about leaving and heading for the front line. We were going to march all the way. We had no choice. We had to hang in there or else we got no food — that's all there was to it! We marched through day and night, for three days. Upon arrival at the front, we were engaged in a nasty battle. We lost quite a few men, not to mention the men we lost en route to the front. While on the road, we had the French on one side, the Germans on the other and we were going down the middle, in between them. That's why we were at a disadvantage. We were being fired at from both sides!

We lost more men, on the road from airplane bullets (about eight inches long). Some of the men saw the planes and others did not. Some were hit before they could say a thing. A man, not far from me, was marching along, when he let out one awful roar as this bullet went right through his face — in one side and out the other. Of course he died instantly.

When we first got to France, from England in 1914, lots of officers were killed either by our men (out of spite) or by the Germans. Sergeant Majors or even sergeants that were rotten to our troops in peace-time (during training) and certain officers were prime targets at the front. It was the troops' chance to fix them and they did. Many were given the chance to become "non coms" (non commissioned officers), but a lot of the men refused, because with an officer's rank, your lifetime was considered short. They were generally marked men.

At the front, in the battle of Mons, in 1914, there were bullets always flying overhead. The word was out, "No talking." It was around midnight. You could just see a ray in the sky like twilight (Verey Light). We scattered — so many went one way, so many went the other way. The other battalions would connect at either end of the ditches. As a result, each end was battling for a certain position.

While under constant shelling we could tell what specific area the Germans were in by the sound of the shells. The Germans sent over a biplane to see what we were up to. Of course they saw us dressed in our khaki. They passed the word back as to our strength. Shortly after that, some very high explosive shells came over. We couldn't hear them — the explosive of the charge — just the explosion of them going over. We certainly knew where they were coming from. While marching from one place to another (and hungry too), we came across a few farms. A lot of the troops broke away from the battalion; over to these farms, to pick the fruit off the trees. They were caught and put under arrest, until a firing party from another battalion put the guilty men up against the wall and shot them. All this for taking some fruit off a tree. If we had left it for the Germans, they would have stripped the fruit off all of the trees.

I remember having three or four skirmishes with the Uhlans. I was lucky to get away! They came out of a field full of small trees and bushes and took us by surprise. We had no idea they were there! They were armed with lances. Some of them carried machine guns with their armament. They even used swords! The Uhlans were wicked blighters! It was the like of them that did a lot of damage to women. They would just shoot the civilian men, but they wanted to have a good time with the women. If a woman would not fraternize, they would cut a breast off as punishment. We were surprised by the tricks they used to be up to.

At the first part of the war there were not any trenches to speak of. We had to dig them. Dig out the dirt and throw it in a pile; then throw sandbags on top; and then we'd nicely have the trench ready, when two of those "bottlebusters" (shells) came along and ruined our work.

We used to have four Vickers machine guns. That was all we had. Two were positioned at the front, one on our flank side, and one at the back of us.

I never saw the "Angel of Mons", let alone any angels! I saw the Huns up there! Not the angels!

I guess they were the nurses; if anything. Anyone who was through the battle of Mons and survived it was lucky. We suffered pain and agony—hell—with no let up—night or day. Many times I said my prayers. I don't know if it did any good, but I'm still here anyway.

Between Ypres and Arras we had to pull ourselves across a river, by raft, via a rope fastened on both sides. I met this other fellow and asked him, "What do you think is the best thing to do?" There was a French man and his wife hiding in the village across the river. The French man carried messages back to us about enemy movements. We went over to find him and stayed rather long. We were as near the road as we dared to go.

This French man owned a shop there and no one cared to bring him back. That was when he got hit. We passed some shops that had wooden awnings. We tore those down and constructed a stretcher. We laid this fellow on it and got him out.

I don't know if anyone recorded any information on him as he deserved the Victoria Cross. He constantly went back and forth with information to the Captains and Colonels, before he was wounded.

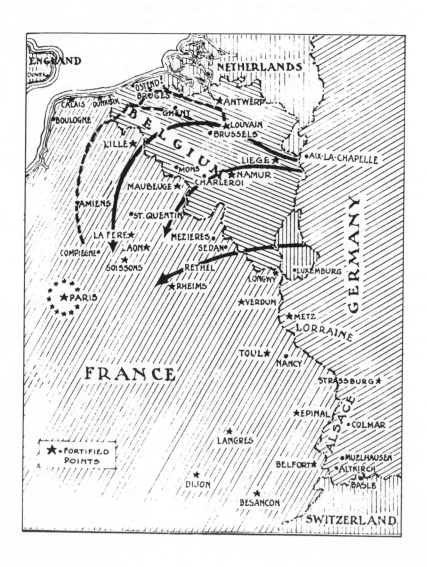

Map.

When we got him back, I said to a friend, "Now we are British soldiers, aren't we! When we go back, we would be so many hours overdue. They'll ask, "Where have we been? What have we been doing?" We had to make up a likely story, because if our officers think we lied, they'd shoot us.

Originally there had been some question as to whether or not this Frenchman was actually French or a German defector. So we took him to Etaples and never did see him again. Of course we told the Colonel exactly what had happened. We got away with being late. We were truthful. We weren't deserting. We were trying to do a good turn. After all, he did a good turn for us, by saving us from walking into a trap.

There was a big battle being fought down in Soissons, so we were rushed down from Liege. It was mainly fought by the cavalry (horses could run faster than we could!) We were quite near the Aisne River. The cavalry would charge in there and slash it up. As a result, a lot of horses came back with no riders. After a few more days, as we marched along, we noticed a lot of stray horses. Something was wrong somewhere. You would not have believed the slaughter. Most of the British horses had been roped together on one line, and the Germans came along and machine-gunned them. They didn't stand a chance.

I told one fellow, "Wouldn't it be a miracle if something came along now and stopped the war. We've had enough of it!"

Lieutenant Albert Winn
ROYAL FIELD ARTILLERY

We had six gun crews divided into three sections in the early part of the war. A German officer was in charge of one of the guns. He had been over to England before the war as an exchange visitor. One morning at daybreak, he was missing. The previous night he had decided that he would go back to his homeland. He had written a long letter to the C.O., thanking him for everything. Then he crawled over 'No Man's Land' back to the German lines. We were in action along side of Hooge Chateau Forest with our eighteen pounders dug in. He knew all our gun positions on our side of the woods and reported them to the Germans. As a result we lost at least four guns. Half our battery was either killed or wounded. He was highly regarded by our men before his surprising departure and yet he went back to his countrymen and did this to us.

Private David Shand
2ND GORDON HIGHLANDERS

After a five hour march from a mission in Lyndhurst to a port
in Southampton, we boarded a ship. For the next thirty-six hours
we crossed the channel which normally took two or three hours to
cross. We finally sighted land, arriving at the coast at Ostend. A
Belgian officer talked with some of us and seemed pleased at our
arrival. He was a little disappointed at our small numbers and he
told us that he didn't think Antwerp could hold out much longer.

When we stopped in Ghent we were ordered out of the train.
As we started forming up on the platform we could see the people
looking through the iron railings at us. Not too many of them had
seen men in kilts. They didn't know who we were. An old Belgian
guy about eighty or ninety came amongst us to tell us he had seen
some men in kilts years before when he was a young man. He said
he had a Highlander photo at home. The people watched us silently
as we started marching out of the station. We hadn't proceeded very
far when we heard someone shouting behind us; it was our friend,
the old Belgian. He must have informed the crowd who we were.
Within a few minutes there were hundreds of allied flags flying. Our
ranks were temporarily broken by the crowd who were supplying us
with beer, wine, cigarettes, foodstuffs, et cetera. The people were
cheering wildly.

On the outskirts of Ghent we saw one of the saddest sights we
had ever seen. As far as the eye could see there were Belgian
refugees coming along the road; some had a horse and wagon with
their household goods piled high; others had dogs pulling small
carts loaded with bundles. Many were walking and pushing baby
prams. They were fleeing Antwerp.

We took up a position about a mile from the city, along a
railway bank and started digging shallow reserve trenches in the
rear. We also started to block the main road. Next morning we
packed up in a hurry and proceeded along the railway in the
direction of the enemy. We heard that the enemy bombarded our
empty trenches for four and a half hours before entering the city.

We then reached the Lys Canal where the Advance Guard of
the enemy caught up with us. Our Platoon had to do the rear
Guard. We crossed the bridge and extended along the bank of the
canal. When the enemy troops attempted to cross the bridge we
poured a murderous fire into them. They hesitated and took cover.
We waited till our troops got quite a distance away before we
retired.

Next we passed through Somergem. Our other Brigade was
marching on a parallel road to us farther to the south. I was doing
the connecting file between two companies when a tall young
woman came alongside of me and started asking questions. She
spoke excellent English. I didn't pay much attention to her at first,
but it wasn't long before I suspected her of being a spy. She must
have thought I was very ignorant from the answers I had given her.
We had only been talking a few minutes when the company ahead
turned on a road to the left. When I got to that point I should have
signalled to my company behind me to turn to the left, but instead I
gave the halt signal; the young woman kept walking towards a
village. Some Frenchmen passed me but we couldn't understand
each other; several French Dragoons came along. One of them
could speak English. I pointed along the road at the woman and
told him I thought she was a spy. I then turned around and gave
my company the advance signal. The last I saw of the three
Dragoons they were disappearing in a cloud of dust. After
sometime I caught sight of the company ahead.

Next we passed over the Ghent Canal where our Engineers
blew up a bridge. Our next halt was Thielt, where we billeted for
the night. On turning out of billets the next morning we saw a
German aeroplane flying very low. A Sergeant of the Scots Guards
formed up about a dozen men in two ranks and gave them the
order to fire. One volley brought the machine down. It landed in
the street. The pilot was only slightly wounded. This aeroplane had
been following us for a long time. The pilot thought we were in the
next village. That's why he was flying so low. In a few minutes
some French airmen loaded the aeroplane on a long truck and
hauled it away.

The enemy were entering Thielt at one end while we were
leaving at the other end. Our Battalion extended across the fields
for rear guard action. We would hang on as long as we could,
exchanging a few shots into the enemy advance guard if they got
too close. We would then retire some distance and repeat the same
manoeuvre again. We arrived at Roulers very tired and billeted for
the night.

Early next morning we were on the march again heading for
Ypres which was about fifteen miles away.

We arrived in Ypres sometime in the afternoon of the 14th of
October.

Only a small number of the population had left Ypres at that
time. Shop windows were boarded up and a warning had been
chalked on the doors about looting.

Several British soldiers who had been cut off at Mons arrived in Ypres. These men had had an awful time hiding in the woods by day and only moving at night. They were helped at times by Belgians who sheltered them at the risk of their own lives.

Early the next day (October 15th) I visited the Cloth Hall. The Cloth Hall was a fine gothic edifice built in the thirteenth century. It had a great sloping roof with Coats-of-Arms painted in gold; all around the gallery were large frescoes painted on the walls depicting incidents in the history of the town.

Shortly after I arrived back at billets we got a lecture about the plan of operations. We were told the French Cavalry were going to cut round the flank of the Germans and try to cut a large number of them off. They were to hold them in front. It seemed to me at that time that we had a better chance of being cut off than the enemy, as their numbers were larger than ours.

Next day (October 16th) we moved out of Ypres along the Ypres-Menin Road. We observed an airplane flying low overhead. Suddenly it started dropping coloured lights. Within a few seconds enemy shells landed amongst the troops on the road, directly underneath the airplane. That happened three times before all the troops in the vicinity opened fire on it. One of the men could be seen hanging from a wing a moment before it was brought down.

The great Cloth Hall in ruins (1916).

He soon let go and dropped to his death; the other man was also killed. Nobody knew of the pilots' identity at that time, but we heard that the next day, the General was furious when he heard the news. It was impossible to find out who was responsible for bringing down the plane, but the artillery got the blame. That was a bit puzzling to us. Two British officers in a British plane, yet they were signalling to our enemy gunners. Our aircraft at that time didn't use that method of signalling, but the enemy did as we soon found out.

Our cavalry patrols had discovered large numbers of Germans in the woods east and south-east of Ypres. In order to cover the town the Division formed a line facing in that direction, about three miles from Ypres. Our battalion lined a ditch at the side of a narrow road which ran through a wood near Zillebeke. After being in this position for about two hours we saw our commanding officer waving furiously to us from our right. It was then that I noticed the Germans; they had formed a large solid square and were advancing slowly over a field between two woods. I don't think the Germans realized we were the main opposing body as it was a long time before they opened fire on us. The bolt of my Ross rifle jammed after firing many rounds of ammunition. I got to my feet ready to use my bayonet when I observed that a man next to me was wounded. I obtained his rifle. Because the ditch was so crowded I put my rifle between two men's heads and fired. The man on my right, who was a Sergeant, immediately jumped up holding his left ear. It took me a long time to convince him that he wasn't shot. I asked a machine gunner near me why he wasn't firing. He said, "the gun was damaged." We had two Maxim machine guns to a battalion (about a thousand men) at that time.

Then the enemy changed direction and seemed to be anxious to break off the engagement.

Later on the same day we went to the assistance of the Border Regiment who were being attacked. One of the Borders on my right was wounded. A Sergeant ordered the stretcher bearers to take the man to the dressing station. The stretcher bearers didn't know where it was. I had seen a Red Cross flag waving from a farm at the left side of the road not far from Ypres, so I volunteered to show them where it was. One man from my platoon accompanied us. We carried the wounded man across the fields as the Ypres-Menin Road was being shelled heavily. We were fired on by a sniper for a long time who would change his position from time to time along a hedge. When we arrived at the dressing station we discovered it had been abandoned. It was still being shelled.

We carried the wounded man to the outskirts of Ypres where we put him in an ambulance drawn by horses. We parted company there with the othr two stretcher bearers.

There was an estaminet near by and we entered it. It was crowded with French soldiers. They were anxious to know how the fighting was going on. We had only been there a few minutes when someone stuck his head in the door and shouted a command. The French soldiers rushed out to the street and formed up. A covered van came along and two men inside started throwing out loaves of bread. My mate and I got one each.

After wishing our French comrades the best of luck we proceeded into Ypres. We went along a narrow street and entered an estaminet about a hundred yards from the square. At that time the Germans started shelling the Cloth Hall very methodically. One shell every two or three minutes.

After wandering about the town for some time we reported to the Military Police. We were taken to a police station where there was an English guard. We were conducted to a large room which was already occupied by about a dozen men from various regiments. I saw a small group of Indian soldiers in the corner talking in hushed voices. My curiosity was aroused when I saw one of them with a large knife in his hand. He was moving his thumb along the edge to see if it was sharp. I discovered from their conversation that there were two German prisoners downstairs in the guardroom. The Indian soldiers were wondering if the Sergeant of the Guard would hand them over. They were speaking in Hindustani. I translated their speech to my mate. We saw two of them leave the group and proceed downstairs. We followed them. They asked the Sergeant of the Guard if they could have the prisoners, because they wanted to cut their throats. The Sergeant, who could speak their language, was very amused. He explained that he couldn't give permission as he had to hand them over to the guard who relieved him. While this conversation was taking place I had a look at the Germans. I felt really sorry for them. They hadn't washed or shaved in several days and their uniforms were splattered with dried mud. They certainly looked very tired and miserable. The two Indians returned upstairs very disappointed. Their comrades felt the same way when they heard the news. I got talking to them. They were glad to meet anyone who had been in India and could speak their language. They wanted to know what part of the world they were in. I drew a rough map on the wall and showed them the route they had taken from India and where they were located at that time. That seemed to please them. More men arrived in the guardroom. Those men were termed 'stragglers'.

In the afternoon we were all paraded and marched up the Ypres-Menin Road. We halted for awhile about a mile from Ypres and helped to bury twenty-two dead horses. After that we rejoined our different battalions.

When my mate and I rejoined our battalion they were resting in a field. Rations were being issued before going to the new position, but there were no rations for us. We were told we had been posted as 'missing' and struck off the strength list — we were just like two outlaws. After marching a considerable distance we took up our new position in a wood.

After several hours we got orders to advance. We hadn't gone far when we ran into a patrol of Uhlans. Very few of them got away.

We continued our advance through the village of Gheluvelt. It was late at night. All the houses were lit up. All the people turned out to welcome us. They supplied us with wine and beer on trays, foodstuffs and cigarettes. After a ten minute stop we resumed our march. When we left this village it was like leaving civilization behind. We continued advancing until we came to a ditch which we lined at the roadside. We halted, dug a trench, and settled down for the night. Those trenches we dug were very narrow and shallow. We spread out the earth and camouflaged it.

N xt morning we were up early. The October weather was fine and warm during the day. A large farm lay about two hundred yards to our left. It wasn't long before some of us went over to investigate. The people had evidently left the farm in a hurry as we could tell by an unfinished meal on the kitchen table. Five people had been seated there. Our attention was drawn to the barking of a dog in an outhouse. The door was locked. When we burst it open a large dog leaped out at us and started licking our faces. We released it from its chain and fed it. There was a dish on the floor, but it was empty. On entering the barn I saw a crowd of our men around some cows, trying to milk them. It took me some time, but I finally convinced them that I could get all the milk they wanted if they let me try. I watered and fed all the animals around the farm. I arrived back at the trench with two pails of milk. My officer in charge of the platoon told me to continue on with the job as long as we were there.

The following afternoon we got orders that we were going to advance again in about an hour's time. Without any warning, shells started falling all around us. We immediately extended across the fields and started retiring. There was quite a distance between each man and as we moved we offered a very poor target to the German gunners. The shells made lots of noise, but did very little damage.

The Germans had their heavy artillery in action at that time. Not long after, the enemy shelling stopped as we must have passed from their view.

After retiring some distance we went farther to the left and advanced again. We had to search all the farm houses in our path and escort the occupants to our interpreter to be interviewed. Then we took them back to their farms again. Sometimes we carried the smaller children in our arms as it was hard for them to walk over the fields. The farm folks rewarded us with milk, cheese, bread and apples. Most of the Belgians were reluctant to leave behind their farms. We continued our advance until it was dark. We halted and dug a knee deep trench. It was in an open field, so we camouflaged it.

At dawn we observed a farmhouse about one hundred and fifty yards in front of us. We had small fires going while preparing our breakfast. Suddenly we heard shouting from the direction of the farm. On looking round we saw two women, an old man and their children running towards us. They were dressed in night attire. They informed us that the Germans were in the house. After conducting those people to safety, a young officer from our platoon told the Sergeant to ask for four volunteers to reconnoiter the position. The Sergeant with his four men, left our trench and approached the farm. They were about twenty yards from their objective when they were fired on. Three of them dropped to the ground. The man on the right took cover behind a hedge and the man on the left found cover behind a haystack. The Germans poured a heavy fire through the windows while the Sergeant crawled towards the haystacks (hayricks); we could see that he was wounded.

German heavy artillery on the move (1914).

Later in the afternoon, our platoon surrounded the farmhouse. We rushed it and entered by the rear door. Our rifle fire had killed about half the defenders. We had some hand to hand fighting with the remaining enemy because they wouldn't surrender. We fought in the rooms and even on the stairs. In a few minutes it was all over. We counted twenty-two dead Uhlans.

Lieutenant Albert Winn
ROYAL FIELD ARTILLERY

There was an old French man breaking up stones on the village road. We were near the Aisne River. The village's church hall was about one kilometre down the road from us. The clock in the church tower was not working at all. The French man was a spy. We had a brigade of wagons and I reported to our Captain saying, "Excuse me Sir, but every time our ammunition goes out to the guns, the hands on that clock go around to the time we have left!" When the Frenchman turned the hands of the clock, the distant Germans would observe the time shown with binoculars. The result was that the enemy knew exactly when we were leaving. All the German artillery would open fire on us at the crossroads in Ypres, because that was our route. The French spy was reported to the gendarmes, was rounded up and shot without a trial.

Private David Shand
2ND GORDON HIGHLANDERS

The Division received orders to try and take Menin, so we were on the move again. Menin was a small village over ten miles southeast of Ypres. Through the dark hours of the night we could hear the enemy guns and transport wagons rattling over the paved streets of the village. The enemy got there a few hours ahead of us. Our battalion and supporting artillery didn't fire all night, so I don't think the enemy knew we were there. As we readied for an attack on the village at dawn, orders came through to retire. The enemy were advancing in large numbers on our left and had pushed back our cavalry. If we hadn't retired when we did we would have been cut off. The Germans didn't follow us at first so we retired to positions held previously.

Our platoon was going along a ditch in a wood when we saw a wounded German sitting in another ditch that crossed ours. He made signs that he needed a drink of water, but our men ignored him. I was last in line so I gave him a drink from my water bottle and bandaged his ankle. He was about forty-two years old, with a little beard—a reservist who had only been in Belgium a few days. A fellow in front of me spit right in his face. That really made me mad. We sat and talked for a few minutes though we couldn't really understand each other. I took his rifle and signalled him to go and join his comrades. He crawled away on his hands and knees. The Germans were two hundred yards in front of us. Before he got out of sight, a Sergeant with another platoon came along. He yelled to me, "Look at that German! Fire on that German!" I said "Where?" I took my time loading my rifle, firing a warning shot near his head. He turned and looked back. Then I fired up in the air. He finally got around a bend in a ditch and escaped.

I quickly rejoined my platoon again. We halted and formed a line along a ditch in the centre of the wood. Suddenly one of our men came along without his kilt on. He had a smile on his face. The Germans were not firing. On asking him what had happened he told us he had been captured. The Germans had stolen his kilt and told him to go home to his mother. Because the infantry on each side were so close together there was scarcely any shell fire. We were in the middle of this engagement when we were ordered to retire. We retired slowly without being followed by the enemy. We had few casualties. Ultimately we returned to the trenches we had held before the advance. We once more passed through Gheluvelt, but what a change! The village in which we had received such a warm welcome was now in ruins. There was a large shell hole in the middle of the road. There were dead horses and cattle lying in the fields. We paused for only a few minutes.

Then the Scots Guard and our battalion went into reserve a short distance behind the firing line. Our Brigade (the 20th) were on the right of the Ypres-Menin Road near the hamlet of Kruisek. We were in reserve for several hours. Next day we were up in the front line again near Zanvoorde. Our battalion was between the Scots Guards and the Border Regiment.

Because we weren't certain of the Germans' position, our 'C' Company advanced in extended order through a wood in the dark. We had orders not to shoot but to bayonet any Germans we found. We reached the other side of the wood without coming in contact with the enemy. As we stopped at the forest's edge for a few minutes, about a score of Germans passed in single file a few yards in front of us. (We later learned that the Germans had advanced quite a distance on our left flank; pushing back the cavalry and infantry, capturing Passchendaele). One man in our platoon got excited and wanted to fire on them, but the officer told him it was only a scouting party so we let them go.

Shortly after that we were passing a farm. Another man and I were posted there to watch for the enemy. The job was a little hard on the nerves as we didn't know what direction the Germans would approach from. We had not forgotten the German patrol we had seen earlier. They could have returned at any time. My mate and I stood at one of the corners of the farm when suddenly something ran between my mate's legs and nearly knocked him down. We heard a pig grunting as it disappeared in the darkness. We had a good laugh at that after we got over our fright. We were at this lonely abandoned farm for about an hour, when our men returned. We were glad to join them again. After wandering about in the dark nearly all night we returned to our new position some distance in the rear.

Word came that the Division had to send out a strong reconnaisance party in the direction of Gheluvelt to find out the Germans' strength. The Scots Guards and our Battalion (the Gordons) were given this task, assisted by the Northumberland Hussars and the Divisional Cyclists. We had artillery support and troops guarding our left flank (1st Wiltshires supported by the 25th Battery R.F.A.). We advanced quite a distance without coming in contact with the enemy.

We came under heavy bombardment. We had several casualties. A young Lieutenant was killed over on my right. His batman was seriously wounded. Blood was gushing out of his mouth. The poor fellow was pointing to his mouth and trying to speak. One man was killed in the hole I was in and two men in the hole on my right were also killed.

The bombardment stopped as suddenly as it had started. It was plain to everyone of us that if we didn't retire soon, we would have been surrounded and cut off. It was to dangerous to retire in daylight. After dark a man came from the platoon on our right and told us to retire.

Our Adjutant, accompanied by a Belgian interpreter, joined our platoon. He informed us that we were nearly surrounded. The interpreter knew the countryside well. He was going to lead us through a narrow gap to safety. He told us to keep together, as any straggler would certainly fall into German hands. It was difficult walking across the fields of growing crops in the dark. The enemy caught up to us as expected. We lined a ditch. Some of us would lie or stand in the open and fire rapidly until the Germans were very close. Then we retired a short distance as fast as we could and repeated the same action over again. Two of our men were carrying a box of rifle ammunition. Another two men were transporting a wounded man on a stretcher. The wounded man told the stretcher bearers several times to lay him down and save themselves. The two men refused. A small group of us surrounded the stretcher to give cover fire, but at last we had to retire quickly. We left the stretcher party to their fate. We were lucky to get away. Only the darkness saved us.

The next day our battalion advanced again. We were about to emerge from the edge of a wood when we immediately came under heavy rifle and artillery fire. If we had remained there any length of time we would have all been killed or wounded. We soon received orders to advance, one man at a time from the left. I admired the way the men would rush forward about a dozen yards and throw themselves flat on the ground. Then they open up—rapid fire. It reminded me of our peacetime manoeuvres.

It wasn't long before we discovered that our rifle fire was more rapid and accurate than the Germans. At manoeuvring in the open they couldn't be compared to us. Our long years of hard military training in peacetime were now paying off. When we retired, we could nearly always get clear but when the Germans retired, it did not take us long to catch up with them. They seemed to be hampered with their packs and large boots, whereas the majority of us were fighting in our shirt sleeves. We had thrown our packs and all unnecessary equipment away. In addition to our regular rounds of ammunition, each man carried four thin khaki bandoliers (holding two hundred extra rounds).

It was a strange sight to see a thin line of British men driving many times their number of Germans ahead of them. All that advancing on our front deceived the enemy as to our strength. We were getting along fine when we were ordered to retire immediately. Later we heard that the enemy had pushed back the left of the line and taken the village of Zonnebeke.

We would drive the enemy infantry back, but they soon counterattacked driving us back. This went on all day.

Private Leonard Wood
1ST EAST LANCASHIRE REGIMENT

Many places that we went to had poisoned water or else the wells had been filled in. Some of the French people were rotten towards us. They used to lock up their water pumps, so we broke them up (after using them) as a form of retaliation. One time my mouth was very raspy. We happened to come upon a ditch, that was full of water. There was a lot of foreign material in the bottom, but what I didn't know. That ditch had filled as a result of a storm the previous night. Anyway, I got water poisoning. I had taken my clothes off to wash in it. This caused me to come out in scabs all over my face and body. The doctors gave me treatments every morning, which consisted of a type of salve or else they would give me a syringe. Later they took a hook to pull the scabs off. Other men were receiving similar treatment. It was a terrible thing to have a parched mouth and not a decent drop of water anywhere. We'd be scared to test water because it might have been poisoned. Sometimes a 'blockbuster' came along, when we did get good water and there would go our water—dixie and all!

Private David Shand
2ND GORDON HIGHLANDERS

One night I had been down at the farm for water. When I returned to the trench I found that everyone was very quiet. I tried to converse with the man on my right but he edged away from me. The man on my left did the same. I started to wonder what could be the matter. The Germans had made an attack on the trench while I was away. I thought this might have been the cause of my comrades' strange behaviour. After awhile one of the platoon told me what had happened. The sentry challenged a man he saw approaching the trench, from the rear. Instead of the man answering properly he started to jest with the sentry. This happened three times before the sentry shot him. The man just had time to gasp out the sentry's name and ask him what he had done, before he died. That incident affected the sentry greatly as the slain man was a friend of his. The dead man was buried behind the trench. From then one, the man who shot him was shunned by everyone.

Not long after, the German artillery laid down a very heavy barrage in the form of a large square. It was later known as a 'box barrage'. Although we were clear of the shells, we were completely cut off from our battalion in reserve. The heavy bombardment lasted for about an hour. It stopped as suddenly as it had started. Whatever the enemy had planned we did not wait to see. We fell back to join our battalion, but discovered they had left. We finally joined them on the grounds of a chateau a little further back.

As our Company marched onto the grounds we were surprised to hear the Battalion cheering us. They heard we had all been captured or annihilated. After spending half an hour on the chateau grounds, we advanced again.

While going through a wood we met many German troops. We could not see too far ahead, owing to the thick undergrowth. The fighting was very heavy. The enemy were being reinforced by fresh troops and heavy guns all the time. We had many casualties, but the enemy suffered more than we did. We captured quite a lot of prisoners there.

One time in Ypres, the prisoners used to surrender in bunches of twenty to thirty men. Our battalion was usually a thousand strong. There were so many prisoners that one guy would escort them all back behind the lines. Then the police took them away.

There was a young German, no more than fifteen that we captured once. He was sitting in our trench. One of our men came over and started taking the little fellow's belongings. The German must have been Catholic, because he had a chain around his neck with a cross on it. This Highlander wanted it. The poor little German started to cry. I was brought up as a Catholic and I figured the kid's mother gave that little crucifix to him. He didn't want to lose it, but he had to hand it over to the guy. I said to the guy, "Don't you take that cross off him!" "Oh," he says, "Yeah, I'll take everything off him." I said, "You will! Well you won't live to see it because I'll shoot you!" I pointed my rifle at him. He took the cross from the kid and I said, "Hand that back." He handed it back. I told him, "Give him back all the other stuff you took off him too. You beat it!" I told the German, "You stay here. You're a prisoner of war now. You join us and I'll take you back."

The Germans began their counterattack, but we drove them back every time. The attacks continued all day and during the night. Owing to the nature of the country, it was very hard for our artillery to locate the enemy guns, but our guns wreaked great havoc with the German infantry. Afterwards we heard that the troops on the left of the Menin Road were not so lucky. The Germans had pressed forward, sneaked through the gaps between our Companies and fired on our troops from the rear. Whole Companies were either captured or annihilated. The Wiltshires suffered the most. Only about two hundred men got clear. Each night attack was more determined and longer than the previous one.

We had lost all our picks and shovels what with changing positions so many times, so we had to dig shallow trenches with our small entrenching tools. We tossed the earth out with our hands. We were south-east of the small village of Kruiseik. It was known for some time that British troops had come up on our left. This enabled the Division to shorten its long thin line, but it did not seem to make much difference to the nature of the fighting.

The following morning we were at the receiving end of a heavy enemy bombardment. Trenches were blown in and men were buried alive. We had one lone gun behind our trench replying to all the German artillery. The Germans meant to take Kruiseik at any cost. They finally broke through a gap on one point of the salient. The Scots Guards, Borders and South Staffords suffered heavy losses. Our Battalion was at the right. We managed to hold our ground. The enemy were brought to a stand-still. The area our Brigade was in was rather isolated and dangerously exposed. After dark, we got orders to retire. The Germans did not follow at first as their losses were heavy. There were about three hundred dead Germans in front of our platoon alone. Our 20th Brigade had defended the village of Kruiseik for five days and nights before it was finally overrun by the Germans.

Our Battalion took up a new position west of the Bassville brook. Next day there was a lull in the shelling. We had not had a wash or shave for days. We thought it was funny, when changing positions, to see other battalions of young men with beards. Our rations were few and far between. Sometimes we found a tin box full of hard biscuits dumped at the roadside. Occasionally they fell into German hands. Some of our men were wearing German boots as theirs had worn down. Our transport trucks were not around for days.

Germans housed in an old church (1914).

At that time (around October 27-28) our Division came under the command of Sir Douglas Haig, who commanded the First Corps. Our G.O.C. had gone home to prepare the Eighth Division for the field. The 21st Brigade held our part of the line. Our other two Brigades were at Klein Zillebeke and Hooge in reserve. There wasn't much shelling on the 28th of October, but that was only a lull before the storm. That evening our Brigade was sent forward again to take over the line at the left of the 21st Brigade. The Grenadiers were next to the Menin Road. Our Battalion was next, then the Royal Scots Fusiliers, followed by the Scots Guards. The Borders were in reserve.

The morning of October 29, 1914, was very foggy. We could hardly see more than about a dozen yards ahead. The German artillery opened up an extremely heavy bombardment at 5:30 a.m. About that time I had to deliver a message to the other side of the Ypres-Menin Road. Several yards from the road I could see men in greatcoats marching along in sections of fours, towards Ypres. When I recognized that they were Germans I jumped into a ditch. The fog was so thick I did not think I was seen. Soon the fog started clearing. The enemy were exposed to our view. There were German troops on the road as far back as the eye could see. That was a very daring thing for the enemy to attempt.

The 1st Grenadiers and our Company on the left charged the enemy as they advanced south of the road and westwards towards Ypres. The Grenadiers were driven back with our Gordons each time by weight of numbers. Because we were on low ground, south of the road, we couldn't see what was happening on the north side where the Black Watch, Coldstreams and Scots Guards held the trenches. It looked like the enemy was going to push us aside and take Ypres.

About noon, Lieutenant Otho Brooke of our Battalion, came up from the right flank with a message. Seeing our situation was very serious, he collected all the men he could from the rear (including Gordons and 1st Grenadiers) and led a brilliant charge.

In a few moments we lost about nine hundred men, killed and wounded. The enemy pressed on, trying to take Gheluvelt but they were driven back, with heavy losses. We heard afterwards that the Kaiser had come to see his troops take Ypres with hopes of taking the seaport town of Calais. The Kaiser and his staff just missed being captured by our yeomanry (the Northumberland Hussars) who crossed some fields to intercept them. The Germans, during this, the First Battle of Ypres, failed to take the town, but we knew they would try again.

That night we went a short distance to the rear to prepare a new position. Next morning we were ordered up to the front again. Then, word came for us to retire. Our platoon was suspicious of that order. We passed back word inquiring about the order. The message only got a short distance along the line when we saw the men on our right were retiring.

An enemy machine gun opened fire on our flank causing many casualties to one of our Companies. Later we heard that a German dressed as a British staff officer had approached the right of our Battalion and given the order to retire.

It wasn't long before we organized a counterattack. We advanced through the Zwartelen Woods, clearing out the enemy who left several hundred dead and wounded behind. We also captured eight hundred prisoners. Our counterattack had been successful, but our Battalion was now reduced to two officers and about one hundred and ten men.

Next day we were lying in a ditch that ran across the centre of a wood. The Germans attacked us in force. We held our fire until the Germans were several yards from our line. Then we fired rapidly.

The attacks would continue at intervals of about half an hour. We knew when we were about to be attacked, by the noise of the bugles, whistles, and the German officers' loud commands. They kept it up all night. They even had a brass band playing! They would get within two or three yards of us. We just shot them down. It was very hard to keep awake. A man near me complained to the lookout man that he had wakened him too early as the Germans were still about fifty yards away.

The enemy were using many fresh battalions against us. When their infantry weren't attacking us, their artillery were. The trees were being stripped of their branches by high explosive shrapnel while the large shells known as 'Jack Johnsons' were falling all over the place. Things were moving so fast and there was so much noise that one lost all count of time. We were retiring one time and the left flank of our Division was exposed. The Royal Scots Fusiliers stuck to their trenches until they were surrounded and cut off. Things were looking very bad when the 2nd Worcesters (who were in reserve) charged the enemy and took back Gheluvelt. They were supported by artillery and the Oxford Light Infantry.

By evening our Division had regained its old position. We were feeling very hungry and thirsty. Our thirst affected us most. We were located on a wood's edge. In the twilight we could see hundreds of dead Germans lying in front of us. Another man and I volunteered to go and collect some of their water-bottles. I noticed my comrade collecting souvenirs at the same time. He asked me to help turn over a dead German officer who was lying face down on the ground. He was an enormous man. In turning the corpse over I put my right hand where his stomach should have been. The sight made me sick. His mouth was wide open and he had a horrible expression on his face. My comrade took his sword which was very finely engraved. We arrived back at our line with as many water-bottles as we could carry; also several small tins of meat.

Time and again the enemy was deceived by our numbers. A German Colonel whom we captured the other day asked one of our officers how many army corps we had fighting against them. When told that we needed another Division to complete one army corps he said that if he had known that he would have given the order to his men to advance and walk over top of us.

On November 5, 1914, our Division was relieved. By that time the fury of the fighting was past. The Kaiser had come and gone. I thought at that time and I still think the Germans lost the war at Ypres in 1914. If they couldn't pass a thin line of troops, then how were they going to stop hundreds of thousands of British reinforcements later on.

We arrived at Meteren on November 7 and went into billets. That was the first rest we had had since we landed at Zeebrugge on the 6th of October. The survivors of our Battalion were reduced to about a Company strong. Out of 15,000 infantry who defended Ypres, only 2,000 returned. Of the four hundred officers only forty survived. The German losses must have been far greater than ours. We found Meteren to be very quiet after what we had gone through at Ypres.

Quite a few of us were slightly shell-shocked but nobody knew what shellshock was at that time. I've still got shellshock to a degree. If a car comes along the road and backfires — I jump! If the landlady comes up behind me and speaks — I jump again. My nerves are so bad that any sudden noise will surprise me. I saw my first shellshock case when down for some rations at a first aid dressing staion. The fellow was lying there shaking — convulsing all over — kicking his arms and legs. The orderly told him, "Try and keep still will you." They guy answered, "I can't! It must be my nerves." The doctor came over. He had never seen anything like it and didn't know what to do. I had shellshock, but never so bad that it made me sick. It would go away. A soldier was useless with it, having heard guns firing and explosions all the time.

We knew our rest wouldn't last long, so we were not surprised when we got orders to move in one hour's time. It started raining heavily as we marched out of Meteren. We moved on again and after a long, miserable march we arrived at the Lys Valley where we took over the 6th Division's trenches.

Our Brigade (the 20th) went in on the right of the line. The 22nd Brigade was on the left and the 21st came in on the centre later on. The Germans opposite us held what was known as *Aubers Ridge.*

The sight of it was very discouraging for us. None of the trenches had been finished. The bottoms of them filled with water and mud. Communication trenches had been started in many places, but had been abandoned when the water flooded them. The enemy trenches were on higher ground, but they were also flooded in places.

The line was quiet compared to Ypres. The enemy did not appear to have much artillery. Most of ours was still at Ypres. Digging trenches kept us busy. Water came pouring in when digging down only a few feet. We had to do a lot of riveting to the sides of the trenches to keep them from falling in. The country was so flat that the water couldn't be drained away. The support trenches were not even finished. In some spots they were only a foot deep. The country behind us was much the same as it had been in peace-time.

If it had not been for the snipers keeping up their continual vigil it would have been hard to believe there was a war on. Those snipers were expert shots as long as their target was still. They weren't so good at moving targets. I proved that fact quite a few times with a small mirror I had. Those were the first periscopes we had. The mirror was about three inches by two inches and covered behind with tin. It had a small loop to fit on the point of a bayonet.

To use the periscope one had to stand with his back against the parapet and raise his rifle until he could see across No Man's Land and see the German parapet in the mirror. To amuse myself at times, and also to tease the snipers, I would move my periscope up, down and sideways. Within a few minutes the sniper would be firing rapidly. A few more snipers would join in with him. When that happened I would pull my periscope down. I knew when to stop. The periscope wasn't hit once. I took it home with me.

One night we captured one of these snipers. His rifle had a big telescope mounted on it. When looking through the sights it would bring a person's head in the distance right up close. No wonder the Germans were good snipers.

We could see hundreds of dead enemy soldiers lying all over the ground in front and to the right of our trenches. They had been

caught while making an attack on the troops we had relieved. After
a battle there would be some men lying around seriously wounded.
I saw men without arms and legs or with their stomachs hanging
out. The stretcher bearers picked up any men with wounds, but the
dead were just left where they fell. A mortally wounded man was
not touched. I turned my guts when I saw these things. I once
looked in a dugout (8' x6'). Up against the wall were some dead
men with their brains and stomachs splattered all over the place. I
got used to it, thinking nothing of it after awhile. We used to say,
"When your time comes — you go." That's all.

Back at Ypres, if we saw a German was going to bayonet us,
we just shot him. I was in hand to hand combat. Sometimes we
used our fists. Some of our men were bayoneted right through. It
all depended on how good one was when using a rifle and bayonet.
We had had lots of bayonet drill back home. If we saw a German
attacking we'd get down and shove that bayonet right through him.
I had to do it to save my own life, but we used to have two or three
crazy guys in our battalion who took a delight in killing Germans.

German dead on Flanders Field. (Public Archives of Canada)

That was their hobby: killing. Most of us tried to make it easy for the Germans. If they surrendered we let them pass; otherwise we shot them. It was either them or us. We were out there and met men that we had never seen in our life before. We tried killing one another. What for? Their men didn't do us any harm. They were the same as us. At first we thought the Germans were heathens, cutthroats and ruffians, until we met them. Upon meeting some of the prisoners we found that there were some nice fellows in the German Army. The Prussians were the worst of the Germans. Like our "Guards" they were big men.

The weather became very unsettled. Winter was just starting. We were getting lots of sleet, rain, and snow. We had to scrape the snow off the parapet in order to make tea. Our rations were quite a distance to the rear. There was one communication trench that was about a mile long and about eight feet deep. There was two feet of mud and water at the bottom of it. It had a hedge along one side of it. That trench had been a natural ditch, but had been dug deeper during dryer weather. It wasn't long before many of us lost our shoes. As Highlanders, we suffered the most as we wore kilts, low shoes, khaki spats and thick hose. The suction of the mud was so great that it pulled everything off our legs. Some men sank to their waist or their knees and had to be pulled out. Small fatigue and ration parties would risk walking on top of the ground, but it was dangerous. We spent many days in our bare feet when the snow was on the ground. Then we were issued with fur lined leather waistcoats. We put our legs through the sleeves, so that the jackets covered our feet. We would have frozen otherwise.

After several days in the trenches we were relieved and marched back to billets.

Next morning we had to turn out for rifle inspection. The Sergeant Major noticed a cigarette end glowing in the dark. He wanted the name of the man who was smoking. The guilty man passed me in the dark. The Sergeant Major grabbed the first man he could find. That was me. About two hours later I had to go up in front of the Company officer. I got a good reprimand, even though I was a non-smoker.

Once while in the trenches we had an impromptu concert. Our machine gunners carried their machine gun on a stretcher, covered with a blanket and walked on top of the ground, behind our front line trench in full view of the Germans. The lines were not far apart. At night we used to listen to the Germans singing, accompanied by an accordian. When they finished a song, we would give them a hearty cheer. One of our men would then play a tin whistle. That man had played for us on many a weary mile while on the march. The Germans would show their appreciation at the finish. The 'concert' would last for hours.

At stand to there would be a few rifle shots fired from each side. At breakfast time we would see smoke coming from the stovepipe chimneys in the dugouts behind the German trenches. That would be the signal for us to light our fires. Just after that, friend and foe would go on top of the ground looking for firewood, water, or souvenirs. We left our rifles in the trench. Some German a little more daring or curious than the others would come over about halfway between the lines. We waved at each other. Only about six men were sent out on either side. The ceasefire would last about an hour or until an officer fired a warning shot. Then we all got back into our trenches again. The 'truce' would be repeated about noon and at 5:00 p.m. It was so quiet at times that our officers would come along the trench, ordering us to fire. We fired up in the air.

One evening a ration party of Scots Guards passed us in the trench. They said one of their men had been killed unnecessarily that day. It happened in the following way: a high ranking officer while inspecting the front trench noticed one of the Scots Guards fire over the parapet and duck down. The officer reprimanded the man on the spot. He asked him if that was the way he was taught musketry. He ordered the man to stand up and take proper aim. While the man obeyed the order, a sniper's bullet caught him in the centre of his forehead.

After being in the trenches several days we were relieved again. Some men were sent from each Company to the village of Sailly to learn how to make and throw bombs. The first men to be picked out as bombers were men who generally went scouting on their own or men the Sergeant Major disliked.

We were known as 'the Suicide Squad'. Those who were picked arrived at the Engineer's headquarters. We heard an instructor had been blown to pieces not long ago, while instructing his class. The first bombs we made were very clumsy and awkward to throw. They were composed of a wooden bat with a handle. A parcel made up of gunpowder, bolts, nuts and odd pieces of iron were enclosed in a sacking. There was a round hole in the centre of the bat. Into that hole a cylinder was fitted containing the high explosives. An eighteen inch fuse was attached to it. The method of throwing the bomb was as follows: some one would light the fuse, then everyone would retire about a hundred yards and lie down flat. The bomb thrower had to swing his arm from front to rear about a dozen times. Then he would throw it overhand and lie prone on the ground.

There was an Irish fellow who knew how to make those

bombs. He had a haversack full of them. When we marched in fours, all guys made a big circle around him. He was left by himself. If he got too near us, someone would say, "Keep away! You've got bombs in that haversack. Keep your distance!"

The Germans threw bombs at us that looked like cloth and powder tied to a stick. If they did not go off we would pick them up and throw them back! Then they went off. The next German kind was better. Made of steel, with a handle on it — called a Mauser bomb. To set it off, we held the handle back, pulled a pin out and tossed it. The handle would fly open and set it off.

We were also shown our first periscopes with double mirrors. We were glad to have them because we could then see over No Man's Land without putting our heads up.

Upon returning to the trenches we found that we were further to the left of our former position. The trench wasn't as muddy. There were lots of bricks handy, so we paved the trench bottom with them. To our right front was the ruins of a convent surrounded by a high wall which was broken down in several spots. The trenches were further apart. Our artillery joined us again from Ypres. We couldn't move much in the daytime, but at night there was great activity bringing up rations, et cetera. A corporal from our platoon was sent down to the dressing station to guide a draft of men up to the trenches. It was the first draft our Battalion had received since we landed in Belgium. Other battalions in the Division were reinforced by drafts, so we were beginning to look like a Division again.

The ground between the lines was waterlogged. There was a thick belt of barbed wire in front of the German trench. Their first, second and reserve line were crowded with men. They had lots of support trenches behind them. It didn't take much imagination when looking over No Man's Land to see that any side that advanced over such ground would be annihilated. We got quite a surprise when we received orders to attack.

On the 18th of December at 4:30 p.m. the Warwicks attacked, supported by the Queens. An artillery bombardment of fifteen minutes duration preceeded the attack. That was all our ammunition would allow. The 20th Brigade was to attack at 6:00 p.m. without a preliminary bombardment. If those two attacks were successful, the 21st Brigade would also attack. Nothing was heard from the Warwicks after they went over until an N.C.O. came back about half an hour later, saying they had been held up at the barbed wire, had lost heavily and needed reinforcements. About a Company and a half of the Queens immediately advanced to help them. It was plainly seen that the attack had failed. No more troops were sent out. Instead the survivors had to get back as best they could. The stretcher bearers went out and started bringing in the wounded. They were not fired on by the enemy.

The Warwicks' losses were eight officers and three hundred men killed, wounded or missing.

The Companies of the Scots Guards and two of the Borders attacked next on a front of five hundred yards. The Scots Guards went over first, but the Borders didn't hear the whistle was used as a signal. The first hint the Borders had of the advance was when they heard screaming on their right. Some of the Scots Guards were held up by the barbed wire and suffered heavy losses from machine gun fire. Others got right into the German trench and cleared a part of it by bayoneting or shooting the defending Germans. Then they blocked the end. The German counterattack wasn't long in coming. but the Guards held on all night. As No Man's Land was about two hundred yards across, a communication trench couldn't be dug in time, so the Guards retired to their own trench the next morning while it was still dark.

When the Borders advanced, the Germans had got over their surprise and met the attack with a murderous fire. A few of the Borders reached the German trench, but they were killed there. The survivors withdrew. The casualties in the attack were, Scots Guards: three officers and one hundred and twelve men killed and missing and three officers and seventy-six men wounded. The Borders: two officers and seventy-one men killed and missing, two officers and forty men wounded. After the attack things were quiet again.

We very seldom saw an airplane in the Sailly area. Planes were only used for reconnaisance at that time so we never shot at them. We thought the aviators were fearless. Our officers used to come around our trenches and ask if anybody wanted to transfer to the Royal Flying Corp. We felt it was safer in the front line trench than in an airplane. Airplanes in flight wouldn't fire on one another. They would pass each other. Then the pilots would wave. We didn't know one plane from another, so we would wave at the pilots. They waved back. They generally flew at two or three hundred feet.

Once a plane was brought down between our lines in No Man's Land in front of our trench. Both sides stopped firing. Our men retrieved the pilot, taking him down the trenches to the rear. The Germans would do the same for us, but co-operation got worse as the war went on.

What worried us most was getting back and forth between the trenches and our billets in Sailly. We had to walk a fair distance on the road when leaving our billets. Then we crossed some fields and entered a communication trench. Our trouble started there. We would sink in the mud again. We had to hold our rifles high over our heads or we would have lost them in the mud. It took a good part of the night to get through that waterlogged trench. Once in the front trench we still had to go quite a distance to the left to reach our position.

One day the relieving battalion was late. We were surprised to hear that they had been back at a village lining the streets for the King. The country behind the trenches looked peaceful. There were very few shell holes and the villages were a pretty sight. When out of the trenches we were either billeted in a barn or in one of those villages.

It was still quiet in the trenches. Each side knew it was no use trying to advance over the mud. We were doing more hard work there rather than fighting. We could look over at the German trench and see them busy shovelling. Once in a while, one of our men would try and shoot one of their shovels if it appeared above the parapet. The Germans would signal back a miss. It was common talk amongst us that the war was at some kind of standstill.

I had been suffering for a long time with a badly swollen leg. One night I got entangled in some German barbed wire, receiving a deep gash on my right shin, just below the knee. I didn't think much of it, so I just dressed it with a bandage. As soon as I sank in the mud, the bandage would come off again. I carried on until my leg was about twice the thickness of my other leg. It turned a bluish colour. At times it was very painful.

I went down for rations one night. The farm we went to was also a dressing station. I had a look inside and saw about twenty men waiting to see the doctor. When the doctor arrived he had quite a busy time sorting out the sick from those not so sick. I finally saw the doctor and explained I was down with a ration party and only wanted a bandage to put on my leg before returning to the trenches. He bandaged my leg and told me to wait for the ambulance.

It was pitch dark when the horse drawn ambulance arrived. Our driver was challenged every few hundred yards along the road by sentries that we couldn't see. We arrived in Merville which was the clearing station.

Private Leonard Wood
1ST EAST LANCASHIRE REGIMENT

I was wounded in late 1914 in Plugstreet Wood (Ploegsteert). I was hit in the back with shrapnel, getting three or four big lumps of flesh gouged out in my leg. The shell was a high velocity one, so I didn't hear it. The shrapnel in my back lodged behind my heart. I was lucky. If you got hit, were pulled out of the line and sent home, well, you were considered lucky. Some other poor suckers went through this and that and it wasn't long until they were pretty near crazy. Some got so bad they couldn't control themselves or couldn't talk! I'll never forget it. I often cry now. It brings back memories of the things that happened over there. Oh...

I was sent home by way of Dover on some private yacht. It was all in white enamel — a beautiful boat. Once in Dover we were questioned as to where we originated from. "Where did you say you lived? How many years were you living there?" and so on. Now if I had said I came from Yorkshire, they'd send me to London, so I told them the 'truth', that I lived in London (laughter); so they drafted me up to Yorkshire!

Lieutenant Albert Winn
ROYAL FIELD ARTILLERY

Around the Ypres area, on Christmas morning, 1914 we (the British, French and Germans) played football in No Man's Land. The football game ended as a draw. There were some Germans (the Prussians & Hanovers) who were friendly with the British. We exchanged Christmas cards and cigarettes, et cetera. We had a ceasefire for hours. All the troops were up in the front line looking out. By midnight, the shells opened up and we were at it again.

Private David Shand
2ND GORDON HIGHLANDERS

I was told that my leg had septic poisoning and that they just got me in time to save my leg. Being young and strong it wasn't long before I got released from the hospital. Shortly afterwards I was back in the trenches again — back at Ypres with our 1st Battalion. When I think of the First Great War, I think about Ypres in 1914.

The Canadian Expeditionary Force 1915

CANADIAN EXPEDITIONARY FORCE (1915)

Lieutenant Ian Sinclair
13TH BATTALION—1ST DIVISION

We were shipped to France and Belgium in February, 1915, landing at St. Nazaire, France. We received a wonderful reception upon arriving at St. Nazaire. Then we entrained to within five or six miles from the front line. We were billeted in people's farmhouses, in villages or any place we could find a hole to put a human being in. It wasn't very pleasant for the population. However they were very friendly.

We stayed in the rear area of Armentieres training with the York and Lancs. Then that British regiment and ours proceeded to Armentieres front line. That was our first taste of action. The first wounded man I saw was a York 'n Lancs man who had been shot right through the face, from cheek to cheek. I suppose it made a complete mess of his jaw. I've never seen anything so swollen in all my life. His face was like a pumpkin. He looked a very sad sight as he lay in the dressing station.

War shows what silly things the life of a soldier hangs on. The night before we left England, one of our men named Knights, who had extraordinarily big feet, was unable to get a pair of boots to fit him. At the last minute, an hour or so before the regiment embarked on the ship, in came a new shipment of boots. Among them were a pair big enough for Knights. As a result he went over with us and was the first person killed at Armentieres. If the boots had not come in he would have been left in England. It shows what one's life depends on.

Corporal Jack Finnimore
3RD BATTALION—1ST DIVISION

On February 4th, 1915, King George V and Field Marshall Lord Kitchener reviewed us in pouring rain. Then on February 16th, after butting Biscayan rollers for four days, the disembarkation of the 1st Canadian Division was completed at St. Nazaire.

Then we were entrained in boxcars for Flanders. My Battalion — the 3rd Battalion, 1st Brigade, were billeted in a school in Armentieres. We had a week's indoctrination in the trenches with British units holding the line in front of Armentieres. That was followed by platoon training during which we took over the responsibility for a definite length of trenches at Festubert. We went in and out of the trenches on four day stints. At night the patrols went out. Worst of all was the listening posts which pushed forward into the 'devil's strip'. It was a strange experience. German flares soared up to curve back to the ground. Suspended by small parachutes the flares sank slowly, distorting the torn landscape with eerie light and shadows. Men caught in No Man's Land froze prone upon the ground until the light had died. It was the lack of sleep that struck the men most. There were casualties but no more than the normal wastage in the trenches.

Armentieres had the two trenches facing each other. The Germans didn't bother us and we let them be. We were just on guard in case anything happened.

THE SECOND BATTLE OF YPRES

Corporal Jack Finnimore
3RD BATTALION

On April 22nd, 1915, the Germans struck at the Algerians on the Canadians' left flank. Contrary to the Hague Convention governing the conduct of warfare, they released the contents of a number of cylinders of chlorine gas which rolled over the Algerian parapets. The men were without protection against the gas. Some died and others were very nauseated. They broke and fled leaving a gap in the allied defences.

That night the Canadians worked desperately to close the gap. The 48th Highlanders (the 15th Battalion then) filled the gap. We only got a sniff of the gas. The 15th Battalion got the worst of it. We were on the right flank and could see the Germans running through the village popping off our men. Then they went around. The first thing we knew they were behind us! We lost thousands, dead, wounded and captured. The historians claim we stopped the Germans from getting to the sea ports in Belgium. We were finished off by Saturday, the 24th of April.

I was wounded on the last jump over between leaving an old trench and building a new one. My brother, F.A. Finnimore, was wounded there just before I was. I started to take his puttee off when Captain Strait said to me, "Come on Finnimore. Look after your section. Never mind, you'll have to leave him (my brother)." A Toronto newspaper back home reported that we kissed each other goodbye on the front, but I only did his leg up. That was all!

Lieutenant Ian Sinclair
13TH BATTALION

Lieutenant Herbert Maxwell Scott, of the 15th Battalion, 48th
Highlanders (later a Captain with the 42nd Battalion) was a friend
of our family. He was also a descendant of Sir Walter Scott, the
Scottish novelist. Lt. Scott died ten years ago in Scotland. Here is
his official account written after his recovery from wounds at the
Second Battle of Ypres:

"On Tuesday night, April 20th we took over the trenches from
the 16th Battalion — Canadian Scottish (They were a mixed bag
from Hamilton, Winnipeg, Vancouver and Victoria) to the north of
St. Julien. The night of the 20th/21st passed without any event of
importance. Wednesday also passed in a peaceful manner except for
a few shells. Thursday, April 22nd was a beautiful day and we spent
the time basking in the sun and writing letters, being impossible to
do any work in the daytime as work attracted shells. About four
o'clock in the afternoon, Captain George MacLaren, Captain Burt
Daniels, Tod Bath and myself enjoyed a glorious tea of Scottish
shortbread and chocolate biscuits outside Bath's dugout; all of us
were very cheerful. After tea we retired to our respective parts of
the trench. (That shows how quiet it was right up to the last
minute.)

Shortly afterwards about five o'clock we noticed a heavy
greenish cloud hanging over the French lines on our left. We could
see the French running back, but owing to the very heavy shelling
to which our trenches were now being subjected, we could find out
nothing more.

During the night of April 22nd and 23rd we heard the
disquieting news that the French had retreated on our left, leaving
the left flank of the 5th Royal Highlanders—13th Canadian
Battalion up in the air. This fact forced the 13th to swing their left
company back at right angles to their original line; at the same time
bringing their support company up under extremely heavy shell fire
and in daylight. Half of the supporting company was wiped out in
doing this.

Later in the night the Buffs (the East Kent Regiment) and 14th
Canadian Battalion (Royal Montreal Regiment) were brought up to
support the 13th, while the 10th and 16th Battalions
counterattacked. We heard nothing of the counterattack until
Friday night. No rations came up Thursday night, only the bad
news. Consequently we spent a very anxious night.

The Germans started shelling again on Friday at six a.m. and
continued until one-thirty p.m. During the shelling they used some

shells which contained a sort of gas causing our eyes to run very badly and making us cough. We could scarcely see a thing for an hour.

During Friday night of April 23rd/24th we received a message from General Alderson (Lt. General E.A.H. Alderson was commanding the First Canadian Division at that time.) He was congratulating us on having stuck it so well, which pleased us immensely. We heard that reinforcements were coming up, though the outlook is far from cheery. However what pleased us most was the arrival about two a.m. of the rations together with the so much needed ammunition. A bag of mail also arrived, but we decided to sort it in the morning which was unfortunate as I suppose the Germans now have it. (A German soldier picked out a letter from my Father to me and answered it, writing my Father after the war was over. He was what they call a 'housemaker' in Germany, a sort of interior decorator.)

We stood to at three a.m. Saturday morning. Shortly after eight-thirty a.m. when it was fairly light we noticed far away on our right, a German balloon which hadn't been there the day before. As we watched it, four red flares were dropped making it quite a pretty sight. Our gaze must have been lingering on this a little too long for when I turned, men were leaving the trenches on our right. A great wall of green gas about fifteen to twenty feet high was on top of us.

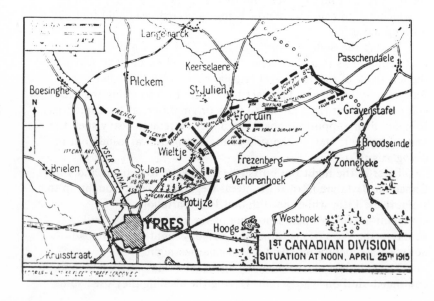

Map.

Captain MacLaren gave an order to get handkerchiefs, soak them and tie them around our mouths and noses. (Some were able to do that and some just urinated on their handkerchiefs.) Some managed to cover their faces. Others, myself included did not, owing to a scarcity of the necessary articles. Even with these precautions it was hopeless to try and stand up against the stuff, so we retired choking, coughing and spluttering. There was a hill behind us. We went up to it in small groups. A few shells burst over us, but not enough to do any harm. Anyway the Germans couldn't see us owing to the gas. At the top we came to one of our reserve trenches held by some of the 7th Battalion (British Columbia) into which we dropped pretty well all in (tired). We hadn't been there long before the shells started coming again. For about seven hours they shelled us most unmercifully: the shells dropping all around, some hitting the parapet, some just going over causing a great many casualties. As far as the Highlanders were concerned we were worthless anyway because we just lay in bundles at the bottom of the trench, choking and gasping for breath.

Sometime in the early afternoon the order came to retire, so having had enough of things by this time they thought of getting me to a hospital. One of my men gave me a hand. Later on another fellow joined in from somewhere, so between the two they coaxed, dragged and pushed me over the most uncomfortable four miles I had ever gone. I wanted to lie down every twenty yards to get my breath back. Finally we reached a dressing station (a Red Cross place run by the regimental medical officer). After passing a good many distressing nights which I was dimly unconscious, I was shipped on from ambulance to ambulance many times in the night until I finally landed up in a hospital in St. Omer where I could at last sleep in peace."

Private Frank V. Ashbourne
3RD BATTALION

We went into the line with a thousand men and only two hundred of us came out of it. Sir John French said that it was our Battalion that stopped the advance of the Germans. 'C' and 'D' Companies suffered the most and were almost wiped out. I was with my brother Bert, shortly before we were separated by the gas attack at St. Julien, on April 24th-25th, 1915. My brother was wounded near Langemarck and taken prisoner of war. During the gas attack at St. Julien we lost the first line of trenches and had to move back to the supports. At the back of those trenches we lay down flat and covered our mouths with wet clothes, waiting for the Germans to come up. They came slowly, thinking we were all dead from their gas, but not so. It drifted slowly over us and showed the Germans about seventy-five yards away. We were suddenly ordered to rapid fire and I don't think that more than a dozen Germans got away alive. We advanced again and regained our front trench with minimal losses.

Private David Shand
1ST GORDON HIGHLANDERS

When the Germans used gas on the Canadians at Ypres we were nearby. We looked back at a village about five miles away. It looked like a fire, because we saw a lot of smoke. We couldn't figure it out because we had passed that village when entering the trenches. We had to go back that way to get out. All at once word came along our trench, "Hurry up! We're leaving in half an hours time." It was daylight. We wondered where we were going. Another English regiment took our place. We never heard the word 'gas' before as the Germans had never used it. So we moved along the railweay tracks around Ypres and stopped at a ditch at a first aid clearing station. There were about two hundred to three hundred men lying in that ditch. Some were clawing at their throats. Their brass buttons were green. Their bodies were swelled. Some of them were still alive. They were not wearing their belts or equipment and we thought they were Germans. One inquisitive fellow turned a dead man over. He saw a brass clip bearing the name CANADA on the corpse's shoulder and exclaimed, "These are Canadians!" Some of us said, "For the love of Mike! We never knew that!" Some of the Canadians were still writhing on the ground, their tongues hanging out. Those Canadians had come along the railway track about a mile from our trench. We saw one young Canadian down on his knees. His finger was on the trigger of his rifle. He was dead. He had apparently turned around and was firing on the Germans because they were in pursuit. There was a big bunch of empty cartridges lying beside him.

Then we reached the front line Canadian trenches. There were no trenches left.

CAPTURED AT YPRES (PRISONERS OF WAR)

Corporal Jack Finnimore
3RD BATTALION

On April 24, 1915 we were soon over-run at the 2nd Battle of
Ypres. A German was standing over me pointing his rifle and
bayonet at my chest. I was wounded in the leg and was not able to
walk. One of the German soldiers handed his rifle to his comrade,
found a wheelbarrow in a deserted farmyard, placed me on it and
pushed me through to the rear lines. If it wasn't for those two
Germans I would have died at the side of the road in a mudhole.

The Germans laid us (the wounded) on some loose straw on
the floor of a church hall until Monday, April 26th. Then we were
put on boxcars with what little possessions we had left. Thirty-five
to forty of us were crammed in one car. There wasn't any guard in
the boxcar with us. They couldn't have stood the smell! Dried
blood was awful.

It must have been two or three days before we arrived at a
place called Paderborn, Westphalia where we were put in a shed
and given our first hot food — sauerkraut and sausages. After that
they placed us in horse drawn carts and took us to hospitals. I was
sent to the Sister House (Nunnery), had a nice bath, with my
wounds attended to, put in a nice soft bed, and treated very well
there.

My stay in the Sister House lasted about two months. When
our wounds were healed we were sent to Sennelager P.O.W. Camp.
The prisoners sent to the Brother House (Monastery) were not so
lucky.

The British P.O.W.'s who had been in Sennelager since 1914
were very good to us. They were receiving parcels from Britain,
without which they would not have survived. They shared their
parcels with us until ours came through. It was comradeship of the
truest sense. If a fellow had two pairs of socks he gave someone else
a pair. We did the same for prisoners who arrived in later years.
There were also some Russians in the camp who were treated very
badly. They were given all the dirty work.

I had taken my boot off and carried it all the way to
Sennelager. I never lost it, otherwise I would have had to wear
wooden clogs. New uniforms were eventually sent to us from
England. They were black. The Germans cut a big piece out of the
back, put a red stripe in and cut pieces from the arms and legs.
Then the people knew we were prisoners. The German slang word
for prisoners was 'Gefangeneniagers'. The sign read,
"STAMMLAGER FOR KREIG GEFANGENEN." (P.O.W. Camp).

Sennelager consisted of three large compounds, each one surrounded by barbed wire fences about eight feet high. There were three fences around the camp. The middle one was electrified. A dog was caught on it once. It smelled up the camp until the Germans turned the juice off. When the dog was cleared away they turned the electricity back on again. A mile away there was a cavalry barracks. A party of prisoners were marched there every morning to clean the stables and groom the horses.

The guards on the whole were just old timers, unfit for front line service. Their uniforms were always nice and neat. They were easy to get along with as long as we did what they said, but they never had anything to give us. Sometimes we saw civilians outside the wire, but the Germans would not let us get too close. Our camps were mainly in the middle of nowhere. The guards wore peaked caps, not helmets.

At Christmas in Sennelager on December, 1915, the Germans gave us a little canvas holder containing a bit of cotton, a needle and a couple of buttons. It was a gift from the Kaiser! We thought it was a good gesture.

About May, 1916, we were packed off to another camp at Minden, which had half French and half British P.O.W.'s. It was closed in more. The huts were crowded. The barbed wire was such that it restricted our view of the countryside. It was not like Sennelager at all. The French were not very friendly. We called some of them stoolpigeons. Our stay at Minden only lasted a few months. Then all the British and Canadian N.C.O.'s were sent to Camp Grossenweeder-Moore.

That camp consisted of two compounds, one for private soldiers and one for N.C.O.'s N.C.O.'s from Giessen and Salter Camps joined us. There were two hundred of us in one compound. That was the first time some of us had seen or heard the fate of our comrades.

Of course, all those moves from one camp to another always tended to disrupt our mail and parcels. Shipping them from one camp to another took more time. Bread would be mouldy and parcels damaged. It was at that camp that they tried many ways to get us to volunteer to go out to work. Had we done so we would have landed in a salt mine or some other dirty job. They had us walking around a field about the size of a football field four hours in the morning and four hours after lunch in small groups of twenty-five men. They stopped us occasionally and asked us who wanted to volunteer to go to work. The answer being no, they asked why. We told them that on the principle of being British

N.C.O.'s we knew that there had been an agreement signed between England and Germany that they would not force either officers or N.C.O.'s to work, but that they could volunteer.

NOTHING is to be written on this side except the date and signature of the sender. Sentences not required may be erased. If anything else is added the post card will be destroyed.

[Postage must be prepaid on any letter or post card addressed to the sender of this card.]

I am quite well.

I have been admitted into hospital

{ *sick* } *and am going on well.*
{ *wounded* } *and hope to be discharged soon.*

I am being sent down to the base.

I have received your { *letter dated*
telegram .,
parcel ,,

Letter follows at first opportunity.

I have received no letter from you
{ *lately*
{ *for a long time.*

Signature
only }

Date _____

A standard Canadian "letter" allowed to be mailed home.

That was before America came into the war. I think Mr. Gerrard was attached to the United States Embassy at that time. He looked after the welfare of British P.O.W.'s. Some of their staff paid us a visit. The Germans put us in our huts. The German N.C.O. wrote down all our complaints and presented them to the Americans. That put an end to the "eight hours a day exercise" as the Germans put it. Instead we got two hours in the morning and one hour in the afternoon, which we welcomed. We would also receive our parcels and mail regularly again.

Once fellow I knew, Buddy Grant from our battalion, was only a Lance Corporal, so he put up an extra stripe to make himself an N.C.O., but the Germans caught up with his tricks. They made us all send back a card from Germany to the British War Office for confirmation of rank. My record came back saying, 'I was a Corporal before I left England', but those who were made Corporals in France never were confirmed. They lost out. When Buddy's verification came back his feet hardly touched the ground before he was shot over to the work camp.

After the U.S.A. came into the war the Spanish Embassy were supposed to be looking after us. We only saw them once. They were not very satisfactory.

A couple of men tried to escape once. They clipped the wire and went their way around, but a guard heard them. The Germans brought them back. They got a month's solitary confinement. That meant staying in the toilet shack which stood over the ground. We took the opportunity to pass them cigarettes when we could.

Then I was sent to Camp Dortmann which proved to be the last one. Things were not too bad there. As in all camps, if you asked for trouble you got it.

The Germans tried another stunt with us at Limburg Camp in 1917. They tried to form an Irish Brigade. We had one or two Irish roughnecks with us, but they wouldn't join it. A letter trying to interest people was circulated in our camp. It read like this:

"Irishmen. Here is your chance for you to fight for Ireland. You have fought for England, your country's hereditary enemy. You have fought for Belgium in England's interest, although it was no more to you than the Fiji Islands.

Are you willing to fight for your own Country, with a view to securing the national Freedom of Ireland, with the moral and material assistance of the German Government.

An Irish Brigade is being formed. The object of the Irish Brigade shall be to fight solely the cause of Ireland and under no circumstances shall it be directed to any German end. The Irish

Brigade shall be formed and shall fight under the Irish Flag alone, the men shall wear a special, distinctively Irish Uniform and have Irish Officers. The Irish Brigade shall be clothed, fed, and equipped with arms and ammunition by the German Government. At the end of the War the German Government undertakes to send each member of the Brigade, who may so desire it, to the United States of America with necessary means to land. The Irishmen in America are collecting money for the Brigade. Those men who do not join the Irish Brigade will be removed from Limburg and distributed among other camps.

If interested, see your Company Commanders. Join the Irish Brigade and win Ireland's Independence.

Remember Bachelors Walk.

God Save Ireland."

I didn't hear of anyone joining it; of course it would have been kept secret anyway.

On March 17th, 1918, the N.C.O.'s who had been in Germany up to three years were all sent to Saltan for a few days while they searched us and all our belongings, which did not amount to much. We boarded the train for Holland and some freedom, landing at Scheveningen near the Hague. There we were allowed a twenty mile radius. We had no way of going home. The officers were sent to Switzerland. During the last months of the war they sent us bread from Switzerland. There were no guards in Holland as it was neutral.

Soon after November 11, 1918, all but a dozen of us were repatriated back to England. Those of us detailed to stay behind were attached to the British Consulate for duties such as cleaning out all the billets at Hague. Then we went up to Rotterdam and we were billeted in the Maas Hotel across from the Maas Railway station where we had to meet all trains coming from Germany, escorting the P.O.W.'s as they arrived, down to the sheds at the docks. They were outfitted with new clothes and made quite presentable before being shipped home. The officers were put into hotels until the boats arrived. That duty kept me in Holland until January, 1919 when I returned to England.

Private Bertram Ashbourne
3RD BATTALION

I was wounded on April 25th 1915 at Langemarck. Not knowing anything about being taken prisoner of war, I did not know just exactly what was going to happen. The fellow next to me was wounded in the leg and his arm was pretty well off. We were lying together and we were picked up by two Uhlans on horseback. The Germans were going to fire at us, with their pistols drawn. Instead of finishing us off they picked us up and took our rifles away. We were escorted into a German trench. They told us that if we did what we were told we would be looked after and taken to a prison camp.

I was nine months in hospital in Germany. The doctor used to come in every day. He would look at my wound and get a pair of tweezers to pull the scab of my wound. He put iodine on it to give me additional pain. It was bad enough being wounded let alone trying to lengthen the time of my pain. It was more torture than anything else. The doctors did not care whether I came through it or not. Fortunately I did.

Eventually we ended up in a prison camp. There were about forty of us in a boxcar. All we had was water. We travelled for a day and a half. Our first camp was at Giessen, in the province of Essen, in Hanover.

We were sent out to work. There were various types of work that the Germans got us to do: sweeping out offices and out in the fields to cut heather, putting it in bundles and pushing it into camp. What it was used for I never knew. That was a pretty tough job. We worked from seven a.m. to about six p.m. When we worked in the fields there were guards all around. When we cut the heather and put it in big bundles by machinery, the Germans had trucks that we had to push on a narrow gauge railway into camp. By the time we got into camp we had just about had it. If we only had a little more food, we could have done more work. They did not have the food to give us I suppose.

Noon meant the Germans brought out the soup. It was made out of acorns without meat. Just bean soup or what they called 'stukgrubben'. It was terrible. There was no body in it. Nothing to help nourish us. The bread they gave us was made out of potatoes and some grain, but it was not very palatable. That was the routine day after day, until we were moved on to another camp.

I witnessed many escapes, but unfortunately not many of them got through. The Germans used to put up big signs, "This is the Holland border!" Holland was probably another twenty kilometres away, so one would naturally just take it easy after passing that 'sign' and the first thing one knew he was pounced on. It was pretty difficult to escape.

It was a terrible life. Day after day, month after month, year after year, wondering if we should ever get out of it. Every Friday the Germans gave us raw herring. We ate every bit of it except the head. The herrings were pickled. It was terrible, but it was a delicacy as far as we were concerned.

We used to get a Red Cross parcel once a month. My Mother used to send me the odd small parcel. They were short of food in England too. So they just sent small parcels containing bits of cake. We would share them with two or three friends: we mucked in together and split it. We could not get books or any reading material. We never knew how things were going on the outside. No newspapers. No nothing. We would sit around and talk to each other. That is all we could do besides prepare for the next day. Rain or shine, it did not make any difference. We went out to work.

The camp had about twenty different barracks. Long barracks about one hundred yards long or more. We had Russians, French, Italians there. I spoke a little German before I was released, but I have lost most of it now.

We used to have a bath once a week. As we entered the bathhouse, there was a fellow with a big box full of what they used to call 'sunlight soap'. It was a soft soap, not a piece of soap, but just like jelly. The fellow with the box of 'jelly' would slap it on your hand. We rubbed it all over ourselves. Then we got underneath the shower to wash it all off.

The defeated Germans took quite a few of us (the ex-kreigsgefangenen) out of the camp, by train, to Bremen, Germany. Then we were taken to a ship and boarded on it. All I had was my prisoner's uniform.

I do not know what happened to the Germans after Armistice Day. I never saw them again. There were no celebrations on November 11, 1918.It was just pure happiness. That is the only word I can use to describe the feeling. We did not think about drinks or anything like that. It was just a case of being free and able to walk around.

It was terrible when I first got back to England. I was there for nine months. I was always looking around to see if anybody was following me. After having guards look after you for about four years, you are looking to make sure you are not being followed.

When I got home a doctor advised me to drink port wine. "It's as good as anything," he said, "It will strengthen you and is good for you!" Port wine was pretty hard to get, so I used to go over to my brother's girlfriend's, after the bar was closed and have a few drinks. We used to go upstairs in the place and there was always port wine. If I had too much I could really get sick on it! It helped!

BATTLES OF FESTUBERT & GIVENCHY (1915)

Lieutenant Ian Sinclair
13TH BATTALION

In the entire 1st Division of twenty thousand men there was
only one company of French Canadians. There were one hundred
and fifty of them. Their officers were nice and we were fond of
them. They were a little odd in their ways. One of them was a chap
called Ercoule Vare who afterwards became the Canadian
Commissioner in Paris after the war ended. When the shelling at
Ypres started, Private Ercoule Vare was given a few hours leave to
go into the town of Ypres. He was having an affair with a Belgian
tart when a shell hit the roof of the building he was in. A splinter
wounded him in the seat. Afterwards the French gave out a bunch
of Croix de Guerre's and Medaille Militaire's to the Canadians for
their gallant show at Ypres. They requested particularly that the
decorations should go to French Canadians if possible. There were
so few French Canadians in the 1st Division that they practically
had to give one to everybody. Amongst those who got one was
Ercoule Vare. He received the Croix de Guerre! When this was
announced in our mess, after it came out in orders what he had
received, somebody said, "For God's sake! Ercoule Vare was
wounded in the seat when he was on top of a girl in Ypres." Eric
McCuaig, one of the comical men in our battalion, admonished,
"Ah yes, but you don't realize. He saved the maiden's life!"
Everybody laughed at that.

The next action we were in was at Festubert which was on the
20th of May, 1915. I did not see much of it because I was hit just
before we arrived in the attack position. I got a bullet through the
leg. We were moving up in broad daylight, so we were sitting ducks.
The Germans were just firing at us and shelling us on the road as
we advanced. At that time we thought that the British staff and our
own staff stupidly wasted lives against machine guns. We had very
few machine guns. The Germans had masses of them. Every time
we attacked we were just mowed down.

Private Ernest C. Robins
LORD STRATHCONA'S HORSE — 1ST DIVISION

We went to Rouen, France from England on the Princess Victoria. She
was a torpedo boat destroyer. After a week's training at Etaples we were
marched thirty miles up to Ypres on soaking wet cobblestone roads.
The first thing we knew we were in the battle at Festubert. Together with
some British mounted units we broke right through the Germans, never

losing many horses or men. Then we turned round and broke through again, only losing six men out of the whole outfit.

The Ghurkas were the ones to fight. They didn't always use a rifle. They had curved knives as sharp as a razor. They wouldn't stand up and go over the top. The Ghurkas crawled along the ground with a knife in their teeth. If one of us admired a Ghurka's knife and touched it, before he would put his knife back in the sheath he had to cut your finger. A single touch from the blade would draw blood. If they threw a knife at a target, say fifty feet away, you could guarantee they would hit it.

Private Frank Ashbourne
3RD BATTALION

At Festubert, one thousand of us went in and only five hundred returned. Again reinforced to one thousand we were cut right down to five hundred and sixty at Givenchy. On the morning of May 6, 1915, I was just going to fry some bully beef when a shell dropped beside me. It seemed to lift me right up in a dense cloud of vile black and green smoke. I was temporarily dazed and choked by the poisonous gases. I found I was wounded in the left side just behind the armpit and on the top of my top rib; also on the left eyebrow and just behind my left ear. As a result I was relieved of further active service as of February 9th, 1916, in Toronto, Ontario. My parents received the following letter from the War Office:

Canadian Record Office
7, Millbank, London, S.W.
May 8th, 1915.

Madam,

I regret to have to inform you that a report has this day been received to the effect that (No.) 9170 (Rank) Private (Name) F. Ashbourne (Regiment) 3rd Battalion, Canadians is reported "Missing".

I am at the same time to express the sympathy and regret of the Militia Council.

Any further information received in this office as to his condition or progress will be at once notified to you.

I am,
Madam,
Your obedient Servant,
 -(signed)-
Major D.AA.G.
For Officer in charge of Records.

While in hospital (the 3rd General Hospital) in Le Treport, France, I wrote home the following letter: (dated May 10, 1915): "I am sure you must all be wondering whether you are ever going to hear from me again, but it has been one of those cases where it was next to impossible to get a line or postcard off to you. Did you get the card, saying I was wounded?

From then till May 4th, I was attached to that regiment, not being able to trace the Q.O.R. They know now where I am, because the ambulance that took us to the station passed through the town where the Toronto Regiment are resting, and I gave some of the boys a shout. I was laid out for awhile with the awful gases, but soon came round. Since then there has been lots of pain, believe me. I think I have still some shrapnel to be taken out of my side, but I will be all right soon, and may be allowed to go and get a bit of my own back.

I wrote a long letter on the 22nd of April but it unfortunately got buried along with my pack, equipment and rifle in the trench when a shell exploded.

Private David Shand
1ST GORDON HIGHLANDERS

When I was a Pioneer in India, I used to help paint signs. You could get lost in the trenches what with communication trenches and all kinds of other trenches leading everywhere. The fellows used to get lost once in a while. I thought it would be a good idea if those trenches were named. We were digging dugouts at the time. We also painted the crosses in back of the billets for those who were killed. Then we took them to the cemetery. I started making signs for the trenches with names like "Fleet Street" and "The Strand". Some officers wanted to know who did it. They were told. They told me to keep on doing it. It was all my idea.

Private Leonard Wood
2ND EAST LANCASHIRE REGIMENT

Upon returning to France in 1915, I was drafted from the 1st East Lancs to the 2nd East Lancashire Regiment. The men in the 2nd were all strangers to me. We landed at Le Havre after a topsy-turvy sea ride. We had not been there more than a week or two when we were told we were going to be on the General's parade.

Once the General appeared, he picked up a microphone and

started 'spitting it out'. He said, "I haven't come to patronize you. I haven't come to praise you, but I've come to tell you that I was very surprised at the way you left England! It surprised me that men under my command should act that way."

The General was referring to the incident when we were up in Kensington Gardens, London, near Hyde Park. Instead of being about three quarters of a mile long, our troops were scattered three and three quarters of a mile along the road, dragging ourselves, some of us quite drunk. I don't know what the civilians thought of us! I suppose the boys thought, "Well, this is going to be the last time we're going to enjoy ourselves", so we enjoyed ourselves! So we were confined at Le Havre while the General told us off.

There was a large battle being fought in Frameries, near Mons. That day we were rushed up the line.

I was with a group that was sent into reinforce the battalion. Quite a few of us arrived that evening. They began sorting us out into Companies.

The next morning, when the whistle blew, the ladders went up in the trench and over the top — away we went. The quicker we went over the better. If we took our time, we were liable to stop two or three bullets. Bullets don't wait for you.

SOUCHEZ, LOOS &
A WAR OF ATTRITION (1915)

Private Leonard Wood
2ND EAST LANCASHIRE REGIMENT
The Germans had the advantage over us at Souchez. They held the hills in that spot. We were deployed below them and lost many men trying to get them out. We eventually placed mines under those Souchez hills and blew them up.

I had to shoot prisoners on one occasion. We couldn't trust a lot of the prisoners. While we were walking over to check them out, they'd have two or three bombs out. That tended to harden us. Just knowing that those were prisoners who were being well fed, sometimes eating better than us, made us angry. They were taking advantage of us, so to heck with that. No more trouble, we just finished them.

One night, in the trenches, someone came and passed the word,

"This way. Come out this way. Did you hear what I said?" We had to go along the communication trench to see if anyone was still alive or if we could be of help. Saying, "If we could help anybody", was a funny way of putting it, because as I shouldered my rifle and followed the trench, on either side there were men lying around, stone dead. I'd tap a guy on the shoulder and ask, "What's the matter, chum?" and he would fall back, dead. We were talking to dead men. It was enough to send us off our rockers.

We used to make a lot of our ammunition up into dum-dum bullets. When they hit a bone inside someone, they spread outward. We made them by shreding the bullets. I used them when I was a sniper in the front lines. I would notice where the enemy fire was coming from and say to myself, "Ah hah, I'll get you this time!" Those dum-dum bullets quietened them down. I seldom missed my target. When you're a sniper you don't play with the enemy. You hit them.

We had a song that started, "Rats, rats, as big as alley cats..." Sometimes we'd look over a trench to see if anyone was coming and we'd see these great big green eyes staring back at us! It was a big man-eating rat. They used to climb over the trench and plop on our helmets, as we lay sleeping. Sometimes we never knew where to hide our food. If we were in a barn, we'd get a rope or piece of wire and hang the food from the rafters. Those rats were wise though. They'd scurry up there and shinny down the rope. Away goes our food! It wasn't a very nice sensation to have a rat flop down on your head or see one skittering around as you are trying to sleep. That's why a lot of the places we slept in were full of lice.

Lieutenant Albert Winn
ROYAL FIELD ARTILLERY

The first time I was under gas was at the Battle of Loos in September, 1915. We were bombarding Jerry. Jerry retired and we advanced, digging fresh positions. We had just got our gun in a new position when we noticed a big shell hole at the back of us. It was the result of one of Jerry's heavy shells. That shell hole was used as a burial ground because some of our troops looked like they were fast asleep. They were sitting up in the shell hole, gassed to death.

When the Germans used the gas at Loos we lost a hell of a lot of men. Then we counterattacked and the wind changed direction in our favour. As a result the gas was going back on the Germans and killing them as well. We were not prepared. We had no respirators or anything like that.

At the battle of Loos where we had advanced, there was a group of buildings that had been flattened by Jerry's gunfire. We heard a round of shots. It was a firing squad. They were sent in because of a court martial. It was for desertion. That was the first time we ever saw that sort of thing. Some men dug a hole and buried the court martialed men and carried on. Their families were notified, but I don't know what they said in the death certificate, whether you were shot for desertion or not. I think they were listed as 'killed in action'. Officers used to desert too. They just seemed to disappear.

We had a group detailed for a burial party. They had to get their identification cards from them as well as their paybooks. It may sound like red tape, but it was necessary to get the man's history for his people. There was a dead officer who had a brand new raincoat ('burberry' or mackintosh) on, one of the most expensive you could buy in England. He was a Second Lieutenant. The cry came up, "Who's going to get it first?" Of course it depended on the size of the man who was there. That was the sort of thing that used to go on.

The 18 pounders had one man pulling the 'trigger'. One man checked the sights which were marked in degrees; twelve degrees on each side. The gun had a limber with ammunition. The crew would hand out the shells. One fellow set the fuses. The Sergeant in charge said, "Five rounds gunfire, range 3,500 (then the fuse man brought the fuse around to the angle that was given), angle so and so", and the fuse was handed to the man who loads. The officer in charge stands back.

The guns were on two 'reliefs', otherwise a man could not keep his eyes open. With an 18 pounder gun or a howitzer, a Sergeant was in charge . After someone had shouted the range, he looked through his viewfinder and adjusted it to the left or right, according to what he hears from the O.P. (Observation Post). He reports to the Captain or Major who is supervising that shoot. The gunner manipulated the gun. We had sandbags to prop up the wheels. Otherwise when we fired the guns, they would recoil and be out of alignment for the target. Every time we finished firing, we had to get the Number Three man to check his target. If it was a church spire on the enemy's side, the O.P. might say, "Range 3,500. Target: church spire" because the gunner could not see what he was firing at.

All artillery men were issued with little rubber earplugs. Those fitted on our gas respirators, which we had at all times, after the Loos battle. The bigger the gun, the louder the noise. Deafening! That is why I'm deaf in one ear and not so bad in the other.

A gunner can overestimate. During an attack there were many times when shells dropped short and killed our own men.

A Canadian Field Artillery Howitzer Battery takes time out for a tobacco chew

Premature bursts were another reason or the ground might have
been a bit spongey. After firing five or six rounds, perhaps a wheel
would sink. That would send us off our target. We had to sit down
and work all those things out. There might have been an old farm
house behind us. We would send some fellows back for some of the
bricks out of the building; perhaps to put under a sunken wheel.
We had all sorts of schemes in order to get on target.

We had a lot of duds. They burst either before their time or
not at all. After two days of gunfire, the enemy knew something
was coming, with a heavy gun concentrating on an area. That was
where we found duds. An O.P. would see them. Sometimes the
shells landed in our own front line, they dropped so short. Later on
of course, the artillery would get hell from the infantry. Like,
"What the hell were you doing back there?" and a few other choice
words. That happened on both sides.

The next morning after being in the line about four or five
days, our signaller put me through to the battery on the telephone.
Earlier the signaller had seen a Red Cross ambulance coming down
an incline on the German side. He said, "Last night it was very
quiet, so I wondered why this ambulance was around." My C.O.
and the powers that be at Headquarters go their heads together and
figured out something was wrong. The following morning we were
told to keep a special lookout. At the least sign of movement we
were to open fire. It was suspected that the three or four Red Cross
ambulances sighted were being used for the wrong purpose. The
next morning those ambulances turned up. Working parties, with
picks and shovels, got out of them. The Germans were using the
Red Cross as a cover. Of course we got about three or four direct
hits on them. We could see the Germans dropping, so we knew we
got them. I got a pat on the back for that.

Private David Shand
1ST GORDON HIGHLANDERS

At Loos, the gas was high at first. Then it would come down
and drift all over the ground. Any guy that was lying wounded was
lucky to escape the gas. One Irish fellow started to leave his trench.
We told him to get back in the trench. He said, "I can't! There's gas
there! There's gas all over and I can't go in there!"

We didn't have masks, but I knew that putting water on the
face and mouth would help. Either that or go up a tree, but there
were no trees within miles of the trenches! Just shellholes. There
was a dead man beside me, so I used his water bottle. I was ready

for the gas. When the gas did come over the top of the trench, before I could get my water bottle ready, I got a couple of whiffs. It was like somebody had a tight hold on my throat. I threw the water over my face.

Then we saw about thirty Germans advancing. They had two machine guns. The Germans spoke to each other, thinking we were all dead. A fellow on my right had cleaned his machine gun. We cleaned the mud off our rifles. When the Germans were closer we killed the whole lot of them. We took their two machine guns. It took me two or three days to get over the gas, though I never reported sick. I could feel it in my throat.

We were out of the trenches for a week. A young officer gave us a lecture. He said, "We're going to take all these villages around Ypres and then we're going to turn around to the left and then come down the coast." I was smiling at him. He said, "Mr. Shand. What are you smiling about?" I stated, "Listen Sir, I've been up and down this Menin Road dozens of times. Every time we go up there our men get killed. Then I'm lucky to get back again. You know what will happen instead of taking all those villages? We'll go up two or three yards in front of our trench." That's what happened.

Lieutenant Walter Moorhouse
4TH CANADIAN MOUNTED RIFLES

We left Caesar's Camp on October 2nd and entrained at Shorncliffe for Southampton where we embarked with our transport on S.S. Maidan, arriving at Le Havre on October 24th. After a circuitous railroad trip we detrained at Bailleul and finished up in hutments called Aldershot camp, surrounded by seas of mud. I saw a cookhouse orderly carrying a side of beef slip on the duckboards and in saving himself shot the carcass off his shoulder into the mud where it disappeared. However, it was soon hauled out, hosed down, and went into the stew.

The O.C. 5th C.M.R. asked me to take him round the line. He was the most intensely serious officer I can remember. As we passed through the front line he picked up a rifle and asked a sentry the cryptic question, "What four things am I thinking about?" I saw a gleam in the sentry's eye, "Four days out in rest billets." The Col. denied this forcibly and, turning to the sentry on the fire step, repeated the question. Nothing daunted he replied "Four long glasses of beer, sir." "No, no!" returned the officer, "I'm thinking of the four principal parts of the Ross rifle — lock, stock, barrel & bolt," continuing with a musketry lecture listened to with amusement by all within earshot.

Private David Guild (1894-)
13TH BATTALION

At Messines the distance between the trenches was eight hundred to nine hundred yards. The Germans were on top of a hill.
We were down in the mud. We used to drive in big wooden posts with a wooden mallet. We stood on an ammunition box, pounding the posts in for the barbed wire. We went out on wiring parties at dusk. The Germans had wiring parties out, so it was a case of live and let live. Later on that changed. We would never hear a sound when out on a raid.

We had a fellow there who was a trapper in northern Canada. In the early morning he used to take off into No Man's Land. He would set snares. Then he always came back with a rabbit for us.

On our right at Messines was a Scottish battalion. I was sitting talking to them one morning in their trench. The Colonel came along. We all stood up, but did not salute, as he passed by. I happened to mention to one of the men, "Boy, That Colonel of yours sure looks like Winston Churchill!" The soldier looked at me with a funny look and said, "It is Winston Churchill!"

ACTIONS OF HILL 60, LONGUEVAL & ST. ELOI CRATERS (1916)

Lieutenant Colonel John Smith Stewart
7TH BRIGADE/C.F.A.

I was up at 3:45 a.m. on April 6th because the enemy had made an attack on the Craters at St. Eloi and drove our men out. The 27th Battalion drove them out of one trench, taking only one prisoner. We did a lot of counter battery work in the early morning. Germans were very busy attacking us. One shell hit near a horse and blew a man in the air. He lost a leg. Most of our batteries fired all afternoon. The 25th Battery fired all night. On April 8th, I got in the staff car and went for Colonel King. We called on General Morrison at Reninghilst and arrived at Eceke about midnight. The 5th Brigade, Northumberland Royal Field Artillery relieved us, but our 25th and 28th Batteries did some wire cutting, firing six hundred rounds south of Pecaham. On April 13th I visited Vermspele and many other places of interest. The ground at Scottish Wood was peppered by shelling during the previous scrap. It sure looked honeycombed. Two days later I went with Colonel

Dodds and some other officers to view a position in the Bollartbeek valley. Germans sent over many shells in the afternoon, otherwise it was quiet there. We are still uncertain as to who owns the front lines around St. Eloi.

On April 21st, the enemy had three observation balloons up. The 28th Battery had one gun hit the night before. One man was wounded. The gun had the shield and buffer springs cover punctured. The enemy shelled Dickebusch for an hour with gas shells. The odor was very pungent, smelling of chlorine and formaldehyde. Four days later the Germans shelled the support trenches near St. Eloi with gas shells. On April 26th, enemy planes dropped bombs just north of Dickebusch. Two prisoners were captured opposite Eloi. One of them stated that they have gas cylinders in the trenches opposite our old positions and intend to use same as soon as wind is favourable. A strenuous bombing attack from the craters lasted one hour. On Sunday, April 30th the enemy sprang their gas attack at Eloi, opposite Mount Kemmel and got into our trenches, but were soon driven out. There was very heavy artillery fire to our right.

Private James Doak
52ND BATTALION

February 27, Sunday: The Chaplain spoke to the men in a very nice way and pleaded with them to watch and pray. Only lasted fifteen minutes, because the men were standing to their shoe tops in mud and slush.

A few yards away were prisoners doing first field punishment, their arms tied outstretched to the wheels of a transport wagon, their toes barely touching the ground. This for two hours at a stretch. It's not right and I have vowed that if any officer ever causes me such pain and humiliation, I will square with him at the first opportunity.

Thursday, March 2nd: Second issue of gas helmets. Fell in at 4:30 for our first trip to the trenches in front of Kemmel Hill. Reached trenches at eight o'clock. We were now in what is known as "The Glory Hole". This was where the 28th Battalion were mined and where whole platoons were buried in the crater.

Only 35 yards separate the two lines of trenches. The 7th Brigade are holding the line and we are in for experience. B Company is with the 49th Battalion. They treated us fine. I stood guard with the sentry till six a.m. Felt rather uncomfortable and was continually ducking when I heard the bullets. My mate told me it was no use ducking a bullet that you heard, as it had already gone. He did not add to my peace of mind when he said, "You'll never hear the bullet that hits you."

Friday night — 10th — Arrived at dugout in the Dickebusch reserve line late tonight after seven mile tramp with full pack and 24 hour rations. Had just turned in when we were called out again to carry rations to firing line. Worst trip yet. Night black as ink, mud and water to the knees. Got back at 3:30. Clothes have not been dry for two weeks. Wonder why I ever left my happy home.

Tuesday, March 14, 1916: Things quiet along the line. Rifle grenade from across the way tore out a sandbag close to my post, covering me with dust. It threw a man size scare into me as well, but a miss is as good as a mile.

Thursday, March 23: Up at 3:30, breakfast at four. Hit the road in heavy marching order at six a.m. Marched about ten miles over bad roads part of the way and a good many of the men including myself are nearly all in. It's a tough proposition for the young lads of 19 or 20. I saw some of them drop out crying by the roadside. Marched the last two hours without a stop. Men are treated like a cross between a pack mule and a transport wagon. My feet are all in for the first time, both my ankles being strained. (En route from Fletre to Ouderdom via Renningheist.)

Saturday, April 1: Near the Cloth Hall at support dugouts, Private Fleet and I were in a 5x6' dugout with the bunk built the narrow way, so that when we laid down we had to stick our feet up on the wall at the bottom. Known as "Border Dugouts", they were condemned soon after.

Sunday, April 2: We have to keep in our dugouts out of sight. Hill 60 is on our right. I went to sleep this a.m. and dreamed I was at home fixing a grandfather clock that had stopped. Thought while I was working I could hear the shells bursting and see them flashing through the open window, so I told my wife who was lying in bed that it was no use fixing the clock as the concussion of the shells would stop it from running. Just then an extra heavy shell exploded and I dodged pieces coming in the window, one of which hit me on the hand. I woke up with the noise of an explosion ringing in my ears and the dirt falling all over me from the ceiling of the dugout. A terrible bombardment is going on to the right of our front.

Wednesday—5: Hec and I up to the reserve trenches today with the company. Lieutenant Hatton was killed early today while inspecting an enemy sap in front of our line. He died instantly. We were shelled violently for half an hour and were covered with debris, but escaped unhurt. Although I thought at one time our chances for getting out alive were nil. Shells blew down part of our front line trenches and Sergeant Mathison was shot through the head by an enemy sniper whom he was trying to locate. I never expect to have any close calls myself and came through. Moving tonight to Maple Copse for four days in supports.

Friday, April 28: Saw my old friend Hugh O'Brien of Fort William yesterday. He looks well, but changed a lot; getting that grey look of the veteran. We are leaving for the line in an hour's time.

Monday, May 1st: Went to front line and saw by the light of a flare one of my pals lying on the firing step. I slapped his leg and was shocked to find that he was dead.

Wednesday, May 3rd: In the evening our engineers blew up a mine that they had laid under an enemy sap. The sap was driving under our position. As soon as the mine went up the enemy started shelling our front line and communication trenches, thinking no doubt that we were preparing for an attack. We had several wounded. One call came from the communication trench. My mate and I went down. I brought a stretcher. My mate fixed up the wounded man. He had to see another case, leaving me and a bomber to carry the wounded out. As we started down, the trench was a regular hell of shrapnel. The other carrier was hit. I was forced to go back up the trench for help and got two more men.

We started again, but in a few minutes the men found themselves unable to handle the stretcher in the narow trench. I went back up a second time. It was getting near daybreak. The wounded had to be taken out under cover of darkness or not at all.

On my way up I met up with another party who had a badly wounded man. The men were unwilling to face the hellish fire in the trench. They were Russians. This time I went to Company Headquarters and told the Captain that I must have help to get the men out.

A Lieutenant and Sergeant from the 1st C.M.R. volunteered to help. The Sergeant, a big six-footer took the wounded man on his back. Sergeant Jack Wallace took another on his back. The Lieutenant and I took the stretcher case. After hard work we got the men out. In my efforts to get the men out I lost sight of the danger.

Wednesday, May 24th (Victoria Day): At six a.m. the enemy were giving us an impromptu concert. They used whistles, mouth organs and bugles. Some of them were singing "Rule Britannia". They kept it up for half an hour, helping the Canadians celebrate the 24th. Fairly quiet all day and evening here at Observatory Ridge.

Wednesday, June 14th, 1916: During the Zillebeke Battle the sky above the trenches reembled a thousand blast furnaces in operation. The noise was terrible. We lay on the ridge for an hour waiting for the signal to advance. All of us knew what the signal was and where to look for it. Two battalions of the 7th Brigade held firm. An hour after daybreak, we were ordered to retire. We had just come through 18 days of fighting.

I was sent out to Ypres with a bunch of walking wounded and one stretcher case. The dead were piled so high in the trench that we had to go out in the open. We got safely through. One wounded man of the party got hit again, but not very seriously. I was ordered to report to my company further down the line, but when I reached the place, nothing was known about B Company so I reported and became attached to C Company in the line.

We went back up the trench, carrying ammunition and water and stayed there until 9:30 Sunday morning. Then they began to sort the battalions out. The 22nd, 58th, 43rd, 60th, King's Royal Rifles, some Guards, the Welsh, the 16th, 42nd, P.P.C.L.I., R.C.R.'s and others were all mixed up.

The dead lay three and four deep in all trenches. In some cases where one man lay alone his body had been trampled in the darkness, almost beyond recognition as a human form in the mud. Bodies without heads were numerous. Altogether the sight was almost too gruesome for human nerves to stand. Although as I look back I know all the men were working more or less mechanically. Sensitive nerves were dead. The men paid little or no attention to their surroundings. The past days had been too gruelling.

Sunday night I went with a party of 100 men to carry out wounded from Hooge. Although we were shelled all up and down the Menin Road we had very few casualties. We brought out the last wounded man to the Mill dressing station on the Menin Road. Here we were given hot cocoa and biscuits. A feast fit for a king, we thought.

All this time I was worrying about getting back to my own company, but they only had one first aid man with C Company.

Tuesday morning I hunted up B Company which was billeted in a Belgian chateau. I was welcomed as one back from the dead by Captain Thompson and Sergeants Brand and Sharp. They had me on their "missing" list.

Captain Ian Sinclair
13TH BATTALION

In April, 1916 I was just doing ordinary trench work when the
Germans started to shell Company Headquarters. That was at Hill
60. We thought we were all trapped because they made a direct hit
on us. So we went outside the building. I had the officers and men
spread out along the trench. We learned afterwards that the
Germans, from their position, could see everything we were doing.
As soon as they saw us move into the open they changed to
shrapnel. A shell burst over my head and I got a splinter of
shrapnel through my shoulder. That sent me to the field hospital for
awhile.

Lance Corporal David Guild
13TH BATTALION

We were in and out of the Hill 60 area for quite awhile. On
April 19th, I was a Private on sentry duty in our trench. The front
trenches were pretty close. We could lob a bomb from our trench
into a German one. The Germans started sending over rifle
grenades. The grenades landed pretty near to us. I was looking over
the parapet, not paying much attention when all of a sudden I got a
wallop in the jaw. I found myself sitting in the trench bottom, so I
got up, not thinking there was too much wrong, and went on sentry
duty again. I had my waterproof sheet wrapped around myself as it
was raining. Blood was running down my poncho and I wondered
what was wrong. I thought something had knocked my teeth out. I
didn't know I had a hole in my cheek. The Sergeant came along. I
turned around and said to him, "I don't know what's the matter. I
can't stop bleeding." He took one look at me and said, "Get down
to the dressing station!" I still didn't know I had a hole in my
cheek.

The medical staff bandaged me up, after a brief stop at
Battalion Headquarters. At field ambulance I was trying to smoke
as I was reading the funny papers. I don't know why. I couldn't
smoke because the air was coming in through the side of my face.
The doctor said to me, "Come on Jock. It's your turn!" He gave me
a shot of tetanus serum which was a darn sight worse than the
wound. I went down to a Boulogne hospital. I still didn't know
what was wrong with myself. One morning the doctor came in. He

put on a pair of rubber gloves. The next thing I saw was his finger through the hole in my cheek. I was sent to England to convalesce for a few months.

Private Craigie T. Mackie
2ND GORDON HIGHLANDERS

In February, 1916, I was a runner carrying messages from battalion headquarters to company headquarters. I went down to the village one cold windy day. I looked into an estaminet. Our support lines were nearby, so I went in the estaminet to see if there were any Gordon Highlanders in it. The Madame shouted at me, "Ferme la porte!" I didn't know a word of what she had said. I asked, "What did you say?" She replied, "Shut the fucking door!" I knew what that meant and said, "Okay. Okay. I was just looking to see if any Highlanders were here." She said, "Yes, there's Highlanders." I never forgot that.

Private David Shand
1ST GORDON HIGHLANDERS

We refused to wear the first steel helmets when they came out because they were too heavy. The ones issued later were lighter. We were in St. Eloi, south-east of Ypres. The helmets were given to us the day before.

Our job was to take up rations and engineer supplies to the trenches. We picked up the rations about three miles behind the trenches. After making one trip between the trenches, we retired for the night. However, after midnight the Sergeant came around and said, "You've got to turn out again." We went out and I said to one fellow, "I think I'll put on my steel helmet."

A shell exploded about two hundred yards straight across from us. I said to one fellow, "For the love of Mike! If another shell comes down here it will be pretty close to us!" Then another shell came swishing over our heads. We ducked down. If I hadn't ducked the shrapnel would have cut me in half rather than wound me in the head as I was pushing the cart. All the other fellows had disappeared somewhere. The cart was smashed. I was left wandering all around there by myself. There were nine big shellholes right beside the little railway track. The German observation planes must have given their artillery our location. Those shellholes were fifteen feet deep, twenty feet across and were three quarters full of water. There was just a small space between each shell hole. A man could have drowned in them.

Wounded and alone, I at least had the sense to turn around and head for my trenches. I kept wandering and falling down. The nearest support trench was about a mile away. The helmet was stuck right to my head. I eased it off. The blood came down my arm, running off of my elbow. Sometimes I crawled on my hands and knees. Then I had to lay down. I had lockjaw because of my head wound. I couldn't open my mouth or speak. My jaws were shut tight! It bothered me more than the head wound. I felt dizzy. I was ready to go to sleep. I said to myself, "If I dpon't get up I'll die here." I lost an awful lot of blood and would have died there too. Then the fellow who helped me with the cart earlier, came over with a stretcher bearer party. They passed me by just a few yards. I could not draw attention to myself, but finally one of them saw me. They picked me up and took me back to a dugout.

The doctor was looking for the shell-shocked and bad cases. One fellow pointed to me and said, "I think we better try and get a doctor for him." I said, "It's no good Mack. I've lost too much blood. I don't think I'll live more than fifteen or twenty minutes." My right eye was banged up and I was deaf in one ear. The wound in my head was the size of a fifty cent piece. It broke my skull. They took fifteen pieces of shrapnel and bone out of my head. An English fellow said to me, "Jock I don't think you're so bad as you think you are." I said, "Don't you think so?" "No," he said. That guy gave me new hope for life. I was letting myself go, as I figured there was no hope for me.

After a month they moved me to England. When I got to Newcastle Hospital the wound in my head was still pretty bad. I had to go through a slight operation. The nurse told me, "You get up. You're going to walk down the stairs for an operation." I said, "My feet haven't touched the ground in about two months." I got out of bed and fell flat on my face.

My wound was still fairly bad, but an old doctor passed me as being fit without even examining me! That was in August, 1916, at the time of the Somme battle. Some men who were deaf and even crippled were being sent to France. I got back to France. A Sergeant came along with another old doctor and said, "Any man that thinks he's fit enough for the trenches go up to that hut there." I did as he said. The Sergeant asked me what was wrong. I told him, "I've got a bad wound in the head. I don't think I can wear a steel helmet. My wound's not healed yet." He asked, "How did you pass the doctor to get out here?" I replied, "The same way I'm passing you and that blooming doctor there! I'm going to the trenches again!" I did go back to the front again too.

Private Leonard Wood
2ND EAST LANCASHIRE REG.

A German had been holding himself off, for I don't know how many days. He desperately had to go someplace. However he couldn't because of the constant firing all around. At that time, I was still a machine gunner. I spotted this German leaving his mates and heading towards a tree away from the trenches. He was right in front, unaware of my position with the machine gun. I thought, well, if I don't get him, he's going to get me, so I let him have it. Down he went. I've often thought back. How would I have liked it, having to go someplace and once there, getting riddled. Awful.

During raiding parties, the Germans seldom opened fire on us. No one fired until the last minute. The same thing with us. For a noiseless weapon in trench fights, we used a stick-like object, like the top of a pick, that came to a point. It was flat on the sides and good for clubbing purposes. We used to surprise the enemy and club them or else use our bayonets. I first used a bayonet in France. If you stuck it in a person, you had to pull it out. You still want to hang onto your rifle, so you put your foot against the victim's chest and yank it out! The poor guy would scream out blue murder, but it would be just the same if he had me!

At an estaminet in Bac St. Maur there used to be an old "hammer and tongues" (piano) of the wind up variety. Two Spanish women ran the place. I looked after the piano. The men used to pay me money to hear me play. I also used to play piano at the officers' mess. The men also gave me drinks, which I lined up on top of the piano. It was pretty hard to play after awhile. All that vin rouge! Bac St. Maur was near Armentieres.

Private Frank Ashbourne
3RD BATTALION

The following day the 3rd Battalion were advancing again. They went south and took Rovrouy. They found a German canteen containing 70,000 cigars and 300,000 cigarettes, which were taken back in loads on ration wagons. That action took place near Zillebeke.

Private James F. Johnson
6TH CANADIAN MOUNTED RIFLES

As a rule there were three lines of trenches: the front line, the support line, and the reserve line. Troops in the front were kept alert at all times.

Men in the support trenches had a chance to sleep and rest in the day time. At night under cover of darkness, we would form working parties, carrying material up to the front line from the points where horses or trucks had placed it. When anyone went into the front line in the daytime he would have to follow the crooked communication trenches for a long way. However, in the darkness everyone travelled over land. The reserve line was further to the rear, and companies took turns in these lines. Of course every man regardless of where he was situated was ready at all times in case of attack. We never removed our shoes or equipment while on duty in the trenches. The periods of time spent in trench duty varied up to ten days or two weeks.

The changing of troops took place during darkness when everything was quiet. All you heard was the rattle of equipment. Of course the noise of shell fire and machine guns helped to some extent in that the noise hindered the Germans from hearing our movements. Whenever they did hear anything unusual, they would open up with whizzbang shells which were fired from small field guns especially designed for front line effect. They also kept No Man's Land pretty well lit up on a dark night by discharging flares from pistols. Men on working parties had to be extremely careful as they were in the open.

The B.E.F. on guard in a trench at Ovillers, 1916.

Barbed wire played quite an important part in trench warfare in front of both German lines and ours, where continuous lines of barbed wire entanglements extended along the whole front. We had not been issued with steel helmets at that time. We had a crude form of gas mask. As time went on we had more and more equipment to carry.

Late in November, 1915, I became ill with bronchial pneumonia. My condition did not improve, but got worse, so I was removed by ambulance, taken aboard a hospital train and went to Number One Canadian General Hospital, near Etaples. It was a large hospital. Most of the wards were long canvas tents with a dispensary in the centre. Most of the patients happened to be Imperials. When I was carried into the receiving station I heard a nurse say, "I am going to have him in my ward as I haven't one Canadian there." Another nurse spoke up and said, "I haven't either." The whole staff was Canadian. I was soon carried to my ward. The head nurse was Sister Jones from Vancouver. She was a middle-aged woman and a very fine nurse. She certainly looked after me. Of course she looked after everyone. The doctor examined me every day.

One day Sister Jones told him, "This boy isn't eating well," so the doctor asked me if I was a teetotaller. I said, "Not exactly." So he prescribed a bottle of Guinness stout before each meal. By Christmas I was able to walk around the ward. On Christmas morning, Sister Jones called me into the dispensary and said, "I have a job for you." She had a supply of wine and brandy. She said, "I want you to look after this and see that everyone in the ward has an appetizer, and you may have one or two if you wish." There were around eighty patients. It must have cost Sister Jones something. I think the doctor helped pay for it. We were served a very nice dinner considering the hospital was generally filled to capacity.

In January, 1916, we were evacuated to England. I went to Bevan Hospital just west of Folkestone, a place called Sandgate right on the beach. We received vey fine treatment from the English V.A.D. nurses. My health seemed to be improving every day so after three weeks I was sent to a Canadian convalescent home situated at Walmer near Deal, a few miles east of Dover. I played my first ground hockey there. The patients used to play the nurses and boy were they rough. I had my shins blackened quite frequently. All of us enjoyed our stay at Walmer.

Since leaving France the C.M.R.'s had been reorganized. Instead of six regiments there were four making up the 8th Infantry

Brigade. Most of the former 6th were in the 5th C.M.R. I left for France again on June 2nd, 1916.

Back in France I did not go directly to the C.M.R.'s, but the trench mortars were just being formed so I became a mortar man. We worked along with the 3rd Division Infantry. The mortar we used threw a round bomb weighing sixty pounds. We generally fired those mortars at around three hundred yards, so we had to have them right up front because No Man's Land varied in distance. We knocked out enemy machine gun emplacements, barbed wire, et cetera.

About the middle of June we went in the line to the right and front of Ypres. It had been a nice city but all that remained was rubble. A few walls of the famous Cloth Hall remained tottering on their foundations. Large German shells were screaming into the town and the surrounding country where our artillery were entrenched.

We waited there till dark then proceeded forward to Zillebeke Lake (dugouts were called Zillebeke Bunds) where there were dugouts just to the rear of the lake, used mainly as headquarters. There was nothing left of the trenches we moved into except tree stumps and holes. That night we carried sandbags, dug trenches and carried all kinds of supplies to the front. Hundreds of men were doing this. Just before daylight we had to crawl into holes like rats. When it was dark we ventured out. We lived like that for about ten days.

The sector we were in was called the Ypres Salient. It was shaped like a horseshoe. We were in the horseshoe when we received enemy fire from three sides. I could never understand why the line was not straightened out but I suppose the higher ups knew more about such matters. We were on that front through June, July and August, the hottest months of the year. Hundreds of remains of bodies both German and our own were only partly buried. The stench throughout was terrible. It was quite a common thing while digging trenches at night to strike a decomposed body which had to be moved. The Sergeant came to me one night and said, "How is your stomach, Foster? I have tried three men on a job ahead and they can't take it." I did the job but I was glad it was a dark night. Every night stretcher bearers were stumbling over rough ground getting the wounded to dressing stations. On top of all that we were all filthy, dirty, and lousy.

While on that front we went into action at Hill 60. The C.M.R.'s were in the front line. We never felt comfortable in that area as there had been many bitter struggles there. Sure enough one morning, just breaking daylight a German raid took place. Four of us were in our mortar emplacements where we had been firing mortars. We were kind of isolated. The Germans each had a loaf of bread tied to their equipment. They passed on each side of us. Corporal Birchill said, "Well, I guess this is it. If they hold out any length of time we will be prisoners." However the troops in support drove them back much to our relief. Before the Germans reached their trenches they suffered severe casualties.

By mid 1916 all our trenches and fighting equipment had improved immensely. Month after month there was more artillery and more of our planes in the air. However, our planes had not reached the proficiency of the German Fokkers.

At Kemmel Hill our communication trench called Poppy Lane went through a nice bunch of trees. Among those trees blackberry bushes were very plentiful; just loaded with berries which was quite a luxury for us. One afternoon one of the boys was filling his mess tin when a shell came over. He was wounded by the shrapnel. When he was in a base hospital the doctor who was taking particulars asked him what he was doing when he was wounded. He replied, "I was picking blackberries." The doctor laughed and said, "We can't give you a medal for that."

Just before leaving that front I received my first promotion as Lance Corporal or Bombardier as called in the mortars. Our Regimental Sergeant Major was a Boer War veteran, and a tall fine looking man with a black moustache which he kept neatly waxed at both ends. Shortly after I got my stripe he detailed six men and told me to take them and clean up our tent lines. Working away with them I saw him standing over beside his tent. All of a sudden I heard him bawl out, "Bombardier Johnson!" I went over and he said, "I gave you six men to do this job and I don't want you to do anything except supervise the details." I said, "Well Sir I think I would have more respect of the men if I helped with the work." He said, "Perhaps you are partly right, but that isn't the way the army looks at it!"

Lieutenant Walter Moorhouse
4TH CANADIAN MOUNTED RIFLES

Machine guns were under the new Bde. M.G.O., Maj. Balfour who started a Bde. M.G. School and range. During this rest period I met my brother Vic several times, who was with the 1st Canadian Field Ambulance. Finally we were moved to Poperinghe and in the middle of March took over trenches in front of Zillebeke and came under the menacing spell of the Ypres salient and in particular of Sanctuary Wood. Typical of the grim humour that infested the Salient was a story told of the advance of a Canadian Scottish unit sent forward to check the Hun's advance during the 2nd battle of Ypres. The Padre was standing by a gate in the ramparts, watching their advance. "Where are we going, Padre?" shouted one of the Scots. "That depends on the kind of life you've led," answered the Padre.

I remember one occasion when we used a 'Caltrop' as a paperweight in the Orderly room. These caltrops in the early part of the war were scattered on roads to delay or prevent the passage of enemy cavalry, a most inhumane practice. A caltrop is of iron, consisting of four spikes with equidistant spacing so that however thrown on the ground, one spike remains pointing upward. These were ancient weapons dating back to a very early period of history.

THE BATTLES OF THE SOMME (1916)

Bombardier James F. Johnson
5TH CANADIAN MOUNTED RIFLES
Around the 1st of September the whole Canadian Corps moved to the Somme front which was about sixty miles south of Ypres. Our unit was loaded into boxcars one morning. We were the good part of the day travelling to our destination. Seldom did troops have transportation provided for them, but when they did it was either boxcars or double decker buses similar to the ones in London. On the end of the boxcar was printed so many hommes and on the other end so many chevaux, but I think we were squeezed in to more than the specified capacity.

The next three months proved to be a very tough consignment for the whole Canadian Corps. It turned out to be offensive battles from both sides. Trenches changed hands frequently. There were no major advances from either side and casualties were very heavy. The ground in the Somme area was different from other fronts. When we dug down a couple of feet the formation was chalk. There wasn't much chance to camouflage as the trenches and parapets showed up very plainly with the white outlines.

Tanks, which were invented and manufactured in Britain, were used for the first time in history and were used with great effect until November when the rains came. The ground became so sodden from the rains and shellfire that nothing could move except horses and men on foot; even that was almost impossible at times. The tanks were manufactured and transported to the front in great secrecy. I don't think anyone had any idea what they were until then. The Germans were a surprised lot when they first saw those big awkward, cumbersome looking armoured vehicles come bobbing over our trenches and into their defense lines, spitting machine gun bullets through their turrets as they came.

We often wondered why these machines were called tanks. We were later told on good authority why this name had been chosen. When the time had come to ship them to the front, they would need a name which could not be interpreted by the enemy. The word "tank" might mean many things such as watering tanks for horses, et cetera.

After seeing the tanks in action I was very impressed. The most serious drawback was mud, which got very deep at times. Their speed was about three miles per hour.

In the meantime, our Division Commander had a request from the 51st Scottish Division Commander wondering if we could spare some mortar men as they needed the support badly. So our unit was detailed for that assignment. We felt it quite a privilege to serve with the famous kilted 51st Division from Scotland which included the Gordons, Argyles, Black Watch, et cetera. They had been known to go over the top headed by their pipers. The Canadian and Scottish kilties had been dubbed by the Germans as "The Ladies from Hell."

Our headquarters was at Englebelmer. The British Royal Naval Division was also in that area. They were preparing to take Beaumont Hamel. Our unit, the mortars, about two hundred men, were the only Canadian troops to participate in that engagement.

The first time we went up the line, we entered the communication trench called "Picadilly" at Birmingham Dump. A dump was where all kinds of supplies were kept and were carried by foot to various positions. The trench was in good repair, zigzagging quite a long way. I was impressed with the white chalky parapets throughout the trench system.

We received fine cooperation from the divisions. They helped carry our weapons in and carried most of our bombs. We could not have carried these bombs in as we were going to fire from twelve hundred to two thousand bombs every twenty-four hours. We did quite a lot of night firing then as there was a ridge in front of us that partly obscured the flash from our mortars. The German trenches were in a shallow valley and we had good observation from our lines overlooking the Ancre River, a small stream! Some months previous to that the Scottish troops had been engaged in bloody action there and we could still see the remnants of their tartan kilts fluttering in the breeze on the wire. Those barbed wire entanglements were terrible barricades. It was generally in the darkness that the troops would miss a gap in the wire and become entangled and caught long enough to get mowed down with machine gun fire. Every few days, under the cover of the dark, we would crawl up and see what we could of the damage our mortars had done. The night before the attack we made our final inspection and found practically no wire longer than a couple of feet left; this time there would be no kilts hanging on the wire.

The attack on Beaumont Hamel took place just before dawn and was a complete success speaking from a military point of view. From my point of view there was and is no complete success in any attack where loss of life and maiming of men is concerned. As soon as our mortars were out of range our unit went up forward to help bring out the wounded. The casualties were heavy on both sides. Our unit did not come through unscathed by any means.

It was during my sojourn there that I saw the first white flag raised by the Germans. Our artillery had been shelling them heavily one aternoon when we saw a German officer walking toward our trenches with the flag held aloft. He asked if we could send word to the artillery to cease fire for an hour so that they could carry their dead back for decent burials. The request was granted and we held our fire and watched the proceedings. According to the Guinness Book of Records, the Battle of the Somme was the bloodiest in history. From July 1st to November, 1916, total casualties numbered over one million and a quarter. Total casualties for the Canadians at the Somme were twenty-one thousand.

In winter time in the trenches we received a rum ration at stand to and stand down. It was a very powerful beverage. One wet night I walked quite a distance to get the rum rations for our section. The officer doling out the ration told me I looked cold so he would give me an extra ration. He said as he poured it out into a cigarette can, "If you can drink this right down and say thank you right after, I will give you another one." After drinking it I spluttered around trying to say something. I was beaten! However, he laughed and gave me a small one. The rum came into the line in sealed gallon crockery jugs. It was marked S.R.D. and was over forty proof. Some said S.R.D. meant "Seldom Reaches Destination." I don't think that was a true interpretation.

Lance Corporal Alfred Eastwood
5TH KING'S OWN YORKSHIRE LIGHT INFANTRY

I never really had any sense of where we were. I've heard
Canadians saying exactly where they were, but I usually didn't
know where the hell I was! I didn't give a damn. Oh we used to
hear stories, "That's the Red Baron or so and so," but I didn't care
who they were, as long as they got the hell out of the way!
Prisoners were taken, but I never was in on that. I saw lots of them
being marched down. We used to hear stories of them being shot,
but I never saw that. I saw a hell of a lot of prisoners on the
Somme.

Lieutenant Albert Winn
ROYAL FIELD ARTILLERY

The first time we saw tanks was on the Somme. Headquarters
was so secretive that we knew nothing about them. When they did
turn up we thought they were heavy tractors for pulling our big
guns! Those tanks would flatten anything.

I remember seeing Von Richthofen in the air. I only saw one or
two zeppelins. They were mainly used for bombing purposes. They
got up to a terrific height. Even with a machine gun the bullets had
to hit in the right part before the zeppelin would explode. The
zeppelin had observers who would send information back to the
Germans. They had machine gunners for self protection just like an
airplane.

I remember seeing one of our aces fighting it out with a
German ace over the Somme. The German won, because he had a
better plane. We could sit on the front line and see these men
machine gunning each other. They could see us. The dirtiest thing I
ever saw was when, after a dogfight, the Germans would machine
gun to death anyone who parachuted from an observation balloon
of ours. This happened many times. The Germans greatly disliked
enemy observers.

Bombardier James Logan
39TH BATTERY C.F.A.

On 15 July, 1916, we reached the Ypres sector. At the Lille
Gate all twenty five gunners in the party collected together under
cover of an earth bank. We were met by a guide from the 11th
Battery C.F.A. to whose position at "Blauwe Poort Farm" in the

Ypres salient our party was bound. After passing the Lille Gate it was necessary to proceed in extended order, as we were under observation by the enemy from Hill 60.

We were distributed among the gun crews and headquarters party of the 11th Battery, to learn how things were done.

The gun pits were known as the "Beehive" type and were constructed of "elephant iron"; that was, quarter circles of quarter inch thick corrugated iron, of which two quarters were bolted together to make the pit the length required. The pits were sixteen feet long and sunk in the ground to the depth of half a gun wheel. The gun muzzle protruded out from the front of the pit. The rear was sandbagged up except for a narrow entrance. All the corrugated iron was covered with two layers of sandbags to make it splinter-proof and turfed over to screen it from enemy observation. The ammunition was stacked around the gun inside the pit. The Sergeant in charge would sleep on the bed of ammunition as it was most comfortable and dry. Two gunners might manage to sleep on other piles of ammunition. The remaining men slept on the ground beside the gun's wheels or under the shield. As quite a bit of night firing was done the beds of ammunition had to be restacked to make them level after each "strafe" before it was possible to lie down on them again.

We received our first real introduction to rats there. One man had all the buttons, which were made of bone, gnawed from a vital part of his apparel, his tooth paste eaten and his tooth brush carried away.

The C.F.A. prepare for action (1916).

The guns were taken out of action on the night of the 24th. On the night of the 25th they were taken into action at Kemmel.

At Kemmel the gun pits were improved upon. They were composed of pit props about eighteen inches in diameter placed upright in the ground for the sides, a beam carried across the tops and rails and trees were placed across from side to side to form the roof. The sides and roof were covered over with earth and turfed. One gun pit was so small that there wasn't enough room for the crew to sleep in it. One of the gunners was hoisted up to the roof nightly on a piece of sheet iron slung on ropes. It was dangerous, however, because machine gun bullets swept over the pits at night. The front of the pit was entirely open. A low bullet could have come in. It was therefore necessary to decide before being drawn up to the roof, which was the better death, to be shot in the head and have the bullet come out one's feet, or the reverse, as the bunk and the machine gun bullets were in the same line.

On the night of October 2nd, 1916, the guns were brought down to the horse lines. The following morning we commenced our journey to the Somme.

After passing through villages like Monchy-Cayeux, Vacquerie-le-boucq and sleeping overnight in a cemetery, we reached the guns near Martinpuich. Our Battery was situated between Sausage Valley and Death Valley.

The Somme had a bad reputation. Two Canadian Divisions suffered 5,509 casualties during the week ending October 4th. The Germans knew it as the "Blood Bath". Its evil name had reached us when we were up north. Under a morning sky the battlefield was a picture of absolute desolation. Not a blade of grass could be seen, nor a living tree, though a few leafless stumps stood fifteen feet from the ground. Martinpuich was practically levelled. Walls stood no more than eight feet high. A few dead Germans lay around the position, with one or two odd legs, which were buried later on.

The Somme "push" had begun on July 1st. Since that date the allies had advanced more than six miles. We were between the 37th and 38th Batteries. The mud was nearly up to the horses' hocks. In trying to improve matters, tree trunks were hauled and laid side by side for the horses to stand on, but it was not successful because the horses constantly got their legs between the trunks, some nearly breaking their legs.

I never saw a "premature" (where the shell explodes as it leaves the gun) in a gun. We had Number Eighty shells made in England for the 18 pounders. Then we had Number Eighty-five's from Canada and the United States. The infantry on the Somme complained that we were firing short and hitting them. We were

firing Eighty and Eighty-five shells all mixed together. We found
out that a Number Eighty shell would fire forty yards further than
the Eighty-five shell would. Something in the manufacturing caused
the difference in trajectory even though the shells were the same size.

THE 39TH BATTERY LAMENT

By F. (Irish) Kane

The troopship Missinabbi left Canada right,
With the 39th Battery all ready to fight
We got in the hold, and oh what a sight!
The cargo consisted of liver and tripe!

Chorus:
Ri Tural, Ri Tural, Ri Tural I Ahe!
The same grub's dished up to us every day.
For they want you to work, and want you to fight,
How in the hell can you do it on liver and tripe?

Some British destroyers escorted us o'er,
In due time we landed on England's fair shore,
In the pink of condition, but mostly air tight
And our stomachs all bloated with liver and tripe.

Lord Kitchener met us and said, "Gentlemen,
You look like some Huns just got out of the pen.
To get on in the Army and get your first stripe
You'll have to quit eating that liver and tripe."

We landed in Witley and then to Larkhill
Where the boys with the Big Feet were taught how to drill.
With guide ropes and wagons they'd wheel to the right
And the breeze from the kitchen was perfumed with tripe.

Sam Irwin and Friday, the greasy old cook
Were lighting the fire with some leftover soup.
Up went the old kitchen as high as a kite
And all they had left was a hunk of green tripe.

Up came Porky Van Horn, a solid wee man,
Cooked up bully and bacon and stew in a can.
He says, "Eat her down boys, and don't think it's cake,
It will blow up the village if dropped by mistake."

In blew Spud Thompson, fresh up from the base
With a drop at his nose and a long moleskin face.
Says, "Suck in your eyeballs, you'll find I'm no fool
When decked in the hump of a Missouri mule."

At last we got settled, God bless the top wits,
Shining buttons and buckles and old rusty bits.
We skinned in the morning and by candle light,
As we sang, "Au Revoir" to liver and tripe.

The men mentioned in the poem were real people. Porky Van
Horn was the cook. Once he was blown up with his cookhouse. He
got stuck in the chimney. Later he was offered Sergeant's stripes by
some officer. He had the nerve to tell the officer, "to shove them up
his arse!"

Lieutenant Colonel John S. Stewart
7TH BRIGADE/C.F.A.

(Diary notes)
We left for the Somme via Dickebusch, Abeele, Tilques, Aire and
St. Pol after four and a half months in the St. Eloi region. We
reached Albert on August 29th. It rained all day. We walked to
Tara Hill where we met the Australians and Lahore C.R.A.'s. We
stayed overnight in Albert as preparations had not been made for
our stay. I slept on the floor of a chateau. We went down to St.
Ouen and travelled via Vignacourt, Flesselles to Septenville. People
in that area seemed to live in communes. The women were hard at
work in the fields harvesting the crops. Heavy artillery fire could be
heard near Albert all day. The next day, September 9th, we went to
the Brickfield area near Albert where the entire C.D.A. 2nd
Division was encamped. In the afternoon one section per battery
relieved the batteries of the 18th Lahore Brigade.

On September 12th, Major Ross and I went to Leipzeig
Redoubt near Thiepval where we got a good view of Mouquet
Farm. We prepared for our big offensive of the 15th. Our howitzers

fired most of the day. On September 15th we fired in support of the Canadian Mounted Rifles as they attacked Mouquet Farm. In the afternoon an advance was made on Martinpuich and Courcelette. The next evening we got an S.O.S. call from the men at Mouquet Farm, but it was a false alarm. I did not get much sleep the other night as I was disturbed by many calls. We took Mouquet Farm and our men consolidated along the lines.

The tanks were first used in support of the 2nd Canadian Division on September 15th, during the storming of Courcelette. I saw Rogers of the 27th Battery killed by a premature of 24th Battery. They had two inside of twelve minutes.

After a week's rest at Albert and a visit with the boys of the 39th Battery, we received word that we would leave the Somme by the 20th of October. On October 13th we were engaged in cutting the wire in front of Kenora Trench for the push on the 16th. On the following day while en route to the 24th Battery I was hit by a piece of shrapnel, but it did not even cut my coat. On October 29th one of our planes was shot down and crashed in Regina Trench. Our infantry attack on Regina Trench was successful. I took a German prisoner in tow who had been wounded and had him act as my escort. On October 24th, still at the Somme, I walked with Major Ross to Hessian Trench, passed Zollern Redoubt and nearly got to Regina Trench. The day was dull and dark. By October 26th we were cutting wire on Grandcourt Trench. There was fairly heavy fighting around Schwaben Redoubt in the early morning.

On Saturday, October 28th, Rifferstein (of the 27th Battery) and myself were hit by a 5.9 shell, going along Kenora Trench. I saw that Rifferstein was looked after. Then I was dressed and carried from the 26th Battery to Pozieres, thence by train to the main road and on to Albert. General Morrison met me on the way and said our work in France had been highly successful. I was sent to Le Havre where I boarded the Asturias (a steamship) bound for Southampton. I was put in Darell Hospital, 58 Queen Anne Street W., London. I convalesced in England until early 1917.

Private James Doak
52ND BATTALION

Tuesday,   August 29th: We left our camp off the Ypres-Poperinghe Road on Sunday morning at 8:30 and arrived near Steenvoorde about noon. We passed through Poperinghe and Abeele on the way. We were overtaken by several heavy rain showers. The billets here are very dirty and crawling with lice. We (the band) made shelter tents in the field with our rubber sheets. We slept in the open. All went well until this evening when a heavy rain set in. Our tents were severely tested by the rain. Hop picking is in full swing. Every available woman and child are employed. It is a very picturesque sight. I wish we were allowed cameras. Our band tents make us look like a bunch of gypsys. I smiled when I read the complaints of some soldiers in Canadian camps. When they reach this country they will learn many things. We kicked at Gresley Camp, we kicked at St. John, we kicked in England and we kicked when we first came over here, but we don't kick anymore. We take what we get and are glad of it. That's the way here.

October, 1916: I passed through La Boiseille without knowing there was a village on that spot. The huge craters nearby would hold a good sized village. Pozieres looks like an old woodyard, not a sign of a house, just holes and debris with a trail through the centre. Contalmaison has one house partially standing. Further up the line the dead of both sides are numerous. Around "Gibralter", a German strong point, the German dead lie in heaps, rotting in the open. The dead are buried and unearthed again scores of times by shells until the bodies are blown to atoms. Such is war.

Less than 100 of our original 52nd Battalion members are left, including three officers. Of course, many of the wounded will be back later.

Bombardier William Shaw
ROYAL GARRISON ARTILLERY/151ST SIEGE BATTERY

We landed and unloaded in the pouring rain at Boulogne on August 28th and entrained for Bethune. Our Battery took up a position at Mesplaux East a few miles from Bethune.

A signaller volunteered to warn us with a tin whistle if enemy aircraft was sighted. Not long after, a Sergeant ordered the sentry to blow his whistle as he spied an enemy kite-balloon. The adjutant of the brigade asked why all the men were under cover and not working. He was told about the enemy balloon. He went speechless with rage and exasperation when he saw that the balloon was British, and way inside our lines. The Sergeant went as red as a beetroot, hid himself as best as he could, and never mentioned kite-balloons again.

Our guns were pulled out and moved to the hilly terrain of Artois and the Somme. The guns were scattered over about a thousand square yards of hollow between Maillet-Mailly and Engelbelmer. A 9.2 howitzer from the 93rd Siege Battery was on our right, a fifteen inch howitzer battery in front and nearby was a South African Heavy Artillery unit of the 125th Siege Battery (S.A.H.A.). The first O.P. there was on the edge of the cemetery of Auchonvillers, overlooking Beaumont-Hamel, where the great battle took place on Sunday, 13th of November, 1916.

A tremendous amount of ammunition was brought up that night. We had two weeks worth stored up for the bombardment. The strafe was started at 6:15 a.m. Hundreds of batteries opened fire. The whole earth seemed to be exploding. Beaumont Hamel and other strong points were captured that day and the British forces took more ground and captured more prisoners than expected.

Afterwards, Doullens became our "resting area". On the 23rd of December we returned to the battery at Maillet-Mailly.

On Christmas Day we had our pudding laced with rum. It was a clear day up until half past three; then there was one of the loveliest sunsets I have ever seen: a great big red ball of fire going down in the west, showing up the shell shattered trees and buildings and desolation. I should have symbolized "peace on earth, goodwill to men" but down between us and the glorious sun was the very antithesis of peace — the shambles of Beaumont Hamel, Aveluy, Thiepval, Beaucourt, Pozieres, Ovillers, Courcelette and other grim reminders. Later on Christmas Day about fifty of us marched through the sludge and mud to a dense forest where the minister stayed. We found his place after an hour's search. He graciously told us that he was very sorry but he would not hold a service because he was too tired. The comments of the men as we trudged home, were not very complimentary to the tired padre.

Shortly after Christmas the Battery moved forward a little near Engelbelmer. On the night of Hogmanay (a Scottish festival), December 31st, 1916, Major Minto gave a bottle of whiskey to every four men in the Battery. When Signaller Forbes received a bottle, he ran off to find a dugout with three teetotalers in it! He was a real canny Scot.

Lance Corporal Craigie T. Mackie
2ND GORDON HIGHLANDERS

It was terrible on the Somme. The mud was like white clay. Our feet would get caked in it. We wore our kilts all the time right to the finish of the war. I think it was better than wearing trousers. We had to wear underwear with kilts. When we got wet, we were wet for a long time. We could hang our wet kilts on the side of a trench until they dried. In the summertime underwear wasn't necessary, just in winter.

I saw the British and Indian (Bengal Lancers) cavalry in action at the Somme, but the German machine gunners just murdered them. They never sent cavalry over again. Up until 1916 the Ghurkas were with us, but they went home. I guess it was too wet and cold for them. They were sent east to help General Allenby's army. We had the Pathans with us. The Ghurkas worried the Germans. When they left the Germans were relieved.

We were at the Somme all summer before going to Armentieres. Shortly after November 11th, 1916, we took Beaumont Hamel. We had been trying to take that since the 1st of July. We took it on November 15th.

We lost a lot of men there what with trench feet and frostbitten feet. There was hardly anybody left, when I was wounded. I made "Blighty" too! I was hit on the left side in the thigh. It was my first wound. A big chunk was taken out of me and I suppose the shrapnel is still there today. I was happy to get back to England.

Sergeant Thomas Peck (1897-)
1ST NORFOLK REGIMENT/5TH DIVISION

When we left England we hated our instructors guts, even though they were probably the nicest guys you could ever meet. They said they would come out to France to see us. We thought they better not if they knew what was good for them. Our instructors saw us off at the train station. They stood on a four foot ramp. As our train departed we boosted our morale by swearing, spitting and throwing things at those instructors. I didn't think there was one guy among us who would have hurt them in France, but once while out on a rest a certain Sergeant Major and a Captain had our guys doing lots of saluting drill. Back at the front they died in one another's arms. Somebody got them. No more saluting drill from those two! I wouldn't say that being an N.C.O. meant your chances of survival were less. It depended on what type of N.C.O. you were. If you "ground the old heel" France was a bad spot to do it. There was always someone in the outfit who would get you.

Our first scrap was on the Somme. We had some 400,000 casualties on a four mile front just on the first day! The first shell hole I jumped in I saw half the fellows I trained with buried in it. From then on my pal and I went through the Somme without a scratch. Funny thing in France was wherever our division was moved, the Germans moved their 5th Bandenburg Division. They were always opposite us no matter where we were. That shows what good intellignece they had. The German was a good fighter. He was taught not to trust us. It was natural as the old Prussian discipline was their mainstay. We were totally different to them. It wasn't the man himself, but the way he was trained!

I saw gas at the Somme, but not in the form of a blanket. We wore those white pull-over masks. The masks were so primitive that when the oxygen inside the mask gave out we had to take them off. If you were near gas, you got a mouthful of it. We were in a sunken road at Longueval. The Germans shelled us, so we went back. The next day more gas shells were directed at us. The South African Scottish Regiment ahead of us were slaughtered. They were lying under the hot July sun, burst open, grease running off them, the stench; legs and arms lying all over. It was terrible.

After I had been in France some time we had a recruit come up who was much older than me. I was just a kid. I tried to advise the guy of "what to do" and "what not to do" in the trenches. He said, "Who are you, telling me? I'm a lot older than you!" I said, "That's fine with me. Stick your God damned head up there then! Get it blown off!" He asked, "What do you mean?" I answered, "Stick your head up and find out if you don't want to listen to me!" That kind of brought him down to earth. It was broad daylight. We were in a jutted-out piece of trench, built above the ground, because of the marshy country. It was all sandbagged. I gave him a good demonstration by lining up my rifle on a big rat. I let the rat have it. "There," I said, "You see that rat?" "Yeah." I continued, "That could be you if you stick your head up over there." The Germans had very good snipers.

One fellow we had was to go on leave. He still had three rounds in his rifle, so he said, "I'll let Jerry have these before I go." He jumped up on the firing step and fired. By the time his third round went off, the Germans had killed him. He never went home.

There was always humour in the forces. It was humorous to us, but not to the victim! Black current jam was a very favorite jam. We didn't get it very often. When it did come, only one section got it. There was a comical kid who was also a good tap dancer in the section who got the jam. The section was squabbling over this tin of jam. He came running out with the damn jam tin, when all of a sudden one of Jerry's old Minenwerfers (German trench mortar shells weighing up to 190 pounds) blew up. A chunk hit him in the back of the neck. I never saw such a God damned mess in my life. He wasn't hit that bad, but between the blackcurrent jam and the blood; he was trying to holler, but he had so much jam in his mouth that he couldn't. Lots of things like that happened.

One night I was slated to go on patrol with a big clumsy

officer. It was a cold frosty night. After the patrol we went into a reserve trench. The orderly said, "Just a minute. I'll give you a shot of rum." He handed me a half filled enamel mug. That was enough to make ten guys drunk. I wasn't going to argue, so I drank it down. Then I headed for my dugout. They used to call me "China". Why I don't know. Later I went to see the Sergeant for another rum ration. I had had enough, but wanted more. He asked, "You've been out on patrol have you?" "Yeah." "Well, I'll give you a double shot." I drank that and went back to my dugout. I had to crawl over six or seven guys to get to my sleeping place. They told me, "We drew your rum ration China. Brooks didn't want his, so we put it in with yours." I drank that down too. I went to sleep in an hour. When I woke up I was a half mile down the trench. I didn't know how I got there. That was pure rum. It's a wonder it didn't kill me.

Bombardier William Daley (1896-)
ROYAL WARWICK REGIMENT/29TH DIVISION

From Alexandria, Egypt we sailed for Marseilles. We went to Bethune on our way to the Somme district. I was in a howitzer battery with the 29th Ammunition Column. My job was to service the trench mortar bombs of different batteries. Sometimes we had to take up square tins of amatol (made from TNT & ammonium nitrate) for the sappers who were tunneling there. In case Jerry broke through we had rifles strapped on our limbers, but we seldom used them. Our unit was opposite Beaumont Hamel on July 1st. Meaulte and Martinpuich were areas we went through every night.

At Training School I was told that a man caught sleeping in a listening post was courtmartialed and shot. The man's snoring gave him away. That's the thanks you got for joining the British Army and fighting for you King and country. You got shot if your nerves were not good enough.

When under fire we didn't have time to be scared. We could hear the bullets singing by. We used to wish for a "Blighty", but never get one. I'd been up the line with the ammunition at night, delivering ammo. We did all our battery work at night. We heard this noise coming and wondered what the hell it was. We saw a great unwieldy mass with both ends of it shaped the same. It was a tank. My horses were scared of it. We passed by like all hell had broken loose, even though there were only three of them. The smell of the fuel and the noise they made was terrible! They were great morale builders. Anything was better than nothing.

Our officers were fine. Things couldn't be run any other way than enforcing strict discipline to get the job done. We took over for the Australians once. I approached one of them, not knowing his nationality (I couldn't tell by his tunic) and said, "Do you mind me moving in here?" "I don't bloody well care!" he said. He was an officer, but there was no distinction. He looked just like any other Private in the ranks by appearance. There was no discipline with the Aussies. My officer was different. He said to me, "Jack's as good as his master," but he added, "It isn't so you know." As much as to say, "Well don't get any ideas." After all those years in the army there was no use crying about the discipline.

I went home to 156 Tineham Road for a nice quiet fourteen days leave. The first night I went to bed and lay alongside my wife. I was petrified all night long. My nerves were so tightened that I didn't move. Later I went back to France.

Captain Ian Sinclair
13TH BATTALION

I was slightly wounded a couple of times earlier, so by the grace of God I missed the Somme. I was blown up, but I recovered completely. Major G. Eric McCuaig was in command of our battalion at the Somme. They were to attack Regina Trench one morning. That morning Eric didn't go over the top. Casualties were so heavy at that time that the C.O. or the second in command would alternate in going over so both would not be killed at the same time. Major W.F. Peterman went over and was killed. Eric waited and waited for some word from the front as to what had happened. They were waiting in a deep German dugout that had been captured. It had been an artillery dugout. One entrance was for troops going up and down the stairs. The other was for sliding ammunition down or pulling it up to the guns. Jock Smith, the base drummer, a magnificent chap (who later became a football star) came back from the front line to Battalion Headquarters. He didn't know about the slide, so he went down it with one leg all shattered from a shell. He slid down and landed at the feet of the C.O. who was in the dugout. I think it was the shortest report that was ever given of a battle. Jock Smith spoke with a strong Glasgow accent. He couldn't stand, so he grabbed a two by four and hoisted himself up to his full height, stood smartly at attention and said, "Sir, We're fucked!"

Lance Corporal David Guild
13TH BATTALION

I was fed up being in England, so in August, 1916, I went to
the doctor and asked him, "Can I go on the next draft to France?"
He said, "Oh, I can't send you with your mouth in that shape." I
only had my back teeth left. I told him I cold report sick at Etaples
and get my teeth fixed there. On that condition he let me go. At
Etaples I reported sick. I found out they didn't fix teeth. They just
extracted and filled them. I went for two more years without teeth
in France. I rejoined my Battalion on the Somme as a Lance
Corporal. Later I became a Platoon Sergeant.

The British soldier was used to taking orders from an officer.
Canadians could take orders from officers, but I always felt I was
sometimes better than the officer. We had discipline all right, but in
my case I rarely had an officer with me. Companies were nearly
always an officer short. That's how I got my own platoon.

Lunch time in the Canadian trenches (June, 1916). (Public Archives of Canada/ PA 166)

Private John (Jack) Stacey
12TH CDN. FIELD AMBULANCE BRIGADE

We detrained at Poperinghe, then on to the Ypres salient and
then back down to the Lens area. We had dressing stations near the
Vimy front. Our main station was at Grand Servin and Petit Servin.
We were also in Estree Cauchie. Our work was to follow up the
infantry. During an attack, different sections of the Field
Ambulance were attached to various battalions. There was usually
one Field Ambulance to every brigade. There were twelve brigades.
There were thirteen Field Ambulances, but the 6th F.A. was known
as a cavalry regiment and was mobilized for that purpose. There
was no use of cavalry, so they applied themselves to field work like
the rest of us.

We had a dressing station in Pozieres Cemetery with a two
gauge railway for bringing out the wounded. At first we used mules,
but we lost so many of them that they wouldn't give us any more.
So we had to push the train cart by hand. We worked between
Courcelette and Chateau. There was a dressing station in the
basement of Chateau. We worked the line down to Beaver Corner.
Then we had a relay station where the stretcher squads took over.
We worked from one point to another while the squads worked in
their designated areas. We had a tent section at Tara Hill with huge
tents for the walking wounded. We gave them first aid and sent
them down to Boulogne.

I got a piece of shrapnel in the back of my hand at the Somme.
The shrapnel wound wasn't serious, so I stayed on duty.

We used to carry all those wounded men out in the open. We
called it the "Potato Field". There were lots of men lost, because it
was the only way we could get them out. Sometimes we had wheel-
stretchers, but they were only good on the roads. They were useless
on a field, so we had four men to a stretcher. Every walking
wounded case received an anti-tetanus inoculation. We used the
Arras-Bapaume Road quite often. We had a dressing station to the
south of Courcelette. The stations were sometimes just old Fritzie
dugouts with out equipment in them. We had to help the sick men
as well as the wounded. There was trench foot and trench leg cases.
I've seen it so bad that men's shoes were cut off because of the
severe inflammation. I've got to give the medical profession a lot of
credit for the handling of the wounded. I only saw one case of lockjaw. No matter what happened, if you scratched yourself it was an
order that you had to get a shot of tetanus. We stuck to it too. It
was a strict order.

It was impossible for the limited number of stretcher bearers we had to handle all the walking cases, so they applied themselves to the bad cases. We organized the prisoners and had them help the walking wounded. The infantry always made sure they were disarmed before sending them to us. Prisoners also carried stretchers as well as other odd jobs. They were pleased to be out of the war. In the case of a man who could not be moved for fear of death, we were provided with a "greelie tube". It was like a toothpaste tube with a needle in it. A glass vial was threaded on top for antiseptic reasons. When we came across fractured femurs, et cetera, we would give them that treatment with some morphine. Then we marked the patient's forehead with an "M". They were left until better equipment could be brought in to move them. Because of that method I think many lives were saved.

Private Ernest C. Robins
LORD STRATHCONA'S HORSE

We moved around all the time on different parts of the front. We were on an isolated post up at Lens on Fosse (French for Mine) 7. I was out on rest at Etaples where the headquarters of the General Staff was situated. I worked serving drinks at night in the officer's mess. They were very friendly. I was well tipped when serving the drinks. They would give me a five franc bill. I came back with the change. They'd say, "Ahh, keep the change." I saw King George V at General Headquarters there. Brigadier General The Right Honourable J.E.B. (later Lord Mottistone) Seely was also there.

Lice did not bother us too much because the horse smell would repel them. A lot of times we switched blankets with the horses. That saved us both from some uncomfortable nights. We were in dugouts once with the 8th Battalion at Arras. We had to cover our heads when sleeping or the rats would get at us. We could feel them running over top of us. "Rats as big as cats" was no exaggeration. They lived on the dead. Oh boy! They would.

We used to eat good. Our iron rations consisted of hardtack, which was like big dog biscuits and a tin of bully beef. Strict orders stated we were to touch it only in an emergency. When we got hungry we ate it anyway. Then we scrounged around for more. Fren Bentos corned beef was good. The four hardtack biscuits were so tough that we had to have mighty strong teeth to bust them. We used to get a spare horseshoe, put the biscuits on a wagon and break them up into edible chunks.

On our run through the main street of a town we would stop at a bakery. One of us would jump off our horse and bring back lots of hot bread and a pound of butter. We cut it up and chewed it right on our horses. It was delicious. "Pomme-de-terre and des-oeufs" (fried potatoes and eggs) was our favorite food at estaminets.

Private William (Bill) Hemmings
11TH CDN. MACHINE GUN COMPANY

Someone told me, "Now look. That man there. You just keep him in sight. Don't close up on him. Just keep him in sight!" So away we went. It was strange country at night. No lights of course. No flashlights — nothing. We passed wrecked buildings; all rubble, stepped over bricks and stones and walked on cobblestone roads. All of a sudden a machine gun opened up on us. The bullets riccoched on the cobbles sending up sparks galore! I looked ahead and thought, "Well I mustn't look back! I've got to keep on going!" So I went forward. The first thing I did was trip over a guy in the road. I thought he was dead or something. He said to me, "Get down you silly bugger! Don't stand up there!" As I jumped down I asked him, "How did you know to get down?" He replied, "Everybody else up in front got down, so I got down!" The next time I didn't need to be told.

At the Somme we used the water cooled Vickers machine gun. It was a good gun. We never had any trouble operating it.

Once in a while a spy would infiltrate dressed in one of our uniforms. I was with a ration party. The Corporal stopped us and said, "There's an officer over there. He's hanging around here and we don't know who he is." I said, "Well why don't you ask him who he is?" "Would you ask him?" I said, "Sure." I walked right over to the guy. He was standing there slapping a swagger stick against his leg. He had a pistol in his belt. I had my rifle. I said to him, "Good evening Sir." "Good Evening." "Would you mind telling me who you are?" He looked up and said, "No, I'm Lieutenant so and so." "What are you standing around here for?" "Well I'm going to dinner at so and so's mess." I asked, "Where's the mess?" It was a hole in the ground in some cellar. He said, "I don't know. He's supposed to take me there." "What time are you supposed to meet him?" "He's supposed to be here now." I told him, "If I were you I'd be on my way. You're going to be in trouble around here. These fellows are all suspicious of you." He said, "They are?" I said, "Yes." So away he went.

I went to our headquarters which was down in a cellar. Our Major came up the ladder and said, "Watch for some officer masquerading as so and so. I said, "I just talked to the guy!" "Well you missed a trip to England," he said. The reward for catching a spy was leave to London. I said, "We'll get him." On my way back I noticed some guy in front of some troops start to run. There was no reason to run as it was dark and there was rubble around. Anderson yelled, "That's him Bill! Get him!" I was a runner, so I took off after him. I didn't go very far. I turned the corner in a trench in what we called a "gas guard" (where the gas warning bell was) and the damned alarm went off. I put my gas mask on and couldn't see anything. Anderson caught up to me and said, "You lost him!" I said, "Yeah I lost him. Someone rang the alarm." We walked on. The gas guard was there, but without his mask on. I asked, "Did you ring that alarm? He said, "No. Some silly so and so rang it as he ran by here." We figured it was the German. A smart guy! He got away with it. So much for London!

One time as I was walking along the road an Australian stopped me and said, "Oh Hi Canada! Give me a pound will you?" They don't borrow, they take! A pound then was worth five bucks. That was five days pay! They would say, "Just give me a pound eh! I want to buy a drink. I'm broke!" If you didn't give it they called you all the names under the sun. I just walked away from them. They were rough. The New Zealanders were entirely different compared to Australians. They were better educated, had better control of themselves and were more civilized. The Australians were hillbillies. I always say that if you put an Australian, a Cockney and a New Yorker beside each other, you couldn't tell who was who from their accents. They are all the same.

Private David Shand
1ST GORDON HIGHLANDERS

The Australians used to live in hotels, not in billets like we did. They would crowd together in front of a hotel. They had lots of money compared to us. If one of our officers came by he crossed to the other side of the street because an Australian wouldn't salute a British officer.

Corporal Frank S. Cooper (1897-)
1ST LONDON SCOTTISH REGIMENT/56TH DIVISION

We moved up to the village of Hebuterne, which was where our attack on the Somme was made from.

The Sergeant would always want two volunteers for this and

that. Every time the Sergeant came around, Campbell, who had attached himself to me, would say, "Shall we go out and buy a tin of jam Coop?" We shared our money and our food. Campbell would always volunteer for the Sergeant. Then he would say, "Come on Cooper!" He would pull me up! I wasn't a willing volunteer, but I had no option. This happened so many times that when the Sergeant was dishing out the rations, we would get a little something extra.

South of Hebuterne, on the Somme, the trenches were mutilated and shot to pieces. We had to dig new trenches. They had to be about six feet deep and three feet wide. Digging was done at night. I had never done any digging in my life, but fortunately Campbell was my buddy at that time. He did his six feet in half an hour. Then he would come over and say to me, "Oh get out of the bloody way Cooper." He did mine too! It was a piece of cake for me everywhere, because Campbell volunteered for everything.

Befriending somebody was always the difficulty in France. You befriended someone and you lost him. I felt very bad after Campbell left. You were friendly with everybody, but you wanted somebody to share your rations. Things like bread were scarce. We were lucky to get half a loaf between us. You needed a mate from the point of view of sharing and dividing up the food as well as having somebody to talk with confidentially. It was always difficult to find a sort of special friend other than those you went out drinking with. It happened many times to me. My friend was taken and I was lucky enough to stay. It was kind of engrained in the old soldier when new fellows came out, to say, "You bloody rookies!" You really wanted somebody who had been through it all with you to be a buddy. However the new men were anxious to learn.

A fellow named Lennox, who came from Aberdeen, was a friend of mine back then. We used to buy a tin of Bird's Custard Powder. In England we used to have apple pie and custard. We mixed the custard powder with Nestle's condensed milk. It was thick, sweet stuff. We boiled it in water and spooned out the custard. We did this in the front line by finding little bits of wood, cut from trench boards and stripped up very small. We waited until it was quite dry, so it didn't make any smoke. We placed the wood piece by piece under our dixie (mess tin) of custard. Soldiers used to come along, see this and exclaim, "Custard in the front line!"

Lieutenant Ernest Hayes
CYCLIST CORPS/MACHINE GUN CORPS

The 14th Division was in action on the Somme near Delville Wood. We were on the left flank of the French who were trying to hold on to Verdun. It was an important part of the front line. The French had lost thousands of men hanging on to Verdun. This was the first attempt to make any inroads into the German held area for some time. I was in charge of two machine guns. I had a Sergeant in charge of one of them.

Whether an officer or a private, we were all in the same boat. I never considered myself a brave person or wanted to see bloodshed. That didn't appeal to me at all in my younger days. Having the responsibility as an officer in charge of some men naturally meant I had to set an example. I found that watching wounded people or seeing people getting killed didn't really affect me like I thought it would. With all that responsibility you get so occupied with what's going on that you don't have time to think of yourself. I never worried about getting killed or wounded at Delville Wood.

After Delville Wood there were no attempts to go any further. The Germans dug in for the winter. Everything was too muddy. Nobody had a chance to move around. The Germans, like us, were only too glad to lay off during the winter months. From September, 1916 on into 1917 it was quiet out there.

Egypt, Palestine & Jerusalem Campaigns 1915-1919

EGYPT, PALESTINE & JERUSALEM CAMPAIGNS: (1915-1919)

Bombardier William Daley
99TH BRIGADE - 22ND DIVISION

Our ship was destined for Salonica, but we were held up in a quay because Greece was neutral at that time. The year was 1915. I don't think the officers knew just what to do, so we waited until dark; then the guns were harnessed and the horses lowered. We were on our way to the country. I got frostbite in my hands and feet. I was eventually sent up the line for treatment. My feet weren't as bad as some cases I saw. A few men had orange coloured feet — severe frostbite! In Salonica I was boarded on the hospital ship Esterias. (She was torpedoed later in the war, but was a B. & O. liner in peacetime.) I landed at Alexandria, was put on a hospital train bound for Cairo, where I ended up in the Royal Mazeria Military Hospital for quite some time.

One day a commissioner visited the hospital with three or four medical men. They examined my medical sheet and since I had had frostbite they put an 'E' on my sheet. This meant a trip to England. Then one of them said, "No. It's no use sending him back there. It's winter — too cold out." They sent me up to Luxor which is on the edge of the Sudan. It was lovely there. I spent five or six weeks at the Winter Palace Hotel. It was once a haven for wealthy Germans. It was situated on the banks of the river Nile. I understand that it was only open five or six months of the year as a winter resort. It had a string orchestra, adjustable wicker chairs and each hotel had impressive French doors. When I woke in the morning the sun was always shining. It never rained. There was a bowling alley in the garden which was full of oranges. A wonderful place!

One morning I put my foot in it. The Australians used to boil little Egyptian chicken eggs every morning in the mess. We shared the hard boiled eggs on our enamel plates, getting four or five each along with the usual bread and butter. One Australian thought aloud, "How does he manage this? All these eggs?" The orderly officer overheard him and made a complaint to his superiors. We were being over-fed. Our names were put on a list. Within a week we were sent to Alexandria. I ended up in Citybish.

A couple of mornings later, while on parade, we were sent to the banks of the Suez Canal. That's where I met with the remnants of the 29th Division who were camped there. They had been sent up from Gallipoli. Lord Kitchener went out and reviewed the situation at Gallipoli and I suppose he came to the conclusion that it was not much use staying there. The 29th Division won great renown for their earlier actions. They were the division that cut a hole in the side of their ship, River Clyde, to escape, while the Turks machine gunned them as they landed. I met one Gallipoli navy veteran who told me of their landing in February and they marched right into the country without any opposition. They returned and reported the easy access to the London War Office. Meanwhile the Turks had put two and two together. They laid wire under the water and enfiladed the shore. Our troops had a hell of a time getting through, only taking about four miles of ground. Therefore the 29th Division was one of the divisions that eventually had to evacuate Gallipoli.

We were sent back to Alexandria; then off to Marseilles. We had a narrow escape with mines going through the Mediterranean Sea. Our convoy had to accommodate the speed of the slowest boat. I was on the Lanonay. An enemy submarine got one of the boats. We could see it listing. We never stopped. The derelict boat was full of French colonial troops. They were quite noticeable in their red pants and blue tunics, tossing out life rafts and shinnying down ropes. We weren't far off the coast of Italy when I saw the great mounds of water go up. Two torpedo destroyers detached from the main route were discharging depth-charges. Whether they got the submarine or not I don't know.

The Suez Canal near Kantara (1918).

I returned from France with the 60th Division in 1917. We landed in Egypt and moved to a camp in El Fedan, between Ismailia and El Qan-Tara. I used to ride in my shorts and sometimes the stirrups would scratch my skin between the saddle strap. We could scrub our jackets by using sand instead of soap. We went down by the side of the canal and scrubbed them clean. Swirling the clothes around in the water along with the sand would do a good job. Then we laid the clothes out and the heat from the sun would dry them in short order. It used to bleach the khaki making it a clean white kind of khaki. Our pith helmets were issued from the quartermaster's stores.

At Salonica I was in D 302 Battery. One morning about eleven o'clock there was a 'woof!' A fast, high velocity shell struck. The next one went over top of us. Wooof! The Sergeant told me, "They bracketed us." Nothing else happened until about 2:00 p.m. when all of a sudden a salvo came from enemy eight inch guns. We had our howitzers in a line of four. The 'A' gun was hit and knocked out. All of us were smothered with the debris. We soon got orders to evacuate. We left and didn't return for a couple of hours. It was a narrow escape because we had ammunition dug in alongside a pit. A shell went right in the pit without exploding.

We took Jerusalem just before Christmas, 1917. We camped at Fromalla where we celebrated a rainy Christmas. It was quite nice when the weather cleared. Then we went to Nablus (Shechem). Before going to France we were changed over to the 74th Division. Our divisional sign was a broken spur in a white diamond with a black background. The broken spur denoted a division made up of dismounted yeomen territorials.

From Alexandria, as a member of the 74th Division, we went back to Marseilles, France. My officer bought a little Arabian stallion from a racetrack in Alexandria and he had it shipped home. The Major didn't like it because we had to make a corral for it. When on the move we had to dismantle the corral, fastening the boards under the wagons. It was a nuisance — a stud horse in a battery with other horses. Of course all the other horses were castrated when they were young. We had the odd mares and I don't suppose a stallion was welcome. My officer, Cliff Dyall, eventually got the horse back to England. How I don't know? I think he sold it to an Arab horse breeder in Essex. After the war, Dyall purchased his own army horse and brought it back to Canada. I was his batman, so after the war, I wrote him asking for a job. He paid my wife's and my fare over. We worked it out. My wife worked in his house, I worked in the barns and he still had his army horse when I was there.

Private Charles Brice (1899-)
2ND COUNTY OF LONDON YEOMANRY

I was only seventeen when I was selected to go to Egypt in
1916. We landed at Alexandria, went to a place on the Suez Canal
(I had a swim there) and then to the firing line. We were under a
lot of firing in the Egyptian hills, but not as much as in France later
on. 'Johnny Turka' as we called the Turks fired quite a few shells at
us. We saw where their artillery had been after they buggered off.
We lived in tents at El Q an-Tara. There were eight to ten men per
tent with their rifles hanging in the middle.

Lieutenant Ernest Hayes
1st/50TH KUMAON RIFLES — INDIAN ARMY

I had to report to the Machine Gun Headquarters in Leicester.
A notice on the orderly board pointed out that they wanted officers
for the Indian Army. There was a shortage of officers because of all
the casualties.

In India we joined the 1st/50th Kumaon Rifles at Rainkhet up
in the Himilayas. A month later we were ordered down to the
plains in central India for further training.

In May we moved to Bombay to join the Egyptian
Expeditionary Force. Our Battalion landed at Suez on June 6th,
1918. By July 16th we arrived at Ludd and became the 180th
Brigade of the 60th Division. We held the line near Palestine
throughout the month of August. All the villages and waterholes
were out of bounds in Palestine.

For a thousand men we were allowed a gallon of water per
man each day. The water was carried in flat metal drums called
"fanaties". There were two drums on each side of a camel,
containing forty gallons of water. We had one hundred camels
handled by gippos (natives). Every day one of our men had to
arrange that the water was picked up. This was generally done at
night, depending on how far we had to go. If anyone was wounded
or sick they were sent out on camels. Stretchers were strapped on.

We attacked the Turks on September 19th, 1918. They were
behind the hills north of Jerusalem. At night prior to the attack,
both the Turks and ourselves would send out patrols to guard
against surprise attacks. All interest seemed lost in fighting. We
went over at the break of dawn. I wasn't with them going over.
When the Turks saw us coming they knew we meant business. They
just threw down their arms. There was very little fighting. They
were glad to get out of the war. I managed to get a German Luger
(revolver) from a Turkish officer as a souvenir.

After that we moved down to Alexandria awaiting instructions as to where they wanted us next. Sports like polo and tennis kept us busy. The war was still on in France.

On November 11th we were still at Alexandria with other English regiments. Everything just went crazy. All tents were layed low. The officers had a big marquee which was pulled down. All the liquor went too. The men got into it. There was lots of shouting. The natives didn't celebrate as much. I don't know if the natives knew what was going on.

What is left of the Turkish transport (dead mules) after the September, 1918 retreat.

After Christmas our unit went down to Suez. A stopover base for troops returning from the far east, like India and Mesopotamia, was set up to iron out the kinks. The troops then took the train to Alexandria, where they caught freighters back to England.

I was demobilized in August, 1919 and returned to my old job at Reeves in London. Because of my overseas experience they didn't consider me a "babe in arms", so I represented them overseas as a result. I opened the first Reeves companies in South Africa and Canada after the war.

Private Charles Brice
2ND COUNTY OF LONDON YEOMANRY

One of the ships in our convoy was torpedoed six hours after leaving Alexandria. All the guns were firing and the searchlights flashing, trying to pick up the Jerry submarine. It was kind of scary, yet a beautiful sight to see. There were about forty troop laden boats in our convoy. Two boats were sunk, one losing between six and seven hundred lives. The escort stayed behind. We could see them trolling back trying to surround the 'strike' area as we went forward. They couldn't drop depth charges with a sub lurking below a convoy. They had to be careful.

One anonymous veteran remembers a Russian ship with so many smokestacks that the troops dubbed it the 'packet 'o Woodbine', after the British slang term for cigarettes.

Sergeant Thomas Peck
54TH DIVISION

The Turks were pushing through Palestine in 1917. We chased them back. Our camps were beside the Suez Canal at Jaffa (Joppa). We were in the lines there most of the winter. We pushed the entire Turkish Army back in about four hours. They were surrounded from the coast, with the Australian Light Horse behind and we hammered them from the front.

Rations in Egypt were very poor. The water tanks that camels carried were called *'fantaties'*. You can imagine what water was like after being sloshed around in 100 degree to 120 degree heat for about a week. At Gaza when we first arrived we found there was not any water left. They gave us tablets to put in our urine for drinking. The enemy could have poisoned the water. Any natural water was brackish. That was one of our main troubles. Little pound loaves of bread were given to us. We generally got two handfuls of crumbs. The bread was all smashed because it was carried in bags on camels. We advanced so fast that the bread and the enemy didn't stand a chance.

The day before the armistice was signed a fellow was dishing out the rations. He had a waterproof sheet set out with little piles of crumbs all over it. Seeing that made us a little desperate, so we raided a village populated with a lot of Greeks. We also tossed Mills bombs into the Mediterranean Sea in order to kill the fish. That's how we survived. Our Division (the 54th) had originally been at the Dardanelles conflict where we lost a lot of men through dysentary. Men were dying right on their toilet seats. Medical supplies were not available.

Barbed wire defences at Suez (1918).

GERMAN RETREAT & ARRAS TO VIMY RIDGE (1917)

Captain Walter Moorhouse
4TH CDN. MOUNTED RIFLES, CMGC

Every effort was concentrated on the coming attack on Vimy Ridge. Technicians made plaster models of the Ridge to scale, with Hun positions, trenches and deep dugouts accurately marked, and every officer and man was given the opportunity to study them.

It would certainly be a mistake to belittle the success of our attack on Apl. 9th/17. However there were certain facts to be noted in order to make a sound judgement, —

1. The Hun was over-confident. France & Britain had failed with heavy losses on Lorette Ridge in 1915.

2. There were great caves that enables us to assemble close to the old line.

3. Once we reached the crest, counter-attack was almost impossible. In fact, we could see the Boche pulling out his batteries.

4. The ground wasn't too bad, and don't forget the force of gravity. It's easier to attack down a slope than up.

5. German dugouts were too deep and too near their front. Our short final barrage didn't give them time to get to their firing positions.

6. It's true that our 4th Div. were held up by the strongly fortified 'Pimple' on our left, but we had M.G. batteries at the crest of the ridge that by direct fire helped to silence the closer Hun artillery.

In fact, the attack looked more difficult than it was. At least many of us thought so as during the summer of 1917 we dominated the salient as the enemy were pushed back towards their stronger line at the mine heads.

However, the possession of the Ridge was a tremendous asset when the 5th Army broke under the German attack in March/18. On making a tour of the Ridge which we were holding at that time we passed at St. Nicholas a battery of our huge 6″ long range guns the muzzles of which were sighted directly to our rear, when we had still several miles to go to reach our forward area. It made us feel a bit cut off as it were, but if we hadn't held the Ridge it might have made quite a difference in the success of the Hun attack below Arras in March 1918.

Shortly after the capture of the Ridge, Harry Symons and I visited the old French trenches on the Lorette Ridge. These had never been cleared and were still well revetted and in fair condition, but with many corpses lying around. The French Mission was engaged in clearing them and were meticulously collecting identity discs, papers and money from casualties that had been there for over a year. We were astonished at the amount of cash, some of it in gold, collected and ticketed for these poor skeletons. We also visited Souchez village where there was literally 'not one stone upon another'.

As the summer passed I had perforce made a study of danger areas during our tours of the line. Gun positions were taboo as also were strong points, trenches, dumps and road junctions. What we looked for and followed were weeds, for these didn't grow where shells fell thick. Thus, day after day I could cover miles of the line with little chance of a shell landing close.

During the summer, "Winston Churchill called at Div. H.Q. on his old Sandhurst friend, Gen. Lipsett. He insisted on going round the Div. front and as the General had to attend a Corps conference, he detailed me (unwillingly on my part) to act as a guide. His last words were not re-assuring. "The man's as mad as a hatter! He'll want to go up into the front line. Don't let him, for God's sake!" He was right! We had a quiet trip and the troops wondered who "the guy in the French helmet" was. We had just got a battery of Heavy Trench Mortars that tossed a missile known as a 'Flying Pig' incredible distances. They had an emplacement near Avion and Churchill insisted on going up to watch them fire. I was reluctantly forced to hand him over to the T.M. officer. When we ultimately got back to Div. H.Q. I, and I have no doubt Gen. Lipsett, heaved a sigh of relief.

About this time we had a rest period in a mining town called Maroc. There was a huge coal pile close to Bde. H.Q., and one day a very excited Chief Engr. officer came to say that the mines owners had notified Corps that the temperature of this coal pile was rising, and something must be done about it. 'What to do!' was the query as the event appeared to be outside his experience. While the C.R.E. was discussing it with the Bde. Major, the D.A. Q.M.G. took a piece of cross section paper and quickly drew a diagram of the coal pile with a pattern of ventilating ducts and show it to the C.R.E. who said, "Where did you learn all this about coal?" "Me?" replied the other, "Why, I'm the Coal Man". This was the slogan of the Standard Fuel Co., of Toronto, and the officer was Maj. Rud. Marshall, son of Noel Marshall, president of that firm. What a versatile lot were our civilian soldiers!

We also had a spell near Camblain l'Abbe when the new Concert Party later known as the Dumbells gave a show. Gen. Lipsett brought an Imperial Army officer as guest and they sat in the front row. You may remember Ross Hamilton, one of the greatest female impersonators of the time. That night he was at his very best and was a vision of fashion and beauty. Ross made a dead set at this gallant British officer and sang in honied voice, "I'll make you love me!" I felt sorry for the poor fellow who was terribly embarrassed and whose face shone like a beacon. Some one whispered to him that Ross was a private in the Field Ambulance, but this didn't seem to calm down his embarrassment.

Bombardier James F. Johnson
5TH CANADIAN MOUNTED RIFLES
In the summer of 1915 the French fought valiently to take Vimy Ridge. They had to give it up after taking part of it. They lost over thirty thousand men in their attempt.

Air activity had increased rapidly. Our planes had improved tremendously. Air combat became more frequent. Dogfights became almost an every day spectacle. On the Arras front we saw the great German ace Von Richthofen in his bright red Fokker leading his flying circus against our airmen. He was well respected by our pilots and considered a fair fighter. The amibition of our airmen was to bring him down alive, but that was not to be, as a Canadian airman, Roy Brown, shot him down in an air battle on April 21, 1918. Other Canadian pilots like Billy Bishop and Raymond Colliishaw were beginning to become famous.

One day in the front line I asked our officer where this ridge they talked about was as we could not see it. There was just a general slope for miles back toward the German lines. He gave me an idea of the topography of the area. He went on to say that a short distance back of the German trenches the rige dropped abruptly about five hundred feet. He concluded, "I hope you will be fortunate to stand atop of the ridge and look for miles into German territory in the near future." While there had been rumours, that was the first real inkling indicating that the Canadian Corps was there for the task of capturing Vimy Ridge.

Just before Christmas, 1916, one morning an officer called me over to the parapet where he was peeking through between sandbags. He told me to take a look. To my surprise I could see some Germans busy receiving their rations. They were about two hundred yards away. Of course, they did not know they were exposed to rifle fire as part of their parapet had been blown down. The officer said, "What would you do in this case?" I replied, "I think this is Christmas Eve." He said, "Oh, yes it is, but in case someone gets trigger happy you fire a shot close enough to them as a warning." I fired about twenty feet to their left. They weren't long in taking cover, but the last man to leave hesitated a moment and saluted. Little incidents like that made me wonder: "Why?" That had been a great opportunity for a sniper. I was glad that they had not taken advantage of the situation.

After a rest at Mareuil we returned to the trenches in early January, 1917. The weather had turned cold, there was snow on the ground and everything under foot was frozen quite hard which was a relief from the mud. It was bad from another point of view. When enemy shells hit soft mud they would partially bury themselves before exploding, but on the frozen ground the shell would burst or turn and scatter shrapnel much further and in greater quantities. Shrapnel seemed to be zinging all over the place. We slept in funk holes dug in the rear side of the trench just large enough for one man. We lined it with sandbags, so it was good shelter from shrapnel and weather. There were also scattered shallow dugouts which would hold several men. They were protection from overhead shrapnel but would not be vulnerable against a direct hit. One afternoon three of four of our crew were playing rummy when a piece of shrapnel came through an opening and pierced one of the playing cards, burying itself in the sandbag wall. Needless to say that card was kept as a lucky souvenir!

In February I experienced my closest call so far in the war. For a couple of days the Germans were firing heavy shells which were exploding in the rear area of our position. We presumed they were trying to knock out our mortar as we were causing extensive damage on their position. After we had fired another six rounds we all heard a shell coming and knew by the sound it was coming close. I was about one hundred feet from the rest, crouching low against the trench. The shell hit our gun emplacement which demolished everything. If that shell had been one minute sooner we would have all been killed. Some of our ammunition was also destroyed by the blast. The concussion from that blast shot through the trenches ripping my tunic down the seam from the collar to the bottom. Most of the seams in my pants were severed, a heavy piece of shell casing buried itself in a frozen sandbag six inches from my knee and a part of a falling sandbag hit me in the head. I was just getting to my feet when our officer rushed in from the communication trench. I had a little cut on my head but it was not serious. The first thing he said after learning no one was seriously hurt was, "What in hell happened to your clothes?" After realizing it was the result of a concussion he said it was hard to believe we were still alive.

As time went on we were wondering when the big day would arrive. The action became more intense. Our artillery were putting up some terrific barrages. Even in December four hundred C.M.R.'s went over the top in broad daylight.

It was a common rumour that the attack on the ridge would take place on Easter Sunday, April 8th. However, the date for some reason was changed to Easter Monday, April 9th.

The frontage for the attack at Vimy Ridge was seven thousand yards. It does not seem a very wide frontage, but it was an important objective. The troops on both flanks were supposed to move up as we advanced to keep the line more or less straight. Four complete Canadian Divisions were used in this attack. The 24th British Division flanked our north side and the 51st Highlander Divison was on our south side. The four Canadian Divisons were in between the British. One thousand pieces of artillery consisting of field guns of about three inch calibre to the big howitzers which fired a twelve inch shell were included in the attack strategy. There were also six inch long barrel naval guns which had a longer range then a howitzer.

On April 9th at five a.m., while it was still dark, the attack commenced. Never before had any of us seen such a barrage put up by our artillery. The flashes of our guns firing and the flaring of bursting shells was a gruesome but fantastic sight. The noise was deafening. Shells were screaming over our heads going both ways. In less than thirty minutes as an exact time our artillery raised their sights to fire deeper into enemy territory. Our mortars were out of range, so we joined in the infantry attack that followed. We had to help the stretcher bearers bring out the wounded who could not walk. It proved to be a big job.

One day we were to start firing. In a little dugout I kept the clinometer used to lay the mortar. I always carried the instrument suspended on a strap in front of me while walking down a trench, so it would not bang against anything. When I walked into our emplacement the fellows were grinning and one said, "Good old Corporal, he is going to give us a drink." I had picked up a water bottle in the darkness of the dugout instead of the clinometer. A day later our C.O. was giving a lecture on general topics and he said, "We do have ingenious N.C.O.'s. Corporal Johnson evidently can lay a mortar with a water bottle."

Early that morning snow and rain fell and continued all forenoon. There was a strong wind with this storm which was in our favour as it blew into the face of the enemy. Nevertheless that did not compensate for the miserable conditions to follow. By noon our artillery were frantically trying to move our 18 pounders and 4.5 Howitzers forward, but they were hopelessly bogged down in the mud. Even our tanks were stuck in the churned up mire later in the day. Our division's (3rd Division) first objective was La Folie Wood, quite close to the crest of the ridge. We reached it about nine a.m. The 1st and 2nd Divisions on our right were making their first objectives by the forenoon. However, the 4th Division on our left was having a bad time and meeting tough opposition, suffering heavy casualties. One battalion lost sixty per cent of its men, another battalion lost every officer. The 1st, 2nd and 3rd Divisions could not move forward to their second objectives until the 4th Division had reached their first one.

Early in the morning German prisoners started pouring in. Several thousand were captured that day. I had seen more on the Somme, but I think the Vimy prisoners were the most dejected looking specimens of humanity I had ever seen. They stood ankle deep in mud, hungry, cold, wet, disarmed and defeated. One of them told me that they had hardly eaten for the past three days on account of our shelling holding up their ration transport. I feel guilty in saying this, but I must confess I was a little envious of these men in one regard: for them the fighting was over, for us the end was not in sight.

There were about two hundred prisoners in one group. Our interpreter asked those who were physically fit, those who had first aid experience, and those who could speak English to step out to one side. Most of them did. After that they were fed, given cigarettes and assigned to different stretcher bearing parties. The few that remained were either to weak or had slight wounds. They in turn joined others who were escorted back to barbwire enclosures where they were transported to various internment camps. During the day I was impressed by the thought that here were men striving to save the lives of men they had tried to destroy a few hours before. The Germans worked hand in hand with us, dressing wounds, carrying stretchers over muddy soaked ground. They were generally adept in first aid. The wounded were picked up as we found them, German or ours. The dead left until all the wounded were tended to. There was not a trace of hate in the heart of any man I worked with that day, friend or foe. Oh the futility of war! Some of the Germans were killed or wounded by thier own guns that day. Surveying the ground we covered I marvelled how a man could live through that utter devastation. However, the Germans in that area had constructed deep dugouts, practically bomb proof. When the bombardment was at its peak most of them would remain inside them. As soon as the shelling ceased they came out to defend their positions. They knew our troops could not advance under our own shell fire.

On April 10th, the 4th Division reached their objective. I will never forget the first time I looked east from the top of Vimy Ridge. From the bottom of the ridge eastward the ground was level

for miles. Towns like Petit Vimy, Vimy and Lievin lay in absolute
ruin. The remains of coal mining tipples coud be seen around
Lievin. Lens, Avion, Merricourt and Douai were visible in the
distance. We could see the Germans falling back in order to
establish new defensive positions. The Lens-Arras Road was lined
on both sides with large trees. The Germans felled all the trees
across the road as they retired. Our troops were busy digging
themselves in and preparing to push farther on. We could not use
our mortars for a few weeks because it was not until June that our
lines were consolidated.

The capture of Vimy Ridge is written in history as the most
carefully conceived and brilliantly executed enterprise of the war.
Our casualties amounted to over ten thousand. Not too bad
considering the numbers of troops involved and the magnitude of
our achievement. However, it was big price to pay to occupy an
area six by four miles square.

The next time we went up the line we were attached to an 18
pounder battery located in Petit Vimy. The batteries were dug in to
the rear of a high railroad grade in front of the village. We
occupied the cellars in the rubble there. While doing our regular
chores of repairing the line, our officers were quite considerate.

Lieutenant Colonel John S. Stewart
7TH BRIGADE. C.F.A.   *(Diary Notes)*
By April 18th we had turned the German guns around and
fired them on the enemy. We located a place for H.Q. at Farbus.
The 1st Division and the XIII Corp made a push, taking Arleux
and other points. On May 5th the Huns brought their 5th Bavarians
to attack at Fresnoy. The Hun strafed Vimy Ridge and our
surrounding countryside. I understand we are to go back to the
Salient before very long.

Captain Ian Sinclair
13TH BATTALION
There had never in history been such detailed planning and
spreading of information. Everybody down to the lowest Private
knew exactly what the plan was from beginning to end. In our billet
we had stone floors on which we spread out our maps. Every trench
and fine detail was marked on them with the officers (us) all
standing around studying them. The maps were distributed all
through the battalion until every company and every platoon had
seen them. The timetable was clear to all involved.

One fellow, Newman of the 48th Highlanders, was hit right through the stomach going over the top at Vimy Ridge. The reason he lived was because they didn't find him for about twenty-four hours. He had fallen into a shell hole. The wound coagulated. He would have bled to death if anyone had moved him right away. I was wounded slightly and ended up in hospital with him down in Boulogne. The doctor used to come to me and say, "How are you getting along Sinclair?" I would say, "Fine." He said to my friend Newman, "I'm not looking at you Newman. You're dead." There was no anitbiotics. If you got infected you died. Otherwise you just had to suffer the pain.

We had some new planes like the Sopwith Camel and the Sopwith Triplane that were held back until just a few weeks before the attack. The Royal Flying Corp wanted to get air superiority. Our flyers took an awful licking for months prior to the Vimy scrap. At Vimy the Camels swept the Hun out of the skies. Everybody cheered when we saw the Germans going down instead of our guys.

We never had anything to do with the Australians. The Canadians and Australians always fought like tigers when they would meet in pubs behind the line. It got so bad that eventually they never put the Australians or Canadians together in the same part of the line. They hated each others guts. You couldn't meet a nicer crowd than the New Zealanders. They were splendid.

Sergeant David Guild
13TH BATTALION

After Vimy Ridge, one of our pilots brought down a German plane. Our chap was flying a triplane. When the enemy plane crashed, he looped-the-loop to celebrate his victory. His wings fell off and down he came, crashing deep into the soft earth.

We had an observation place at Double Crassier that we took over from the English. It was mining country, near Maroc. There were big tipples there. A tipple ran from a mine occupied by the Germans, to our front line trench, where slag was dumped. A big mound ran parallel to the tipple. Our artillery knocked the Germans off the opposite end of that slag heap. We occupied the opposite end of it and the Germans could have just as easily knocked us off it. The Germans heaved bombs at us, because they knew we were changing men around. My men ran out of patience sitting there, so one of our guys heaved a can of bully beef over. The Germans thought it was a bomb, so they took off. We did not have any trouble for about five days. They came back later on. They could see all over our territory and we could see all over theirs. The slag heaps were about fifty or sixty feet high. I don't know why the heaps weren't both blown up.

Private George Black
8TH BATTALION — IMPERIAL BLACK WATCH

At the Arras front, on a Thursday morning, five a.m., May 3rd, 1917, I was wounded. On my way back, a Captain Taylor said to me, "Get back to the front line!" I had been shot through the right knee and I hobbled back on my way to the divisional front lines. On the way there was a big shell burst. I remember the heat of the shell so well. The next thing I knew I woke up inside a big, deep shellhole under the brilliant sunshine. I had been in that hole from Thursday to Sunday morning at ten a.m. A Sergeant from the Seaforth Highlanders carried in seventeen men that Sunday morning. The Germans never fired a shot at him. That's how I got out. The Seaforths were in the front line with the Black Watch. I was sent to England to convalesce where I had two operations on my leg.

Earlier, at the Vimy show I saw the Canadian Black Watch. We were used as a working party for the Canadians when their Engineers dug a mine shaft there. We laboured carrying sandbags out of the long mine shaft. I appreciated being with the Canadians very much because they had the best food I ever ate in all my soldiering. They blew up a huge crater at the crossroads of the Arras-Baupame Road. The Germans could neither go backwards nor bring up reinforcements.

Corporal Craigie T. Mackie
2ND GORDON HIGHLANDERS

I saw some of the men lie down in a trench there and hold thier feet up to see if they could get wounded.

Oh we suffered form the cold and lack of food. We were supposed to get a half a loaf of bread between ten or fifteen men. Most of the time we never got any. When we were in the line we just got biscuits, bully beef, jam, pork 'n beans and, towards the finish, lots of butter. We could always chew the biscuits so we never got hungry. We never saw any potatoes. Behind the line we got rations of bacon. We soaked our bread in grease. Then we got stew. That's all we ever got was stew. Greasy, bloody stew. Lots of times we never had water to drink. Sometimes an officer ordered us not to take a drink until fresh water was carried in. The water came in Jerry cans (gas cans) and was always tainted by gas. We couldn't drink water out of shellholes because it was all full of blood and piss and shit. Water was a terrible thing.

Sergeant Thomas Peck
1ST NORFOLK REGIMENT/5TH DIVISION

In the Arras sector we could see the deal on at Vimy Ridge every night. We were eventually pulled in to assist the Canadians. Our unit was made up of what they called, "Kitchener's Army" and the 1st K.O.S.B.'s (King's Own Scottish Borders—2nd Battalion). They went over with the 13th Brigade of Canadians. We were in support. After taking the initial enemy lines, we pushed the Germans back to the Hindenburg Line. I was wounded at Avion near there. A German threw a bomb at me and it landed between my legs. Lucky for me that it didn't go off! The second bomb that came over, went off and took a chunk out of my leg. That same day a German was caught out in the open in front of us. Some men beckoned him in, but no way! The poor German misunderstood us and picked up his rifle. That was the end of him.

The day I was wounded a German prisoner travelled all the way back with me. He wouldn't leave me. He had stopped a bomb on the side of his face and was quite a mess. The funny thing was that I went in the Canadian dressing room, then they shipped me out, putting me on a hospital train. I looked up from my bunk and who was looking down at me? It was this damn Jerry! He had trailed along with me, but I didn't give a damn where he went. I didn't bother with him. I was more concerned about myself, but he followed me like a dog. We couldn't communicate because all he could say was "Kamarade" and I could not speak German. I got back to England and eventually went to Egypt.

Corporal James Rourke
1ST FIELD COMPANY/CANADIAN ENGINEERS

At Vimy we did everything; digging trenches, laying cables, and mines. If the trenches were blown up we fixed them. We worked day and night.

The ground was all chalk. When we did tunnel work we could not pass the sandbags full of chalk up until it got dark. We had an eight hour shift in Vimy all winter. The day shift would come on at eight and work till four. All they did was fill sandbags with chalk. The next shift was from four to twelve. Each shift had a certain section to work on. In the morning we covered the chalk so that the Germans would not see our work. Candles provided the necessary light. The engineers did the blasting. We did the digging. In the tunnel we were down so far that we never really heard the shelling.

Sergeant Len Davidson
7TH BATTALION/CDN. ENGINEERS

We were known as sappers. The infantry would always ask, "What the hell is a sapper?" It originated from the British Army in Gilbraltar putting in dugouts there. The work on granite and limestone was very difficult. One guy came along and told them, "You know. We're a bunch of saps to do this." That's how we got the name "sapper" or we would say, "digging a sap". Then they'd ask, "What's a sap?" The infantry always had the idea that the Engineers, living behind the lines in barracks were living the life o' Riley. Of course we were!

We worked putting in bridges across different trenches for the 18 pounders to go over. We had no idea what the score was. We knew something big was coming up because we used to have to leave Berthonval Farm at four a.m. in order to do our job. At night when we entered the trenches they were oozing with three feet of sloppy mud. That's what we worked in.

On the morning of the Vimy scrap we had been working on the bridges and we were dead tired. When I returned to my unit I had to see that the men got their rum ration first. It was in a little brown tin that they used to sell cigarettes in. The men got a darn good shot of it. I often felt that that was one thing that kept them going. The Quartermaster, George Miller, gave me the rum. I said to him, "Holy gee am I soaking wet." He said, "Well I'll give you a double shot." I climbed into bed and went right to sleep. Directly behind us was a fifteen inch Navy Howitzer. It was the one that signalled the attack. It was only about a hundred yards away from our billets in the woods of Mont St. Eloy. I never even heard it.

We had to thank the Germans many a time for saving our lives, because when we got to our billets in the rear, they'd shell the daylights out of the forward trenches. One night in particular we went in through the communication trenches. The officer would lead the fatigue party in and the Sergeant would bring up the rear to see that there were no delinquents hopping away. The Germans started shelling us. They were so methodical, sending a salvo over. We would set our watches. In say, five minutes it was all quiet. We would run like the very devil and miss the next salvo coming over. Five men were sent through after each salvo, until we all got through.

The German dugouts in Vimy Ridge were like little cities. They were loaded with water, soft drinks, and wine. The German was issued so many cigars a day and we were issued cigarettes. One brand called "The Beauty Queens" were so strong that if we smoked them we would cough for about a week aferwards. The experience was good.

When holding a Mills bomb you just had to make sure you didn't let go of the lever. Then you could do almost anything with them. If you let go, the detonator would go and set it off within four seconds and bingo! We got the men down in the trenches and explained how to throw them like a baseball and all that. I had this eighteen year old nut Bradshaw. He got one, threw it and the bomb hit the parapet. The bloody thing fell down into the trench. He put his foot on it. Bradshaw blew his foot off and was sent to Blighty. One of the V.A.D.'s in England, a Lord's daughter, nineteen, saw him and eventually got married to him. He was set for life.

Private Harold (Pat) Wyld
CANADIAN FORESTRY CORP

We weren't in any major battles because we were a construction company. We followed the infantry as they pushed the Germans back.

We had to keep going all the time to keep the airstrips operative, so the planes could come or go. We did it with horses and scrapers. We filled in holes and leveled them off. The second day we were in France old Jerry found us and bombed the daylights out of us, scattering the horses all over the countryside. It took us three days to gather them up.

We had a camp of German prisoners as labourers. There were four big lights on each corner of the camp to show any enemy bombers that they were Germans. The German planes managed to bomb us without hitting their own men. The next day when the prisoners came to work, they were laughing. They said, "Oh scared eh! Scared eh!" Once one of the prisoners went to go to the toilet in the bush. I called him back. He turned around, but didn't come back. He started away again. The Sergeant Major came around a corner and ordered, "Shoot that man!" I put a shell in the breech. When the German heard that he came running back. I was almost courtmartialed for disobeying an order. I couldn't shoot an unarmed man running towards me. Most of our prisoners could speak English.

Lieutenant Ernest Hayes
MACHINE GUN CORP/14TH (LIGHT) DIVISION

We worked our way from the Somme to Arras, going in and out of the trenches, reinforcing them and getting occasional leave. Our troops were hidden in caves under Arras prior to the Vimy Ridge attack. We took "the Harp" on the edge of Arras. It had to be captured before we could go forward. The Canadians were on our left.

Certificate awarded to Lt. Ernest Hayes (Machine Gun Corp).

I was looking out just above a shellhole. I had just figured out our angles of fire, when suddenly I didn't know what hit me, but it felt as if somebody had kicked me in the stomach. I lost my breath for what seemed a minute or so. One of my men said, "You're hit Sir." I really didn't know what had happened.

At an operating room on the coast the doctors probed around and removed some of the bullet that had been smashed to pieces. The reason the bullet was smashed was because I used to wear my Colt 45 revolver in front of my waist. It was easier to take out that way. The sniper's bullet hit my revolver. I was lucky. The bullet came out the same way it entered. I still have the revolver.

When on leave at my parent's place on the south side of London near Surrey, my brother Reginald visited. He was then with No. 45 Squadron, R.F.C. as a 2nd Lieutenant. He flew in a two seater Sopwith as an observor. I asked him what happened if one of their planes was shot down in flames? He told me he would have to get out on the wing of the plane. The pilot banked the plane sideways. This helped the plane plunge so the flames would go away from the fusilage.

The next day after Reg got back to France he went out on a mission and was shot down in flames near Ypres. Apparently the Germans flew over near his squadron and dropped his identification discs and pocket bible. They were sent to my parents. It proved his body was found, though we never discovered where he was buried. After the war we had a plaque put up in remembrance of him in a church in Belgium.

Private William (Bill) Hemmings
11TH CDN. MACHINE GUN COMPANY

I was a Private. I could have been an N.C.O., but I turned it down. The rank wasn't worthwhile. Nobody wanted it. We didn't look at the war as a daily job. It was something to be done. Then we were going to get out of it. Some men were promoted ten times, then knocked down to Private again, because they had a job and had said, "To hell with that" and they would lose their stripes again. No one really cared.

Private Robert Parnaby (1898-)
ROYAL ARMY SERVICE CORP

We became reinforcements of the 52nd Siege Battery, transporting two guns and we also supplied ammunition. At Merivale none of us had had a day's infantry training. We couldn't salute properly or shoulder a rifle! Once when driving up the road the brass wanted someone to "Mount Guard". It was comical. They lined us up with our rifles at the shoulder and we didn't know how to manage ourselves. The officer yelled, "Mount Guard!" We didn't respond. He sternly said, "Dismissed. Go down to that ditch and come back with your bayonets on your rifles." We were too busy being truck drivers to bother with infantry drill. In late 1917 I was transferred to the "Flying Column". Consequently I saw every part of the front.

A truck was our home. We were always on our own. It was a crime to run out of oil and grease. No matter how tired we were or even if we had driven a full day, the rules were implicit: the truck always had to be mobile. It had to be filled with oil and petrol before going to bed. Once I asked my Sergeant where the "store" was. He said, "Down the road. What do you want there?" I said, "I must fill up with petrol, oil and water." He said, "You get into bed. I'll look after it for you." He carried it all by himself. They don't come any better than that.

The tires on our trucks were solid, so there were never any flat tires! Our speed limit was eight miles per hour, but we could do about twenty m.p.h. However they were governed at eight m.p.h., so we took the governors off.

One of the trucks (lorries) used in Private Robert Parnaby's days (1917).

Private Alexander Wilson (1888-)
4TH CANADIAN MOUNTED RIFLES

We were crowded in at the front, shooting the Germans. we
killed a lot of our own men because the guys that were ahead of us
were wearing German greatcoats. We couldn't take a chance, so
bingo! German greatcoats were generally superior to allied coats.
They shouldn't have been wearing them.

Private John (Jack) Stacey
12TH CDN. FIELD AMBULANCE

We sandbagged this Fritzie dugout because it was facing the
wrong way. As we worked on it the enemy sent a shell over. They
must have thought we were outting in a gun pit. The explosion sent
up shrapnel, mud and everything else. Of course as soon as we
heard it we flopped down. Something hit me in the fanny. I
thought, "here's my Blighty," but when I was in the dugout I
checked my pants and couldn't feel any blood. I was just hit with
stones!

The Australians were good scrappers. One fellow was out
looking for his relative and he asked a "Tommy" who was on guard
duty, "I'm looking for an Australian camp number so and so. Do
you know where it is?" "Yeah. I know where it is. Go down the
road and you'll see the camp on your right. You'll see their hats
with the crack in the middle and they'll be calling each other
bastards!"

There was a good sense of humour in the war. It's hard to
describe. It had a quality all of its own, destroying despair and
sparking hope, under stress and strain. You would get a half dozen
guys together and there was always one guy who would keep things
going. It was so damn easy to get down. A Scot named Hughie
Carruthers, accompanied two other guys and myself to an estaminet
in Barlin, just outside of Grande Servin for some eggs and chips. It
was payday. We all decided that Hughie would do the ordering.
While waiting to place our order, we rehearsed the French word for
eggs with Hughie, which was 'des oeuf'. The Madame appeared and
asked for our order. Hughie proudly told her, "Oeuf! Oeuf!",
motioning to us. Hughie was quite pleased with himself as the
Madame departed. Not long afterwards, the Madame returned
carrying a great, enormous platter with a dog bone on it. She said,
"Misieur, your parles-vous Francais come les petite chien! Woof!
Woof! Woof!"

Private Ernest C. Robins
LORD STRATCHONA'S HORSE

We used to fire phosphorous bullets in our machine guns, so
we could trace the trajectory. The Vickers fired at a rate of seven
hundred rounds a minute. The bullets were on a belt webbing. The
Lewis gun had about eighty odd rounds in the pan. We carried
about forty boxes of ammunition in each limber. Our fire power
covered all the necessary angles to keep the enemy at bay.

At one village we went into the showers in the coal mines. Girl
miners were there too. We were stripped stark naked under the
showers and some naked females came right in. They didn't worry
about exposing themselves over there.

It was my job to fire a Lewis gun in our sub-section, as anti-
aircraft. One day a German plane was being chased down from the
sky by one of our planes. I kept shooting and shooting at the
German plane. The officer whistled at me. I didn't know what to
do. Then I realized that they didn't want me to shoot at him. Our
plane was trying to force him down. The enemy plane finally circled
and landed. Our officers wanted to capture it because it had some
new parts on it that they wanted to study.

Bombardier William Shaw
ROYAL GARRISON ARTILLERY/151ST SIEGE BATTERY

The Canadian Corps achievement, commanded by General
Byng, was one of the most outstanding feats of arms during the
whole course of the war. It brought imperishable glory to the men
from the great Dominion in the west. It was hailed as a great
Canadian victory and proved that the officers, rank and file of one
of the newest of armies were as good as those in armies which were
steeped in the traditions of Moltke, Blucher and Frederick the
Great. The Canadians captured five thousand prisoners, one
hundred officers, fifty guns, one hundred and twenty-five machine
guns and a large quantity of other materials.

On account of the quick advance and the congestion of traffic
around the ruins of Roclincourt, telephone wires could not be laid
from our battery positions to the O.P.'s on the ridge. With the use
of large flags and a telescope near the officer's mess, signals were
sent ot a similar visual station located on an unused tank on the
ridge. From the tank the messages were relayed by field telephones
to a captured German gunpit, which was being used as an O.P. It
was good work on the signaller's behalf and proved that the visual
method of communications still had its uses and advantages.

On May 3rd the great battle of Oppy Wood took place. We

put up a stupendous barrage. Many divisions were engaged, but Oppy Wood remained the limit of the British advance until March, 1918.

Bombardier James Logan
9TH BATTERY/CDN. FIELD ARTILLERY

Usually we had one blanket. Some nights we pretty nearly froze. I told my partner I would get a couple more blankets. He said, "What are you going to do with them?" I said, "I'm limber gunner. I'll put them in the gall darned cover of the gun." So I hid them underneath the gun. The officer never got wise. We had two extra blankets for almost a year. They never did find them!

One day General Stewart (then a Colonel) came to visit us. We all knew him well. One of our men, Ernie Fleetwood, had a father who was good friends with Stewart, back in Lethbridge. Stewart asked Ernie, "How are things going Ernie?" Ernie said, "Not bad. Not bad." Then Stewart asked, "How's the grub?" "Rotten Sir. If it wasn't for the other batteries we'd be starving to death." Old Major R.T. Young was with Stewart and the Colonel asked him, "How come Major? The grub is sent here to feed these men." After Stewart left, old Young said to Fleetwood, "You know you can get in trouble saying something like that. I've a notion to push it too." Ernie said, "Go ahead. Colonel Stewart and I are old friends. Just go ahead and see how far you get." We had steak for supper that night. We never got a poor meal from then on.

The Canadian Garrison Artillery send a message to the Hun. November, 1916.

A German prisoner once said, "The Frenchman fights for his country, the Englishman fights for his King, the American fights for his flag and the Canadians fight for souvenirs."

We used to write slogans on the shells quite often, like, "We want the Kaiser!" or "Help!" All kinds of stuff! The shells exploded on the enemy side, so we knew the Germans would never read them.

We had an old Clyde horse called "Bully-Beef". It didn't matter where you were, he would tromp on your feet, balk or wouldn't let you ride him. Being a gunner, I was elected to ride any spare horses, including Bully-Beef. One morning at Poperinghe I got out onto the middle of the road and Bully-Beef bucked. He would not move back or forward. Even if hit with a club he didn't seem to feel it. He would not even grunt. I was mad at him. A big army truck came up the road and had to stop. He couldn't get by. I told the truck driver, "Hit him!" The driver said, "I might kill him.' I said, "It will be no loss if you do." He started the truck moving, but it didn't hit the horse very hard. He knocked Bully-Beef his length. After that all I had to do was get him in front of a truck and he would go.

BATTLES OF HILL 70, MESSINES, 3RD YPRES, — Passchendaele (1917)

Bombardier James F. Johnson
5TH CANADIAN MOUNTED RIFLES

Towards the end of September the Canadian Corps moved from Vimy to the Passchendaele area. It was a small town to the west of Ypres, occupied by the Germans. Heavy rains set in. Our purpose was to take Passchendaele Ridge. It was just a rise on the ground. All the area between us and the ridge was low-lying ground. These were the worst conditions the Canadian Army had ever contended with. It was almost impossible to dig trenches in that mire. The Germans had fortified their area with large cement emplacements known as pillboxes. Our pioneer battalions had previously constructed a plank road up towards the enemy. That was the only way our horses and mules could bring in ammunition and supplies. Mules were better than horses under fire. They kept plodding along and did not panic. I felt sorry for those dumb animals. Many of them were killed or wounded. The Germans made use of our plank road as a target! Tanks were hopelessly stuck in the mud. I slept in a tank a couple of nights. The Germans started sending over their cumbersome, two-engine Gotha bombers. In daylight they flew under an umbrella of protection with fighter planes. The planes came over low and their bombs were quite accurate. The only redeeming feature of the mud was that it saved a lot of lives because the bombs or shells would bury themselves before exploding. As the days wore on our casualties were getting very heavy. I lost all track of time there, but I know not many days had passed when a piece of shrapnel pierced my gas mask cannister. The officer told me to take a man with me and go back to headquarters to get a new mask.

Upon arrival at headquarters we were informed that there were no new masks, but we could pick out one from a large pile that had been collected from casualties. The mask I selected later turned out to be defective.

About two nights later, for the first time we could hear small shells popping around us. We knew they were not high explosives. We were soon ordered to don gas masks. It turned out to be the first gas attack of its kind. Previous gas came from cylinders with chlorine. This gas from shells was the blistering mustard gas. We kept our masks on all night, but just around daylight I became sick to my stomach and had to remove my mask. I replaced it as soon as possible. By that time I was feeling pretty groggy. Blisters had started to form on my legs and neck. One blister on my thigh was about eight inches long and four in width. We could see the ground around us covered with a yellowish green. Later I was ordered on a strecher and told not to move until I had a thorough examination. My gas mask had had a slight leak which caused the internal trouble. Early in the forenoon I along with many others were carried out to the plank road where all the stretchers were lined up in rows to await ambulances. There were hundreds of us in line. It was not until late afternoon that my turn came. The German artillery had been shelling a battery behind us. One of their shells dropped short and landed right in the midst of the casualties.

The ridge was taken toward the end of October, but at a terrific price. Sir Robert Borden, then Prime Minister of Canada, announced in the Ottawa House of Commons afterwards, that "the operations at Passchendaele cost the Canadian Corps twenty-four thousand casualties and all there was to show for these losses was a few square miles of ground." On top of that, after the Canadians left the area, the ridge fell back into the hands of the enemy. The achievements of Vimy and Passchendaele could not be compared in terms of victory.

Bombardier William Shaw
151ST SIEGE BATTERY — ROYAL GARRISON ARTILLERY

On the afternoon of June 6th, 1917, Captain Hill of the 285th
Siege Battery told us to be ready to go over the top.

At three: ten a.m. on June 7th, an hour before dawn, nineteen
mines went up on the Messines-Wytschaete Ridge. Simultaneously
the greatest bombardment of the war opened up.

By six a.m. our party came to a German observation post
which was somewhere between Onreat Wood and Oostaverne
Wood. From the front it appeared to be an old farm building, but
behind the old brickwork it seemed a veritable fortress: a two
storied concrete emplacement with walls ten feet thick. The roof
was much thicker. The top served as the O.P. proper, with a very
narrow slit for the telescope. It was smaller than the bottom 'room'.
The first floor dugout was the last word in luxury and comfort so
far as front line conveniences were concerned. It must have been en
enemy division or brigade headquarters because we found eider-
down quilts, wine glasses, cigars, cork and gold-tipped cigarettes,
silk pillows, lots of blankets, two pairs of double periscopes and
large scale maps of the Wytschaete front with range finders made of
aluminum.

Quite a few counterattacks were made to retake Messines
Ridge, but none of them were successful. After four days forward
our party got orders to return to our own batteries, which we did.
The victory on the Messines-Wytschaete Ridge was one of the best
organized of the war. General Plumer, who was in charge of the
Second Army, was a master of detail and thoroughness. For fifteen
months sappers had been at work tunnelling under the enemy lines
so that the mines could be set.

About thirty thousand of the enemy were killed, wounded or
captured in the Messines battle. It was the beginning of the battles
for the liberation of Ypres as the Germans had held those heights
since November 1st, 1914. The ridge soon swarmed with British
observation posts. Our guns were soon pounding shells onto the
enemy concentrated points, batteries, dumps and villages which
were visible from Messines and Wytschaete. From July to October
1917 six separate attacks were made to drive the Hun out of the
Ypres salient, culminating in the capture of the famous
Passchendaele Ridge by November 6th. The Canadians and
Australians played a prominent role in that victory.

Corporal James Rourke
1ST FIELD COMPANY — CANADIAN ENGINEERS

We were under gas at Hill 70. At night we entered the trenches in preparation to go over the top at five a.m. Every shell falling near our line was a 'dud'. We didn't know it at the time, but those shells contained pineapple gas. That is what it smelled like. As a result of all the duds, we thought, "Well he's got a carload of bad ammunition." The next thing we knew it was gas. That was how we passed the night!

We took Hill 70 the next day, Monday, August 15th. The entire battle lasted another ten days. Prisoners were used as stretcher bearers. I was wounded going over the top. A shell blew seven of us up. I became a walking case with a shoulder wound. The stretcher bearers dressed me. Then I took my equipment off and got the hell out of there! I didn't wait to get any more! I got down to a casualty clearing station where I saw some Americans, from their first contingent. I was given a needle to put me to sleep. First thing the next morning the doctors came around to wake us up. They were clearing us for a draft to England. The doctor who approached my bed had a beard. I had never seen a doctor with a beard. I thought, "Holy Jeez! Have I been taken prisoner?" The doctor was an American. I stayed in hospital for three months over in England. Then I went back to France.

Worn out German P.O.W.'s look on as Canadians tend to their wounded

Private Thomas Rattray
10TH BATTALION

Many fellows died at Passchendaele because they lay wounded and nobody caried them out. It took three to six men to carry a man out. We used to take turns as observer in an O.P. just above the trench. I was lucky it was my turn. All my chums were killed down in that muddy trench. We did not know what hit us. I was the only survivor, though I did receive chest and leg wounds. Six men carried me out, walking up to their knees in mud, lugging me out. Some old German dugouts in the reserve line were used for the wounded. An officer was killed while trying to put a tourniquet on me. I layed there a long time before the stretcher bearer party had arrived. The mud oozed over me.

I noticed how full the dugouts were of wounded men. A lot of men died right in the dugouts. There wasn't enough room for myself and some others, so we had to lay outside. That was luck, because I was among the first to be put in those horse drawn ambulances. Mud spattered everywhere as we worked our way down to the hospital in Etaples. My uniform was a mess. My legs had blood poisoning, which the doctors tried to stop. They wanted to take my leg off because it swelled to quite a size, but I told them, "Leave it on or take me with it!" I convinced them to leave it on. Then I was sent to England.

I never got rid of the lice until quite awhile after my placement in a V.A.D. Imperial Hospital. I was covered with bandages, which could not be removed for fear of harming me, so the lice lived in those damn bandages. The nurses washed us, but they could only do so much. There were tubes perforated through my legs and thighs. They drained down to the floor in order to get the poison out of my system. It was kept running all the time. I was the only Canadian in the hospital. It was run by private donations. All these rich girls waited on us. There was only one man in the whole damn place. The girls there, whose fathers were influential in the civil service or army, would do anything for us. It was like an old school and was located near the shoreline. The waves used to come up on high tide and hit the side of the building. The girls would take me out in a wheelchair and run me up a hill for a quarter of a mile at Folkestone. Thirty years later, one of those nurses came to visit me in Canada! They were wonderful!

Mrs. Ian Sinclair *V.A.D.*

I was in the Voluntary Aid Detatchment. We called ourselves
V.A.D.'s like others who were called W.A.C.'s or W.R.E.N.'s. We
were all situated in British hospitals. My hospital had a Canadian
staff, but the house was loaned by Lady Margaret. It was near
Folkestone. Four wings were added to the house for wards. The
staff lived in the main house. We were so close to the coast that
when the casualities from the ships came in, we got them directly
from the front line dressing stations. There was no in between. They
were really a mess. The wounded were shipped out as fast as
possible. We were one of the nearest hospitals. The wounds were
terrific. Our surgeon was a Canadian, trained on Harley Street and
came down once a week to operate. One of our young M.O.'s was
Doctor Tisdale, who has become a very famous doctor in Toronto.
All we had for dressings was saline solution. Nothing else except a
thing called P.C.A. (Phenal, camphor, and alcohol). If the wound
was simply filthy we used to dress it, but after a few days the
P.C.A. was so strong it would sluff everything away, so we used it
to clean up with. Once the saline was used there was not one darn
thing left. The chaps died from infection simply because there
wasn't anything to stop it. We could not put iodine on a stump.
That was too strong. The best treatment was saline. It was amazing
how extraordinarily effective it was when you think that they got no
injections or anything at all. Morphine was used, naturally, but not
antibiotics. An awful lot of the fellows died from shock. Even after
having blood tests and plasma they died of shock. There were a
great deal of amputations. When they were sent through they were
more or less marked for it.

Major Ian Sinclair
13TH BATTALION

The horrible Passchendaele thing was the next battle I was in.
I managed to get through that almost without a scratch. We were
taking over a front line position up amongst the shellholes and
water. I went to headquarters with the Canadian Scottish of which
Lieutenant Colonel Cy Peck V.C. (16th Battalion) was the
commanding officer. He and I shared a little dugout there. We
could barely squeeze in it. We had a field telephone to keep in
touch with things going on behind us. Just as we were taking over
the dugout a shell landed in amongst the battalion we were relieving.
Some chap's tin hat was blown off and his helmet came sailing
through the air, hit my nose and squashed it flat. The M.O. fixed me
up, so I didn't have to leave the line. That didn't count as a wound.

Sergeant David Guild
13TH BATTALION

Passchendaele was just a sea of mud. If it wasn't for the
duckwalks we would have drowned. I admired the old English
Labour Battalions. They were laying planks down for roads. The
trucks would come over and a shell would blow up the road ahead.
While the debris was still falling, that gang was in there with planks
repairing the road.

Lieutenant Geoffrey Marani
24ND BATTALION

There were strict orders when we moved into the trenches to
stay low. The 22nd Battalion had been in the line just in front of
Neuville Vitasse. Mercatel and Telegraph Hill were in the same
front. They found things a little quiet around the support line, so
they decided to get out and start a baseball game. There was a
wonderful view because Neuville Vitasse was at quite a height.
Other troops got out and became spectators until there was quite a
crowd present. Then the Germans let them have it. There were lots
of casualties. That was the French Canadians nature. They were fed
up with that slow motion stuff in the trenches. Our orders were no
more playing baseball.

Corporal Craigie T. Mackie
2ND GORDON HIGHLANDERS

There is nothing wonderful about war. It's terrible. Just murder,
poor bloody murder. In 1917, the British Army fought in
the 3rd Battle or Ypres from August to November. We were there
to take Passchendaele. We went through mud and hell with either
duckboards or corduroy roads to walk on. We lost hundreds of
men each day in casualties; wounded, killed or prisoners. The next
spring, in March of 1918, the Germans went in and took it all back
from us in about two days.

What they had us in Ypres for I don't know. There was no
worse place to fight. It was the worst God damned place to fight.
There were hundreds of other places we could have held the
German Army. To make matters worse, the French Army revolted
at that time. They were shooting amongst their own men.

I'll never forget the 4th of October, 1917 when we went over
the top. Seven of us had grown up together, went to school
together, played soccer together, joined the army together and only
two of us came out alive. That hurts.

The Germans had wonderful trenches and dugouts. The latter were twenty-five feet deep. The British Army didn't dig that deep because we did not intend on staying there. We were there for bloody years! We used to jump from trench to trench cleaning out the Germans if there were any of them left. We would throw bombs over into a trench. Then we would jump in with a bayonet fastened on our rifles to shoot or bayonet whoever was occupying the trench. We usually looked for prisoners, so we didn't kill them all. This German I encountered wanted me to shoot him, but I couldn't do it. He was only a young man. We were all young then. He had a bad stomach wound. I couldn't kill him. He was sitting in the corner of the trench. I was the number one bayonet man of the bombing raid back then. The Sergeant was behind me, two or three men back. When he came around he said, "Why don't you shoot him?" I said, "No. Why? Will you shoot him?" He said, "No." The Sergeant got his head blown off about ten minutes after that from a German "potato-chopper" that landed on his chest. He was a good guy too. Oh no, I couldn't kill a wounded man. It's not hard to kill someone with a rifle because you just shoot. The German was speaking words of English, pointing at his stomach saying, "Kill! Kill! Kill! Shoot! Shoot!" Of course with a stomach wound you don't have much of a chance. We didn't have penicillin at that time. A stomach wound was slow death. Agonizing I've heard. Poor devil.

We did eventually make an attack at Cambrai, but I was in hospital in November, in London, England. I was very sick with gangrene in my thigh. They were going to take my leg off, but the wound was too high up. It wouldn't have done any good. They were talking about it and I told the doctor, "You just leave my bloody leg alone. If I'm going to die, I'll die with my leg on." I asked if it was gangrene and the doctor said, "Yes, gangrene, son." I said, "It won't make any difference because it won't stop anyway." But I guess I was in good health then. There was a nurse named Maggie Piper. I'll never forget her name. It was about a month later, nearing the end of November and she was working on my leg all night! When I recovered consciousness I said to her, "Have you been working on my leg Maggie?" She said, "I am tonight." In the morning, she said, "You know Craigie, your fever is gone." I said, "yeah, I thought that." I added, "You're still here?" She said, "Yes. I've been working on your leg all night to see if we could stop the gangrene. I think we've stopped it. I wrote and told your Mother that I think you're going to live. I'm leaving for Salonica today. This morning." I never saw her again. Maggie Piper. I'll never forget her name. I went back to France again shortly after that.

Captain Walter Moorhouse
4TH C.M.R./CDN. M. GUN CORP.

In the late fall of 1917 we moved into the St. Jean-Wieltje area
for operations towards Passchendaele. Here we had a spot of bad
luck when a bomb dropped in the 7th M.G.Co.'s lines. This
Company was regimental in its routine under all conditions and was
just sounding 'Feed' when the bomb fell. Each man was standing at
attention, a feed bag held with elbows horizontally in front of each
horse. Fortunately for the men, the bomb landed in rear of the
horses, of which 25 became casualties, while only three men were
wounded. Then came an horrible task, that of burying the horses.
The depth of a spade in that soil reached water and other horrors.
However, Maj. Bill Lytle of a Pioneer Coy. nearby came to our
assistance, and 25 watery graves were soon dug beside the
dismembered carcasses. Splash, fill in, and soon the major part of
the equines was hidden, though a fair proportion of the 10 legs still
protruded. We took over from the New Zealand Div. machine-
gunners, — positions only, — there were hardly any men left to
man them.

Passchendaele was indeed a scene of strange and terrible
happenings and strange anomalies. You might see men in full
equipment sitting on the duckboards in the rain, fast asleep under
shell fire. Many during the attacks were mired and drowned in
swamps filled with barbed wire. On one occasion Hun prisoners
loaded belts for us voluntarily, while waiting for escort to the rear
area. A Canadian M.G. officer, severely wounded, was carried for
miles on the slippery mule tracks by 6 German prisoners without
escort. No one would have been any the wiser had they left him to
die in the mud and they would have had an easier and safer trip
back to the prison cage. One feature of the Passchendaele campaign
was the absence of cover. except for immediate need or when
possible as a shelter from the rain, cover was forgotten and
everybody stumbled in the open. The bad footing lent a sort of
aimlessness to one's gait and added to the general inanity of the
scene. In no other campaign of the war was one so conscious of an
insistent undertone of helplessness.

I had an opportunity to re-visit Poperinghe, our old stamping
ground and crossing the Square, saw to my astonishment a Belgian
Captain of artillery whom I recognized as a Mr. Hoogstael who had
been the head of the Belgo-Canadian Construction Co., which had
done several jobs for us before the war, at the outbreak of which he
had been immediately called back to his Battery. We had a bottle of
wine in an estaminet and he told me his battery was to the north of
us near Dixmude facing a horrible area called the Houlthust Forest,

which I had looked down on from the Passchendaele Ridge. He told a grim story of how he had gone up as Observation Officer to an O.P., and on his way found he had left his gas-mask behind. When he had done his time as F.O.O. he started back through the shattered woods when he heard the unmistakeable plop of gas-shells. There was no wind and the gas began to cover the ground in waves. He picked out a suitable tree and quickly climbed up above the gas cloud. Shells kept coming in and as the cloud rose higher he kept climbing up until the cloud seemed to be stationary, and moving like waves, completely obscured the ground. He strapped himself with his belt to a limb and prayed for a breeze. Dawn came and he thought he had fallen asleep, but with the dawn came a light breeze that swept the gas away. He got a blazing from his Battery Commander but had the last word. "Mon Commandant" he said, "you have in your Battery at least one officer who will never, — but never, — forget his gas-mask again!" He told me also that his family in Brussels had phone communication all through the war back of the Allied lines.

Two Canadians wearing gas masks examine a Lee-Enfield rifle (March, 1917).

His story reminded me of one told by Gen. Byng, our Corps. Commander. He and his orderly left their car and as they were going across country to advanced Bde. H.Q., he realized that he had come without his gas-mask. Seeing a soldier returning from the line he sent his orderly to borrow one, which the runner reluctantly handed over. When they reached the dugout, a Bde. officer in his shirt-sleeves opened the gas curtain and climbed into the trench without helmet or respirator. The General thought it a good opportunity for a lecture on gas protection. Addressing the Bde. officer he told him it was not only important to carry a mask, but be able at once to come to the 'ready'. Suiting his action to the word he opened the satchel and pulled out, — "a pair of socks" and the General added ruefully, "and dirty ones at that!"

Private Leonard Wood
2ND EAST LANCASHIRE REGIMENT

At the Third Battle of Ypres (Passchendaele) in 1917, we were called out for two nights on a work detail. Our job was to get all two-by-fours, hammer them together, and take them up to the front. They were what we called "trench boards" or duckboards. We used them in extremely muddy areas, like bogs or shellholes. Some were so wide that you'd drown if you tried to get across. We set them up the best we could.

Corporal Alfred Eastwood
10TH WEST YORK REGIMENT

By July, 1917 they started issuing chevrons. Four blues, three blues and a red, so the quartermaster came around and said, "When did you join the army Eastwood?" "1913", I said, "'13? You mean '15!" "no, I don't, I mean '13." He said, "The war hadn't started then." I said, "No, but the British Army was going on a day or two before that!"

Private Robert Parnaby
ROYAL ARMY SERVICE CORP

We were noted for being scroungers. One of our truck driving fellows had a piano right in the front of his truck. I asked, "Where did you get that?" He said, "Right down the road at a farmhouse over there." People always accused us of pinching the rations. We had to take the rations up in the "Flying Column" at 2nd G.H.Q. It was mainly bully beef. We had a six foot fellow named, "Tiny". He said, "I wonder what's under that tarpulin over there? I'm going to have a look!" He lifted the sheet and found bags of sugar. He put one bag of sugar over his shoulder, went overland to the truck and got away with it. The authorities thought that someone had sent us to pick it up, so we were all right for sugar! We shared it with everyone.

Private William (Bill) Hemmings
CANADIAN MACHINE GUN CORP

Our Company was at Tyne Copse near Passchendaele. The Germans looked right down on us. One day he looked down too close! Some German fighter planed dived on us with machine guns blazing. At the same time their artillery was directed our way. Inside a couple of minutes we had almost six or seven casualties. What could we do. There was no where to run. There wasn't a tree left in the area! We had to wind our way in and out of our position in the trenches. There was a pillbox overlooking us. Otherwise there were no buildings at all. We lived in the water.

I saw the photographer who took our picture at Tyne Copse, but I didn't know who he was. He was under observation from the Germans. He was lucky to get away with it. The Germans probably thought, "What's this guy doing?" You can baffle the enemy that way sometimes.

In the First World War you either went forward or got shot. During barrages I did see shell shock victims. We took over one of those little pillboxes at Tyne Copse Cemetery, so the Germans knew we were in there. Sometimes we used the pillboxes as headquarters. When a shell hit near us we got the noise of the crash reverberating on steel and concrete. A terrific pressure from the concussion would press against every inch of our bodies. The pressure was just as bad outside the pillbox. That damages some men, some more than others. They don't have a mark to show, but they are hurt. There was nothing wrong with a fellow who couldn't stand it. Some were just more mentally prepared than others. It was like a man who has led a scholarly life all of a sudden getting involved in a gang fight. It could be quite a scary experience.

Sergeant Len Davidson
7TH BATTALION — CANADIAN ENGINEERS

After the Passchendaele scrap we put in a gun emplacement about half way up Gravenstafel Ridge. The Germans waited for us to put in that anti-aircraft gun emplacement. It was such treacherous country. I knew a fellow there who won the D.C.M. for saving a mule's life. If everybody knew (as much as I do) about those phoney medals!

Colonel John S. Stewart
7TH BRIGADE — CDN. FIELD ARTILLERY (*Diary Notes*)

I visited the batteries on Abraham Heights the day before our attack on Passchendaele. On November 6th at six a.m. our attack commenced. The 1st and 2nd Divisions captured all objectives and held them against counterattacks. General Morrison phoned saying we had done very well. On November 7th orders were received to push beyond Passchendaele. By November 11th, 1917 the infantry were secure around Passchendaele. I heard General Burstall is to command 4th Division while General Watson is in England. On December 3rd, voting commenced for the Dominion Election. They are making a dead set against Frank Aline in Edmonton and Laurier in Ottawa. Everyone over here is supposed to vote for the Union Government. I do not agree with the complusory tactics as far as voting is concerned. Colonel Gordon told me he is very interested in the voting and says it will be a calamity should the Government be defeated. I voted on December 5th.

THE ROYAL FLYING CORP (1917-18)

Squadron Leader Charles H. Linn (1899-1978)

I joined the R.F.C. in Calgary in 1916. By 1918 we were known
as the R.A.F. (Royal Air Force). There were no machine guns on
our Curtiss planes. One time on the runway at Long Branch, which
bordered Lake Ontario a humorous thing happened. Those biplanes
were simple to operate. Stunts, like loop-the-loop were not
permitted. The men did not wear leather coats, or hats, nor did they
wear long, flowing scarves. During an attempted landing of one of
the two seater Jennies, instead of a perfect landing, the plane
careened straight into the lake! Fortunately, both the plane and its
passengers survived.

Private John C. Laing (1900-)

I joined up at Toronto in the Royal Flying Corp in March,
1917. The training in Canada was in joint cooperation between
England, the States and Canada. England sent over the instructors,
Canada provided the flying fields and the United States supplied
pilots for us, and the rest of the Commonwealth. It was quite an
exciting life for me!

Enough machines (planes) were broken up. The ambulance was
the busiest machine on the field. There would be five or six planes
standing on their nose at almost any given time. The planes didn't
have brakes. Some didn't have wheels. They were put together with
bailing wire and wood. There wasn't much to them. They were all
Jennies. They had a four hundred pound engine. It had twin stacks
and two cockpits. The fellow seated in the rear (if he did not have
earplugs) would have bells in his ears for days, when the exhaust
came out. We could never get used to the open exhaust, because the
cylinders and ports were exposed to us. The Jenny (JN4) couldn't
do much. Sixty miles per hour was wide open. They could take
sixty easier with a tail wind rather than with a head wind. The
shocks of the Jenny consisted of the front axle which was just tied
on with half inch elastic wrapped around and around. They were on
about four inches and pulled apart. We could hear them snap.
Those were shock absorbers.

Through all this I got my first airplane ride. Flight Lieutenant
Coates, from England, came over to the ambulance one morning
and said to me, "Come on. I want to take you up and show you
your little butcher wagon from the air." Twenty minutes before that
we had picked up a body from a plane that had spun down out of
control for about four or five thousand feet. It dug itself under
ground pretty well. The corpse of the pilot was just like a rubber

man when we pulled him out. All his bones were broken. I didn't know if I should go or shouldn't go with Coates. I didn't know if I could refuse or not. So I went with him and he taxis theb plane up the two mile field. He went right down to the bay at the end of it. I didn't realize then that I was getting the ride of my life! He ran the plane wide opne for one hundred to one hundred and fifty yards and then we took off. It wasn't six feet over the ground when he headed straight for the hangar that the ambulance was parked beside. I was sitting there looking at all those hangar windows coming closer. The only thing going through my mind was how many of them we were going to take out! The joy stick hit me. It shot up so fast that I grabbed hold of the exhaust pipes. I burned myself and let go of them quickly! I was strapped in. I was sure we would hit. The weight of my body pushed me on the joy stick. I had never been so scared to death! The height never bothered me, but with a high wind and sitting in the open manouvering, it was rough. We flew over the same spot the accident had occured. Coates put the little Jenny into a spin just like the other poor guy had done. At first we were going around the ambulance. After awhile the ambualnce seemed to be going around in a circle. I guess that was one of the first flights of anyone from Oakville. That was in May of 1917.

At Leaside there was a flying field. There were about twenty-one flying fields in all for the R.F.C. I flew on other occasions. The second time I went up we sucked in a hen on our propellor. It went over the top and pieces came down all over us. We had a pancake landing too. The biggest job was changing the propellors. When we got up to Camp Borden they were flying in the sand there. I could hear the planes whistling as they flew over from four to five miles away. When the propellors were out of balance it slowed the planes down. They were pretty huge propellors for the size of the plane. I had a really good friend who had his right leg cut off from trying to start a plane's propellor. We used to work like a team. The plane would be brought out. If the motor was cold we'd have the pilot sit in the plane and warm the machine up. He'd call out, "Switch off. Switch on. Petrol on. Suck in." He'd put the choke on and pull it two or three times. He stopped when he thought there was enough gas in it. Then he's say, "Contact." You'd pull on the propellor. If you stuck your leg up it was gone. We had to stand with our feet together and sort of push ourselves away from the plane. It was awkward. Some mornings I would start six or seven planes up, after rolling them out of the hangars, because I was qualified. I never had any trouble with them, but some guys lost half a hand or foot because they didn't get back fast enough.

I saw one plane try five times to tackle a field landing. It finally went up on its nose, catching on the corner of the wing and landing flat on its back. Then somebody flying right in behind him got all excited and crashed right on top of him. One fellow steered his plane seven times into the ground and never got a scratch. He walked away from every crash. We thought he was a jinx. Actually he was one of the better pilots. We didn't have parachutes until the last year of the war.

In October, 1917, our planes were all cleaned and stood on their noses in hangars. We didn't know where we were going. Everyone was pretty excited. Some thought we were going overseas, but we eventually found out we were going to Texas to get out of the snow for the winter. They were training American pilots there. We were at Evermond Field in Texas with the 87th Squadron, C.P.S. That was the only squadron that had its eighteen planes all serviceable in one day, which was some kind of a record. The shamrocks on the planes were green. The rest of the plane was all white. Eighty-four Squadron there, had orange and blue on it. Another unit had black planes. In the spring of 1918 we were still in Texas.

Canadians trained in these Curtiss Jennies at Evermond Field, Texas during the winter of 1917/18.

I was discharged on my own request after serving about a year and a half. In April, 1918 the R.F.C. became the R.A.F. I was in civvies when the war ended. I was in Canada on November 11, 1918.

Flight Lieutenant Arthur C. Hardy (1898-)
15TH SQUADRON

In France we were situated half way between Douellens and Amiens at a place called Aveluy Wood. It was near Vergalon Farm. We lived in dugouts with connecting tunnels that were dug out of a huge crater. The dugouts were safe from German bombs unless there was a direct hit. We flew an R.E.8 (Reconnaissance Experimental). I was a pilot. I had a gunner/observer with a circular rotating mounted machine gun in the rear cockpit. He could point them up or rotate them anywhere, but not down. Only on a slight angle down. Our job was to locate enemy positions and send back information on them.

Our airfield wasn't large. There were just hangars set up, but in order to use the field we had to taxi across the road over on to 59 Squadron's airfield and do our taking off and landing there. When we finished we had to cross the road again and put our planes back in the hangars. The planes were pulled back on ropes. We never had much to do with the 59 Squadron. Our Squadron was casualty prone just like the "Flaming 59th" was! I saw some of our planes shot down when I was flying. It was a hell of a mess.

We did see observation balloons which were quite far away, back behind the enemy lines. One of our jobs was going on bombing raids, but primarily we went to shoot down enemy planes. It was our job. I think it was wonderful the way we shot a plane down. It usually took around fifteen rounds to bring a plane down. I shot down about five or six planes. My observer was always with me, but being a pilot and knowing where I was going and what I wanted to see, I took over the observing job. He became my rear gunner. If there were too many German aircraft approaching we beat a retreat as fast as we could. If there were only a couple we would engage in a little bit of a scrap. They would look for our blind spot to shoot at. I usually flew out of formation on lone patrols. It was dangerous. I went over enemy lines many times. I saw the German soldiers fire up at me with their rifles, but they never hit me. Our altitude depended on how close we wanted to observe the enemy. Usually it was about fifteen hundred feet up. I went on dawn patrols. We never had any superstitions or good luck charms.

Once I ran out of gas and had to land in No Man's Land. The boys in the front line trenches came over to help, because my gunner was wounded by enemy planes. I left the plane behind. We went with them into the trenches. That was in 1917. Another time I landed behind our lines. I was so damn near out of gas that I had to fly fairly low to the ground looking for a suitable spot to land without crashing. I landed on a flat field just before running out of gas. I rolled forward until the plane stopped. Not realizing what I had done, I had stopped right on the edge of a great big gravel pit. There was a twenty-five foot drop. I was about ten feet from the whole God damned business going into the gravel pit!

Then German planes which were mostly Fokkers in our area, had camoflauged colours. Our R.E.8's had a yellowish fusilage. The wings were brown. The upper wing extended over beyond the lower wing. If you dived too fast or pulled up too quickly the ends of the wings would fly off. Then you'd spin into the ground and that was it. I've seen it happen, but thank God I never experienced it. Some of my best friends were killed that way.

When I was referred for the D.F.C. I had to go before William "Billy" Bishop, who was from Owen Sound. He was the boss, so to speak. Things were reported to him and so on. If any medals or decorations were given out he was the man to see. I never did get the D.F.C.

Lieutenant Russell H. Williams (1897-)
59TH SQUADRON

In my early training near Owen Sound I crashed my Curtiss Jenny (JN4) into some rural telephone wires. I didn't even see the wires! They dulled the edges of the plane's propellor. That was the only damage done. A few days later I flew the same plane again. I was practising my spin, spiralling downward. I didn't come out of the spin fast enough. Just as the plane started to nose up, it hit the ground. I wasn't hurt, but the propellor was a shambles. I kept a piece of it as a souvenir. Later I had it made into a clock by having the face of the clock set in the hub of the prop blade.

We trained on the F.e.2B. in England. It had a stationary engine and was a two seater. The propellor had two blades whereas the R.E.8 had four blades on its propellor. The R.E.8's performed four major tasks. One was the flying up and down the line on our side, keeping an eye open on the enemy side for any activity going on and reporting it. Artillery observation was another job. One other was photography and the other was low flying when there was a battle going on. In addition to that we did carry six bombs. There were three bombs on the under portion of each wing. They were twenty-five pound Cooper bombs. Every job that we went on except photography we took the bombs with us. We did not take bombs when flying low over a battle either. There was a good reason for this. We flew so low in order to identify troops. My observer identified them by recognizing their helmets. The uniforms on both sides looked the same colour from up there. It wouldn't have been good to report that enemy troops were there if they might have been our own! Then the artillery would open up on them!

Each twenty-five pound Cooper bomb had a fan arrangement in its tail. We had to be up high enough when we released them, so that the wind's speed would pick up and turn the fan a certain number of revolutions before this would allow the percussion cap to go off. Of course at one hundred and fifty or one hundred feet above the troops there wouldn't be a chance of the bombs working properly. If they dropped they would have been duds. It would have been a slim chance of them exploding.

When I was assigned to Squadron 59 I went into Flight "C". In that flight there was an observer named Lieutenant E.J. Hanning from New Brunswick. He was an officer from the Canadian Engineers. I worked with him. He was a mighty good observer. He undertook the training of all the new pilots who came into the squadron from England.

When we were flying, Hanning as an observer, would tell me, the pilot, what to do. If he saw a group of fighter planes (they usually flew in groups no greater than six; unless they had more than one Flight) and I didn't recognize them, he would point them out to me. If he doubled his fist then they were enemy planes. It was up to me from then on to keep an eye on them. He would go about his observations. There was no concern if he didn't double his fist as that meant they were ours. That was one way of communicating.

If I wanted to turn he touched me on the right or left shoulder according to which way he wanted me to turn. I was to judge how fast I should turn by the amount of pressure he put on my shoulder. A light touch meant a slow turn. A fast touch was a different matter, but nothing to do with turns anyway.

When the observer stood up and wanted to speak to me the wind would hit him in the chest or belly and bounce back over across the ears, so there was no trouble hearing him when we wanted to speak to me about something. I couldn't answer him back because the wind would be in reverse, so I could only answer by a nod of the head, yes or no, whatever the case might have been.

When communicating with the ground the pilot had the job while airborne, of unwinding a wheel at the side on which a tremendous amount of wire footage was coiled. At the end of the wire was a lead weight. There was approximately two hundred feet of wire. I never measured it though. When I was rewinding the damn thing it felt like a lot more than two hundred feet. It starts with a small spiral on an axle. The pilot unloads the wire. In his cockpit was a small shelf with a keyboard on it. The observer had a similar arrangement in his cockpit. The observer did most of the signalling as far as ground communications went.

On photography flights there were between one and five planes sent out. Usually three of them went to photograph one area. The number of planes used depended on how wide an area they wanted to cover at a time. The cameras were under the seat of the plane. There was a bit of a wire and a wooden plug about three inches long, with the wire attached to it. To expose a plate I just pulled up on the wire. There were twenty plates carried in the box. The pilot had to take an interest in a sense from the point of view of getting good results.

Ten thousand feet was the highest altitude we photographed from. There was photography done at higher altitudes, but that was done by planes like the D.H.9's. They did it from twenty thousand feet. That meant they could go about thirty miles behind the enemy lines and take their photos. If they wanted the planes lower they told us. When we did observation work we were about five thousand or six thousand feet up, depending on how clear the day was. It was very cold for the observers at ten thousand feet. They had to stand up in that cold. Sometimes I'd wonder how they could have managed it. One fellow I flew with often was Lieutenant G.W.A. Green, from British Columbia. Herbert, as we called him, was in the Canadian Artillery. He was a damn good man. He stood up and took that wind. A lot of people would get down on their little piano stool, which was in the observor's cockpit. Sometimes I wondered if he wasn't going to go through the floor of the plane. He stomped his feet. It scared me a bit in that respect, but I couldn't blame him because I knew what he was going through. The pilot was sitting there fairly comfortable because he was out of the wind. There was a little windshield that pretty well covered my head. If I went to look over the side at something it was a wonder that the wind chill factor didn't take my head off.

In low flying during a land battle near Bourlon Wood, right after the Passchendaele show, the ground communications system was different. We didn't use the wireless. The observer had a bag with a weight in it (rocks or something). At the end of it he wrote on his pad about his observation. I would see him looking down, peering over the side. Then he's be glancing at his map which showed locations. He made notes of what he saw, like enemy movements and so on. He'd tear the notes off and put them in the sack. We kept repeating this while flying in and out of the lines until we filled the sack with messages. The small bag had a three foot long line of coloured streamers attached to it. The observer signalled me by touching me on the spine. He was ready to go to the receiving station. We approached it and when we got about fifty feet above the ground, at the right moment he tossed it overboard. He didn't want to tangle it in the rudder at the back, so he gave a real good throw. We got out of the way really fast. A man from the receiving station ran out and retrieved it without any problem. He ran it back in. Then we turned back to flying over the trenches again to repeat the procedure.

At the end of the Passchendaele show we were flying along one day. Up in front of us and to the left there was considerable activity going on. I got interested in the battle, not watching where the machine was going. Then all of a sudden I got the damndest crack on my left shoulder from the observor. He wanted to turn and turn fast. It was almost automatic for me to pull over to the left, simply because his punch was so damn hard it pulled me down anyway. There was no lapse of time! I automatically stuck my left foot out so that I could make the left turn. I looked to my front. If not for the sharp turn I would have been headed straight on for one of those observation balloons. It was tethered to the ground. I was headed for the basket. I hadn't noticed it in the air before. There were two 51st Highlander fellows gripping the edge of the basket. I wasn't any further from them than fifteen or twenty feet when I made that turn. They didn't have parachutes. They were staring wide eyed at us. I don't blame them for being scared. I would have been scared in their place. As far as my wing tip was concerned I missed the basket wires by only a few feet. It was a close call.

The Germans probably did shoot at us from the ground, but we never knew it. We couldn't hear it and took no notice of an individual rifle even though there was a slim chance of them hitting the plane. I think they shot at us out of exasperation. If we startled them with a bomb they were probably glad to retaliate. We didn't think of them as individuals on the ground. They could have been mummys or dummys. There was no feeling to kill or wound them or otherwise. We came back not knowing if we conflicted a casualty on them or not.

I was due to go on leave on the morning of February 17th, 1918. I was very anxious to get going because I had a brother who had had a skull wound at Passchendaele. He was about to be sent back to Canada. I wanted to talk to him before he left England for home. An orderly knocked on the door, came in and told me I was to report to the orderly room. When I reported the only man present in the orderly room was the recording officer. I was detailed for a certain job that day.

The job was to fly over Baupame on a photographic mission for at least ten minutes. Upon completion I was to fire off a Verey Light pistol. It was a blue one that morning. It enabled our fighter planes to identify us. They started us off first, because the fighters could get up faster. Before a flight the observor was always assigned to a pilot. This time they altered that rule and let me pick anyone.

I saw gunner Eagan. I thought I'd pick him because he was a nice fellow and it was a tough job. He was no good against the cold though. He wouldn't be sending down messages anyway. I had heard two fellows in the mess complaining about what a poor observer he was. He was the least valuable to the Squadron so I took him.

We left the aerodrome, getting over to the other side of Cambrai where I started my photographing. I kept track, counting each plate that I exposed. I was almost over the outskirts of Rheims. Over the wing ahead, I could see the centre of the city. At that moment I had eighteen out of twenty of the plates exposed.

German pilots relaxing before going on patrol (1917).

When the Germans saw our plane in the air they communicated to their aircraft by sending up six anti-aircraft gun bursts.

That warned the German fighters that we were a lone R.E.8. I immediately banked the machine to the left, kicking out my left foot. I was belted in. I turned to look over over the side. As I did do, I was hit in the chin. I could feel it.

By the time I saw the enemy plane I would swear that he wasn't more than twenty-five feet above our plane. He had been firing as he descended on us. That bullet had caught me. As I turned I felt another bullet go by my cheek. The first bullet was more like a nick you get while shaving. No more than that. I was astounded to notice that a number of the flat steel wires between the lower and upper wings had been ticked by bullets. They snapped just like that! I used to think they were stronger.

From the moment I noticed that several of the wires were broken I thought to myself, "Jesus! I've got to slow it right down or the wings will come off. I've got to handle it easily."

So I slowed down to the minimum flying speed. It was about fifty to sixty miles per hour. That was fifteen to twenty m.p.h. less than my previous speed. I decided to try and get to our side of the lines. According to my estimate I was about seven or eight miles from our side of lines. I thought of my brother who was killed at Passchendaele. I didn't want another telegram going home to my parents. My 'dandruff' was up too, because I was still damn mad about the orderly room interfering with my leave. I guess if you get upset enough it sometimes works favourably for you. Otherwise I may not have made the attempt to get home.

I was keeping the left wing down, so that the right side of the machine was exposed upwards. A few nights before I had been doing some night flying to keep in practise for takeoffs and landings. At one point I looked over the edge and saw the exhaust coming out of the right hand side beside the pilot's cockpit. You would never notice it in the daytime, but at night I could see a foot long flame coming from the exhaust. It would be simple for a bullet hole to get in there. If the petrol leaked out and travelled the four to six feet to the flame it would take a second to get there. That would explain our nickname, the "Flaming 59th Squadron", because so many of us went down in flames. I was determined to keep the machine turned up that way so that if we were hit on the right hand side, the petrol might not leak out. The petrol tank was on the left side. I figured every German down below would be looking up at my plane, so I straightened the plane out for a moment. I leveled off. Then I snapped the picture. My nineteenth photo was exposed when I turned left over Rheims. I thought they might like an angle shot of the roads and the city. Then I tiled back to my left again. As soon as I reached the second strands of barbed wire I reached over and switched the engine off. I planned to sideslip or crash into our lines. I was just above the eight thousand foot mark. To my surprise the enemy planes left. I saw them head off safely. They must have figured I was a goner. I think they left me because their ammunition supply was getting low. If they met up with any of our fighters they would have been in trouble. Besides, fighter planes on both sides could only spend about an hour or so in the air. They used up their petrol climbing and diving at terrific rates.

I banked the plane around until I could see our "A.L.G.", which was a small ground area kept clear for emergency landings. It was about one city block in size. There was one per squadron. The neighbouring squadron had one, but I didn't know where.

I estimated the A.L.G. was five miles away and that I could just make it there if the wings stayed on. I was hoping I wouldn't encounter an air pocket. There wasn't much chance of an air burst. You might say, "all was quiet on the western front"! I had dropped to a little over five thousand feet when I had turned. I had hoped that if any of our planes were flying that they would have the good sense to keep away from me because I didn't want to get in their wash. I didn't think my plane would hold together in their wash. A "wash" is the air coming from behind a propellor, just like the wash from a motorboat going at a good clip. A lot of holes were visible in the fusilage.

I thought my gunner was dead. I had heard his groans earlier. I had told him, "Damn it! Shut up!" Then he didn't moan anymore. The enemy planes had a definite pattern. They fired on us from farther back after I had slowed down. That gave me a better chance to side-slip them. The enemy had to pull out very fast when descending. They would get a few shots off, then pull up. I upset their pattern.

We looked at my gunner, Eagan. I was surprised to see that he was alive. Between the two of us we got Eagan out of the cockpit. Then the other men arrived. I left it to them to help him. He's still living as far as I know.

I became a curiosity in the hospital. I began to wonder why. First, a medical officer, rank of Lieutenant looked at me, then a Captain. The Captain brought a Major, until eventually a group of men accompanying a Colonel came to see my wound. None of them had asked me how it happened. The Colonel said, "The only way that the bullet could have missed his hip bone is that the wicker chair at the back of the seat must have deflected the bullet as it came through." That was a ridiculous diagnosis. I was on the verge of telling the Colonel differently. Then I thought, "No my God if I correct that Colonel (he was a bugger) he will send me to a hospital in the south of France." I wanted to get to England as fast as possible. I had corrected a Major a few days before for something not so obvious as that. By that time I thought that maybe it had some bearing on why my leave had been upset. Some of those Majors and Colonels could get awful touchy at times. That was the attitude that pervaded among individuals at certain times when they had a bit of authority, no matter what business they were in. It's human nature for some. They are a small purportion who at a certain point don't want to be talked back to or corrected by anyone that they consider inferior.

In Canada there was little or nothing reported about the R.E.8's in the papers, which surprised me. It was all about the fighter planes. One time in Canada after the war had ended, someone asked me, "How many planes did you shoot down?" I said, "None." He turned away from me as if he had found a bad smell. People were so intent on statistics like that. His nose actually went up in the air!

THE GERMAN ARMY

Leutnant Johan Farkas (1898-)
NUMBER 32 REGIMENT — GERMAN ARTILLERY

We were a fighting unit of the Austrian-Hungarian Army. I was nineteen when I was called up for the war in 1917.

We had two kinds of guns, the eight inch and twenty-two centimetre guns. The twenty-two centimetre was a heavy gun and difficult to load. I was eighty miles from Paris once. We were shooting the big thirty-two millimetre gun. They hit a cemetery and blew up all the poor dead men. Coffins came out of the ground! Bones and everything. Another shell hit a church. After that we found that it was too much trouble to use the big artillery guns. I was only in France long enough to catch my boat to Italy. There were about fifty of us on the ship. I saw most of my fighting in Italy.

I was wounded in three places in the back once. They were small pieces of shrapnel. The doctor removed them with pinchers. One piece was about an eighth of an inch from my lung. The doctor told me, "Any nearer and you would have been finished." I was in the hospital for six weeks after that. It resulted from a British airplane strafing us while we were destroying a barn. Three of our men died instantly from head and chest wounds. About fifty minutes later the German planes came along and shot down three British planes. It was quite a dogfight. I was taken behind the lines on a stretcher. We got all kinds of cigars and cigarettes to smoke. Some types of cigarettes were banded with tobacco leaves instead of paper. There was no shortage of them.

When I got back from the hospital it was my job to use a spyglass and sit getting the right range on the enemy through it. I signalled the artillery by raising my hand. Bang! One time I saw some infantry target. My gunner landed his shells right between the men. It was like a scythe cutting down grain. Those people had never done anything against me. I had to shoot them. Why? I felt so sorry. They were the French.

Another time the English used gas. We found yellow corpses. A highway of dead men. We did not have time to clean off the highway. We drove over dead men and everything. I felt so sorry. It made me sick. The big wagon we were in drove right over the heads of the bodies, splitting them open. Later we cleaned it all up.

The English and French had lots of chocolate and other good stuff. They left it behind. We were very hungry. An officer ran over and warned us, "Don't touch it because it's poisoned." We destroyed it. There was wine and whiskey, but we didn't touch it!

French airplanes made a musical sound like a violin. We could tell by their sound, which was ours and which ones were French.

I was in the German Army for one and a half years. By golly, that was enough for me. No one wanted to fight after that. Our heart wasn't in it anymore. Many of us spoke of going to Canada or America after the war. We were between Italy and another country when we heard of the armistice on the wireless. We were loaded in open boxcars like animals. The soldiers there kept a close watch on us. We were all very glad to be going home. I ended up going back to Budapest, Hungary where I originated from.

GERMAN OFFICER'S DIARY (1916)
Discovered in the field by Major Walter Moorhouse

May 24, 1916: There is no doubt that something is going to happen. One sees so many artillery officers. This morning there was a General of artillery with several officers at Tenbrielen. The "double hill" 60 (Hill 60), in front of the 120th Infantry Regiment is to be taken. When we are in possession of the commanding heights, a further advance is to be made.

May 25, 1916: It is incredible that after two years' war, in which so much experience has been gathered, so many stupid things are still done. The Battalion carried out manoeuvres this morning at the strong point at Tenbrielen. Excellency Count von Pfeil was there. The attack has to be made as naturally and realistically as possible, e.g. losses are to be notified? Why? In order that the Divisional Commanders may see for once at least, more or less what it looks like. And still, when anything is being done which every musketeer in the front trenches does right of his own accord, which his human instinct shows him how to do, then we hear, "But, gentlemen, here — never mind what you do in the trenches. Here things must be done according to the drill book."

For example, they say, "At Doberitz we used to fill tent squares with straw and throw them on the undestroyed barbed wire." But where do we get straw from here, where the men hardly have enough to sleep on? Why don't they come and see an attack from close by? But it has always been the case, the man who draws the most pay is right.

I must say it is a shame when a Lieutenant hears almost every day, "you get 310 marks to do your duty". We in turn might say, "You didn't get 1,000 marks to play peace-time tricks of this kind, things which a Lieutenant understands better than a man who sits behind the lines in a bombproof concrete dugout."

Such things are not calculated to raise morale and stimulate the spirit which should always be maintained. The men have their eyes open too. When Excellency Count von Pfeil came, "One can see he gets his twelve rations."

May 26, 1916: Went into the trenches and relieved a Battalion of the 11th Reserve Regiment.

May 30, 1916: At six a.m. we are sent to rest at Wervicq. It came as such a surprise that we don't know what they mean to do with us; whether they are going to use us as reserves for the attack on Ypres which must be expected soon, or packed off to Verdun. The order of the day of the Corps expresses recognition of our excellent bearing in trench warfare against superior forces, and believes that we shall win further successes there, whither the Emperor calls us.

June 1, 1916: the attack is to begin early on the morning of June 2nd at seven minutes past — (the hour will be known shortly). The 11th Reserve Regiment is presently held in readiness in our regimental section. It has a free hand and if the situation is favourable, will take the enemy's first line. The objective is the capture of the first two trenches and where possible of the third line. In doing this the subordinate commanders will have a free hand. In all circumstances Hills 59 and 60, which lie in front of the 120th Regiment must be taken. A mining company is attached to the 120th Regiment (it comes from a Silesian Regiment which is in reserve.) Farther to the right, the 125th and 121st Regiments will attack under the command of General von Stein.

There is a colossal amount of artillery and trench mortars. Our Division has, in all, 95 guns (including 21cm. etc.) Lt. Col. von Watter is in command. The Regiment has 2 heavy, 8 medium, 10 light and 2 Ehrhard trench mortars (Minewerfer), 10 breech-loading mortars. By these together with the artillery, now the front lines and now the rear lines will be carefully bombarded for pre-arranged periods, reckoned in quarters of an hour. At times the trench mortar fire will stop, and the artillery will lift its fire on to the support trenches. It will continue thus for 4½ hours, and finally there will be "drum fire" on the front trenches. The attack must be successful, if 200,000 shells have to be fired. The mines are timed for two minutes past —.

Our 111th Bn. & 127th is in Brigade Reserve in the "Kaiser-Lager" with the 120th, the 111th Bn. in Divisional Reserve in TENBRIELEN. The 1st B.N. 127th is in Corps Reserve at WERVICQ.

2.6.16 The attack was completely successful — we are in possession of the important "double hill." I gather the 121st and 125th had no easy job.

3.6.16 In yesterday's, 718 prisoners were made, including 1 General and 1 Colonel. A splendid success.

One is proud of the victories which Germans and Austrians, Bulgarians and Turks win on all sides. Our enemies, after their continual failures, must soon recognize their helplessness and the uselessness of their sacrifices, and make an end of it.

8.6.16 The Bn. went into the trenches this morning unexpectedly relieving the 120th. the 1st Coy. relieved with 2 platoons in newly constructed trenches; 1 platoon had to be kept in the rear, as there is no room in front. The 2nd and 3rd Coys. are in our former first line position ("Chailsheim-on-Durlesbach"); the 4th is in support at ZILLEBEKE where one platoon of the 2nd Coy. still is on account of lack of room. One platoon of the 4th Coy. moved back still further into the "walkheim". So a whole battalion is being sent into the front line for the sake of 2 whole platoons. the sectors are now considerably smaller and it is really a miracle, with today's heavy bombardment, nothing has happened. The English fired all day, and only with heavy calibre guns — I should put them at 22-24 cm. Our artillery has orders to shoot as little as possible in order that the English may be able to dig themselves in peace. We hoped that they would creep up close to us, in reality they are about 500 yards off, so that they can bombard us very heavily, of course, without danger to themselves.

Nothing more is to be seen of a large part of our old first line position only traces of the position; everything is shot to pieces, one shell hole after another, beams sticking up in the air, dugouts completely fallen in, parts of the trench buried.

12.6.16 The 125th is next to us. I heard that a whole squad of the 125th said they would not go forward any more; they had better be shot out of hand, then there would be no need to carry them back. The artillery fire is, indeed, absolutely fearful, but I should not have thought such a refusal to obey orders possible, and the rumors which had found their way to the 127th that the men of the 125th would not go forwrd any more, are thus confirmed. Perhaps the personality of the Commanding Officer (Stuhmke) is partly responsible. Some of the 119th are doing the same; they expressed themselves freely in the same way. Men of the 11th Bn. 125th lay in dugouts to the rear. After all, it can be understood, with such awful artillery fire, which has been raging since the 2nd by day and night.

13.6.16 The catastrophe happened to-day; the "double hill" was lost back. Since 2.30 this morning — then the English opened a fearful artillery fire. At five o'clock the Coy. was moved from its support position at "Gronenburg" up to BOBLINGEN. Only the 1st platoon, however, managed to get there. The two other platoons stayed behind, as connection was lost. I myself went forward to look for Lt. Pfleghar, but could not find him till 8.30 when the 1 Bn., 125th, and 2nd and 4th Coys. of 127th were to attack. It was quite irresponsible, how many *superfluous* people were pushing about in the communication trenches right up to the front line. Men of the 127th and 120th, pioneers carrying up hand grenades, men of the 125th...The 2nd Coy. 127th was supposed to be on the left of the 125th, but I could not find it. The attack would naturally not be made. The 120th went forward, the 125th came back; while the English artillery continued to fire ceaselessly with light and heavy guns. I looked for someone of the 2nd Coy., 127th but could find no one.

At 9.30 the attack was attempted for the second time, but again could not be made. We could not contend with such a mass of heavy artillery. The strength of the fire showed clearly that the English had brought up a fair number of new batteries. It may be remarked that the English are firing ammunition of the most recent date; 8.2.16., 1.3., even 16th May are said to have been found.

The greatest mix-up gradually prevailed. The men drifted this way and that in the communication trenches, discouraged and convinced of the ill-success of the attempt, especially since our artillery, particularly the heavy, seemed to have given out completely. The English meanwhile fired like mad, so that there is literally no position, the trenches are quite destroyed or levelled, one shell hole joins the next, and besides this fearful devastation, the dreadful spectacle of the many dead, and the number of missing, depresses everyone.

Now that the English had enfeebled us by artillery fire, and reoccupy their trenches, and can sweep us with machine guns from the hill, they are content.

14.6.16 Excellency Count Pfeil expressed his sympathy with the troops for their heavy losses. He regards the retirement as a necessary consequence of the heavy artillery bombardment and declared his unshaken confidence in the troops.

How cuning and sly the Englishman is. In order to be able to work without danger, last night they sent up rockets with two green stars, a pre-arranged German signal that our artillery are firing short. The artillery, seeing these two stars, lifts its fire beyond the British trenches. They allowed themselves this bad joke yesterday, when they were again in their old position, and our artillery thus served us very badly for the second time, after having failed to support us with a single shot during the English attack, and only fired later, probably when they had got their boots on, the proud artillery. First the English artillery fire — and now our own artillery fire, the only logical effect of which can be to draw fire (at present all heavy fire) on to our front trenches — I did not notice much co-operation between the two arms.

15.6.16 When I think of the losses of the last few days, it is striking that there were very few, almost no slightly wounded, but only severly. The nervousness of the men has increased to such a degree that they saw ghosts and perceived Englishmen in the pioneers who were placing wire entanglement in front of the position that was to be constructed, and hurriedly ran back, first one by one, then all, in a stampede and panic.

16.6.16 The 26th Division has, up to the present, 800 dead, the number so far buried. That is a huge number, without the missing and wounded. The Division is commanded from to-day by Lt. Gen. Von. Moser.

18.6.16 At 5 yesterday morning, the so-called "Gallipoli enterprise" an hour's bombardment of the enemy's trenches in front of the 120th — took place.

1.7.16 As there was a favorable wind for the English, "immediate readiness to receive gas attack was ordered."

2.7.16 Our fellows grumble at the amount of work; now nothing is right, of course, everything is wrong, especially the food. We get enough food and the men simply cannot take things easy. I hope it will be better at WERVICQ.

14.7.16 The voyage of the German merchant-submarine "Deutcheland" to BALTIMORE will be discussed throughout the world as a unique event. Here is joy, *triumph*, gratitude, there consternation, envy, thirst for vengence.

15.7.16 Work is being carried on feverishly in the first line on the construction of concreted dugouts. Even officers of the Corps Staff are inspecting the position and the places where the dugouts are to be made. Their interest is welcome; it has lasted long enough. We have always been told in long Divisional and Brigade orders, that during a bombardment the men must go into shell-proof dugouts. Nonsense. When there are none. We need such dugouts, because we must at all costs hold our front line.

It was the policy of the Germans to bury their pilots where they crashed (1918).

Part II

26.7.16 It is now certain that we are to move. His Royal Highness Duke Albert of Wurtenburg took leave of the 1 Bn., this morning. Nothing, however as to a possible theatre of war could be gathered from his short address...At 3 o'clock the Bn. marched off from TENBRIELEN to MENIN. The 123rd and 124th are here. The general view is that we are going to Galicia. The 26th Infy. Div., is also preparing to leave.

29.7.16 Yesterday morning at 6 the Bn. unexpectedly left by road for LAUWE, entertained there and detrained at BOHAIN. Marched by way of PREMONT to SERIAN...By motor-lorries to HEUDICOURT...It is the 2nd Army General Gallwitz.

30.7.16 What we hear here is incredible. The troops here had only *one* front line position, instead of a second and third, as we had. And this ommission has cost them dear. Flung out of their only position, they are now lying on open ground. On the other hand, the transport wagons were protected with concrete, but not ready to move; some of them had broken axles, wheels, etc. The experiences of the Champagne battle had not been taken advantage of in any way. This was the reason why so much transport was lost. Further, the transport was not armed, so that enemy airmen were able to cause enormous losses from quite a low altitude.

At 7 o'clock the Bn. marched on to EQUANCOURT, which is full of troops and transport...The 123rd and 124th are up front.

31.7.16 The 1 Bn. goes into the trenches to-night and relieves the 22nd Bavarian Regt. The 111 Bn. stays at EQUANCOURT, the 11 at FINS...The Bn. was moved up by way of ETRICOURT, MANACOURT, and Government Farm into the little wood of BANCOURT — into the north-eastern corner, as the western edge is under artillery fire.

1.8.16 Tremendous confusion prevails generally at the front. We cannot get to our position. Lt. Pfleghar, who has been from the Company to Bn. H.Q., says that the Battalion Commander knows nothing at all. Men are lying all mixed up, Jager, 22nd, 23rd, 19th, in holes and shell-holes. Saxons are lying there too, with whom the field police have a tiresome job, as they have to fetch a great many out of the cornfields. So it is no wonder if nobody is in front. In EQUANCOURT a man said when questioned "yes, I went off and came back again." It is a fearful mix-up, and as there is no order and supervision, no methodical counter-attack can be made. Our airmen are rabbits, not one shows himself over the lines.

2.8.16 Yesterday evening at 11 the company marched off, after having been scared out of its bivouac in an unpleasant manner by shell fire at 10.15. The 3rd Company had several killed and wounded. It was a long march, during which touch was lost several times, so that the men in the rear nearly always had to double. We passed through MANCOURT, left COMBLES; which was burning and was still being continuously bombarded on our right, went along the ravine and reached the slope half way up which the position is situated...Two companies of the 111th Bn. are in reserve at COMBLES; two more, and the 11 Bn. are in the little wood which we left yesterday. The French airmen fly scarcely 600 feet above our lines, *while not a single one of ours shows himself.* We cannot fire, for if we do, immediately we get heavy artillery fire, so we have to put up with it — lying in a trench, in broiling heat, thirsty, and waiting till we are shot to pieces or buried, or if God will, come safely out of it...We have brought with us preserved rations. There is no water. At the best it can be got in COMBLES which is generally under fire.

3.8.16 We got coffee from COMBLES yesteraday. No light matter for the men who fetched it.

The soil here consists of lime and chalk, good for digging in but there is very great danger that a man who gets buried will not come out again. Luckily I found another yesterday afternoon. The French only fire with heavy calibres — 12cm. to 30 cm. they fire all day long with perfect accuracy, with aeroplane observation, while not a single one of our airmen is to be seen; the French airmen are masters of the air. They brought down a German yesterday morning, too; that is disgusting. When we read the French communique we put a question mark after these claims, but only for the sake of illusion — it does really happen.

4.8.16 ...We experienced the most accurate barrage fire possible; it was a lesson and a proof to us all of what will happen to us if we either attack or defend. Unfortunately it again caused us some losses, so that I have now had 2 killed and 8 wounded in my platoon in the last four days...

I received the news that my dear good Werner was killed on the 27th...I was filled with rage towards the English, by whose impious hand he died.

6.8.16 ...The Bn. is relieved in rather difficult circumstances. Unfortunately we again had some wounded. It is incredible that the Bn. is going into the same wood which was fired on when we were leaving it.

Our airmen are so inferior that they do not hold the field even as far behind the front as this. Our standard of airmanship is far below the French and English. In consequence we cannot go a yard outside the protecting foliage of the wood; enemy airmen are nearly always cruising around the bit of wood and signalling. We are here frankly inferior — we may confess it to ourselves, or not. "Germany ahead in the air" is not the case at all. That is why we have these enormous losses at the front too. No one shakes off the pests which stick to us continually all day and till into the night. This moral defect has a bad effect on us all. Ultimate success depends only on the combined use of all weapons at our disposal, which is lacking here. It is all the more surprising that we shoot down so many enemy aeroplanes — but they are always the same ones.

7.8.16 Great air activity, which is gradually getting on our nerves. The wood was fired on at 10 p.m. so that we had to clear out...The Bivouac, unfortunately could not be moved futher back... 8.8.16 The English and French attacked at 5 a.m. on the front held by the 123rd, 124th and 127th, and were everywhere repulsed; the 124th were assisted by the Bavarians. the 124th Regt. took prisoners 7 officers, and 346 men, the 127th some prisoners and 2 machine guns. In order to keep the Company together if the bombardment of the wood is repeated, every squad to-day constructed a trench. Yesterday one man of the Company bolted as far as EQUANCOURT; there the Town Commandant arrested him and telephoned to the Bn. The fellows are making the Regt. a laughing stock. Another roundly declared that he would not go into the trenches any more. All Capt. Goz' representations were unsuccessful. The number of men reporting sick is also mounting up. Lt. of Reserve, Schenk (F.I.) reported himself sick-foot trodden on. Some of our men are absolute cowards, who take every opportunity to get away from the company.

9.8.16 Protestant Church parade at 10.45. He (the Chaplin) evidently with intention, dwelt on loyalty and courage, and spoke of fear and cowardice...Let us hope that we shall not be more than another week on the SOMME.

10.8.16 The 2nd and 3rd Companies relieved the 4th and 6th in COMBLES shortly after midnight. The men are in trenches which lead through the houses, in places cellars. The officers and all the higher staffs are in the catacombs, which were only discovered when the civil population took refuge in them when COMBLES was bombarded. They have 3 exits...They are about 15 cm. (45 ft.) underground. COMBLES presents a picture of the most fearful destruction and barbaric fury. We are partly to blame, as we have emplaced many guns in houses in the eastern part of COMBLES, but the north-western part has also suffered severly.

12.8.16 Up to this morning about 20 men had reported sick in the last 2 days, and some of them have been placed on the sick list. This is because the men, with the best will in the world, have no opportunity of taking things easily; they are simply overworked and overstrained. In spite of all the men in the front line must be fit to fight and fresh...

There was an attack. The French...partly occupy MAUREPAS alone with us. Only on the front held by our Regt. were they beaten back after severe fighting. The 1st and 3rd Companies each put in 1 platoon...Several officers fell, and even airmen took part in the fight with their machine-guns from a height of 300 ft. Men came back with wounds in the head inflicted from above...

13.8.16 I went in front of the DOUAGE wood to reconnoitre a position in which many retreating Bavarians might be collected, who had to retire from MAUREPAS to COMBLES...12 p.m....Left to relieve the old position.

Apparently at that point, August 13, 1916 was the German officer's last entry in his diary, because he was killed in action.

THE GERMAN AIRFORCE

Oberleutnant Alfred O. Wolter (1896-1978)
NO. 56. GERMAN AIRFIELD UNIT

I was drafted into service in late 1915. My Mother and Father tried to keep me out of the war as long as possible. I worked at their bayonet making steel factory. The government ordered us to make bayonets. We had no choice. My parents would pay so much at a time in gold to the government in order to keep me from going to war. It was who you knew that kept you out.

I trained for a time and by early 1916 I was involved in active service on the eastern front. We operated our Feldflieger Abteilung 56. (Airfield Unit) up around Lida, Russia where it was very cold. Food was in short supply. My parents sent me parcels all the time with foodstuffs in them. Once two soldiers went searching for food around some farms. They found forty-eight eggs. We had furloughs in places like Breslav and Cologne. Our stations were moved from time to time, so we didn't get to know everyone very well.

On one occasion I met Rittmeister Baron Manfred Von Richthofen. He was a small fellow. We were only acquaintances, meeting when our air groups got together once in awhile. The Red Baron wasn't known so much for how many planes he had shot down as he was for his nobility. We had drinks together. I used to play the piano and violin for entertainment. Many times our unit would have sing-songs.

Most of our transportation was by train or by horse drawn wagons. We also had the occasional ride, bundled up in a German officer's staff car. Our plane's hangars were sometimes nothing more than tents, which could be loaded on the wagons. The horses were used for dispatch riding too.

At age sixteen every able German had some form of military training for about six weeks. Reinforcements were needed. Lots of men that were good for nothings in peace-time, came out like men after the war. It was like day and night. The military made men of them. We were very sports oriented, playing lots of football and getting involved in gymnastics.

The German footsoldiers used to have to go on long route marches. After being well worn out they were ordered to sing on their march back into camp. The officer wanted to keep up their morale.

I flew an Albatross at times. Our bombing raids were among the first of World War One. We used to fly our planes over the railway tracks, using a train's lights to guide us. Those were our bombing routes when flying in our Rumplers. All we had was a compass to guide us back. It was very cold flying those planes. I was a pilot. A gunner or observer always accompanied me in the two-seater planes. I shot down one French plane, but I felt bad about it afterwards. One of my best friends was forced to jump from his plane. It was on fire. I found his body on the ground. He

Alfred O. Wolter's rear gunner in a German Rumpler plane (1917).

was only two and half feet high. His legs had gone into his abdomen. It was horrible. Once I was badly deafened in one ear when a shell exploded near my plane as I was flying it. I was put in hospital for weeks afterwards. Another time a couple of German soldiers were standing talking to each other. Suddenly a shell came over. One of them just disappeared. He was blown to bits!

One time at a station, many of us were relaxing by our airfield. All of a sudden our Hauptmann (Captain) yelled, "Here comes the enemy! It's a raid!" They were British planes. He screamed, "Allus out! Everybody out!" I refused to go out in that. I would have been killed. The men who ran out in the open were shot down almost immediately. Our officer had been drinking, so in a fit of glory he ordered us to fly up and attack. Our planes were shot down before we even had a chance. The officer was courtmartialed for his stupidity.

I never saw any of the champagne or girls like there was in the movie "The Blue Max" (1966). I enjoyed it though, as I did shows like "Snoopy and the Red Baron" and "Those Magnificent Men in Their Flying Machines" (1967). I wrote my own pass out of the German Airforce on Armistice Day. I was glad to be out of the war. I did not like war. I just wanted to go home.

THE FRENCH POILU (1917-1918)

Sergeant-Major H. John Wickey (1899-)
412TH REGIMENT

I am of Swiss origin. Having completed an agricultural course in college, I went to work in France. At that time there was a mild form of war hysteria. Many of the students, some Swiss and others from bordering countries decided to join the French Army. Being somewhat hot headed and much to the dismay of my parents in Switzerland, I decided to join. The nearest recruiting office was near Lyons. It was October, 1917. Those of us who were willing to sign for the usual five years were incorporated in the Foreign Legion; a few who wanted to join up for the duration of the war were incorporated in other Regiments. I was assigned to the 412th Regiment of Infantry which was part of the 58th Morroccan Division. We were occasionally brigaded with the Legion. Our emblem was a sort of crescent. I was only eighteen when I joined up, but in those days I knew of nothing better to do.

After the usual indoctrination and basic courses I was drafted back to the 412th Regiment as a machine gunner. During my first week at the front I was perhaps a bit too 'high and mighty'. Sometimes I was compared to the size of my shoes. A French Sergeant-Major (when I was just a Private) came over to me and said, "Jean, (my French name) if you want to get along well in the French Army there are two persons you must respect and obey. One os your Sergeant-Major and the other is your Major!" That was the best advice I ever had. After that I never had nay trouble.

The French military school stressed that the main point was to "Attack! Attack! Attack! Always attack!" That was the theme of the day. Following the battles of the Marne and the Somme, the French were almost decimated as a result of those mass attacks. Usually it was against a German machine gunner for only a few yards of ground gained. The French loss was tragic. In 1918 we were told to be more wary. We were sent in small groups here and there. One group would go forward and another took up the rear.

I took part in one large assault once. I just went over the top and advanced. I remember seeing a wounded German soldier. When I passed him in No Man's Land, he got a hold of my leg. I tried to kick him off. He wouldn't let me go. I had to go! I couldn't stop because my section was coming behind me. I felt bad about that.

There was a mutiny in 1917 among the French troops. The Foreign Legion was called upon to guard the French and prevent them from infiltrating other units. I never actually took part in it.

I found the French officers to be very good up to the rank of Major. The ranks superior to the Major were somewhat distant. The general field officers and subalterns were very paternal and always took good care of their soldiers.

I won my first Croix de Guerre when one of our officers lay very badly wounded out in No Man's Land. We had our machine gun on an extreme side of the front line trench. We were firing. A calm set in for about ten to fifteen minutes. I don't know what came over me, but I crawled up to the officer and brought him back to our trenches. I returned to my machine gun post. The officer survived.

Whoever was selected to be in command of a trench raid would ask for volunteers. It was a case of, "You volunteer — you volunteer and you and you. We were briefly told what the raid was about — the objective. We were to wear only light equipment, darken our faces a bit, and carry a few grenades. I had a pistol. A knife was in my puttee. We were told the time of departure, then given a specific route and told how far to go. That was very important, so that the sentry did not fire at us! There was always a password or some kind of sign when in No Man's Land. The men in the front line trench were advised as to our operations. It was seldom that we returned the same way from a raid, because of the danger of snipers sighting us. The enemy machine gunners sighted on any open space in the barbed wire. I was in charge of one or two raids as a Sergeant.

Once on a raid we 'bumped' into a German patrol. We made for each other. The first thing that happened was that my blood ran cold and icy-not being the bravest of the brave you know! I was in command of the patrol, so I had to do something and fast. With revolver in hand I said, "Let's go!" One of my fellows bayoneted the first German. I shot one. He fell. Another German attacked me. I ran at him. My foot caught somewhere. I fell to the ground. I had my revolver ready as the German lunged for me with his bayonet. I shot him from underneath. He fell dead, but his rifle and bayonet went through my arm. One of the Germans was very badly wounded, so we left him there. We took a slightly wounded German officer back with us. We had lost one man with two (including myself) wounded. Most of the time we never took anyone back. Their own men picked them up later on. On raids you don't bother with a corpse. You get in and out fast! I won my second Croix de Guerre for that action.

Booby traps were prevalent in the last five or six weeks of the war. We were in pursuit of the Germans, so they often left a grenade, bomb or some other contraption to blow us up with. Poisoned water was the worst form of 'booby trap'. Steel hooks left in oats for the horses was horrifying. We found many dead horses on the Belgian border. I had been on leave two weeks previously. I returned to the unit about one week before the armistice was declared. We knew that something was going to happen, but what it was we were not too sure. We kept up our trench fighting until November 11th. On the morning of the armistice the R.S.M. (Adjudant Chief in the French Army) came to us and said, "Keep down. Don't show yourselves too much." Being a machine gunner, I was on the extreme flank. The word to stay low didn't get to us, so we kept firing right up until 10:00 a.m. About half past ten somebody came and told us that the armistice had been signed. There was complete silence for about five minutes. No one in the trenches really knew if it was true or just another false alarm. The Captain came over saying, "Let's go." So we got up on top of the trench, put our helmets on top of our rifles and shouted, "Hurrah!" Then we were regrouped and sent back to the base for a new uniform, a bath (delousing), a haircut, and another needle.

In December, 1918, at Hirson, the regiment was inspected by General Petain, Commander in Chief of the French Army. He decorated our flag with the 'Fleur Raguerre', which was the colour of the French Military Medal. A few of us were awarded either the Croix de Guerre or the Legion of Honour. A paternal army, our General kissed on both cheeks, when presenting a medal. I received a palm (bar) to my Croix de Guerre, which I had earned in June, 1918, following the tough and bloody battle of the Ourck River. Then the regiment proceeded to Laon.

The German "Big Push" 1918

THE GERMAN "BIG PUSH" (1918)

Major General John S. Stewart
C.R.A. 3RD DIVISION — C.E.F.   *(Diary Notes)*

On March 15th, I went forward to the brow of Vimy Ridge
with General Lipsett to see the raid put on by the 5th C.M.R.'s.
The raid was successful. We got nineteen prisoners and had few
casualties.

On March 25th the Huns were shelling Paris, which was
seventy miles away. We withdrew most of our guns to the top of
Vimy Ridge. The withdrawal of batteries and dropping of S.O.S.
lines is keeping things busy. The Huns attacked early on the
morning of March 28th, making an inroad into our trenches, but
the 56th Division held the Red Line.

Corporal Frank S. Cooper
1ST LONDON SCOTTISH — 56TH DIVISION

The night before the attack was the first time that food was
sent up to us to be cooked. The cooks had to prepare some rabbits.
Rabbits were eaten a lot in those days. We said, "Oh boy! Rabbits!"
They were packed in open crates without any wrappings. During
the night the Germans saturated as with gas shells. We'd hear the
"plook!" then the damn gas bell was rung in order to warn us. As a
result those damn rabbits were saturated with gas, so we were
forbidden to eat them! Our rabbits went "west"! We had hardly got
over the disappointment of that when the Germans started laying
down a barrage.

We were in part of the Hindenburg Line, which was an
elaborate system of trenches. The Germans, having lived in them all
that time, were very familiar with them. They chose to attack us
there. They knew exactly where all the dugouts we were occupying
would be located. They bombed many of our dugouts there.

Major Walter Moorhouse
CDN. MACHINE GUN CORP

In March/18 the Boche made his great attack on the British
5th Army south of Arras forcing our line back to the gates of
Amiens. The Cdn. Corps then was moved back to Vimy Ridge
where we were scattered on a wide front like currants in a boarding-
house bun. We had an opportunity to iron out the kinks in the
organisation and administration of our new establishment. We did
this both in and out of the line so that by July we had absorbed a
mass of new trained personnel from the M.G. Depot at Seaford,

and achieved what we assumed to be Gen. Brutinel's purpose in his masterly plan to make the Battery of eight guns and about 125 all ranks a tactical unit that could operate on its own. We were lucky to be in the Avion area as there was a bad epidemic of Asiatic Flu in June, and our troops south of Arras suffered heavily.

Bombardier James Logan
39TH BATTERY — CANADIAN FIELD ARTILLERY

Prime Minister Borden came right over to our guns. Some of the other members of parliament came too. Sir Robert Borden was a nice fellow to talk to. He just asked questions, asked how we were feeling. His party wasn't gone five minutes when the Germans started shelling our battery.

A Belgian village in ruins (1917). (Public Archives of Canada)

Lieutenant Albert Winn
ROYAL FIELD ARTILLERY

There was a soldier who once overstayed his leave. He had run
off with a young girl. When he was rounded up, his fellow troops
were back in the line again. He was court martialed for cowardice
(desertion) and taken out and shot. This was the first time I had
attended a court martial. There was a Captain as chairman (or
Chief Judge) and there was a Major. I was the Subaltern. They
gave us each a plain manilla envelope. Each of us had to write
down a sentence on it according to what the Crown wanted. I put
down "two years". The others wrote, "Shot at dawn." I got a hell of
a lecture from the Captain for not sentencing him to death. This
happened at other times. The offenders were always shot at dawn.

I was also in a trench mortar section. We were called 'the
suicide troop'. All the men including myself were volunteers for the
trench mortar battery. We used to get an extra two-pence a day,
because we were doing a perilous job. The trench mortars were
nearer the front line than the artillery, which was immediately
behind the first lines. The mortar shells would go over our
infantry's heads and into the enemy lines. The idea was to cut the
German barbed wire before an attack. We could only fire our
trench mortars when the artillery were sending over their barrage,
because everyone was getting under cover with all the shells coming

King George V escorted by Canadian officers, near Arras (1917).

over. Therefore we could fire our mortars in safety and see the bomb dropping on target, cutting the wire. If we missed at our point of fire and zero hour was say, at the end of the week and half the barbed wire was not cut, it meant that the infantry were stuck on the wire and were just mowed down. The artillery used 'firearm bombs' during bombardments to keep Jerry's heads down. The 18 pounders could fire at an extreme range of seven thousand yards. The trench mortars had a spout on them and fins. We had a gunpowder bag to put in it, then screw in the shell and just pull the trigger. Long before that, we had the range set and the angle right. To get the proper angle from a trench mortar, to the enemy's barbed wire, so we could get the infantry through quickly, we could only work it out under artillery bombardment.

I remember a target on the Somme in 1918 called High Wood. It was a little forest all on its own. Jerry's dugouts in there made it like a little town. We were all digging around the roots of the trees in that forest. Zero hour was say, five o'clock. We opened up and Jerry opened up. The Germans had their observation officer out. We were using trench mortars. The shells landed in the "Y" shaped ravine there. Their battery was rung up and we were shelled by the German artillery. Two of our men killed. I ordered, "Get under cover! Get under cover anywhere!" to the other men. We were under heavy bombardment, when I noticed a slight movement from one of the men I thought was dead. So I said to my Sergeant, "Look here! I'm going out to try and help him." The Sergeant said "Don't go out!" to which I replied, "Now look here. In case I'm shot, you ring up the Battery." I got over to this chap. The calf of his leg was hanging out, so I pulled him right along. He was yelling and screaming. I got the shaft handle of a pick-axe. I put the shaft under his leg and fastened bandages galore. Then I shouted to one of my men, "Run back there and shout for a stretcher bearer!" I knew there were men in reserve for that purpose. The stretcher bearers arrived and took the wounded man to the hospital. Then there was a lull in the shelling. I told my Sergeant, "Now Sergeant, I'm going forward to see if we are able to move to see how far Jerry has advanced." In this case we all had to fire our trench mortars at a certain range. I said, "To be on the safe side, add twenty-five yards on each gun!" So I crawled forward and found a little hole in the German lines. I discovered that it was not necessary to add twenty-five yards. In the meantime, my second in command had been up to see how we were getting along. My Sergeant told him what I had done. I won the Military Cross as a result. My C.O. had an M.C. on his spare jacket, so he took it off and said to me, "Here Winn, you can have mine."

High Wood was on the other side of the "Y" shaped ravine. We lost a lot of men there. We had to lob the bombs into the ravine and we were successful. We lost a gun, but eventually captured the wood and dug in. Jerry retreated.

Bombardier William Shaw
151ST SIEGE BATTERY — ROYAL GARRISON ARTILLERY

Gun pits were prepared in front of Arras in the vicinity where the Arras-Douai Road crossed the Arras-Lens railway. On March 20th every man in billets was warned to be ready to move very quickly. Kits were packed. The lorries and caterpillars were held ready in case of an emergency. The gun guard was doubled. Arras was crowded with troops of all kinds. At about five a.m. on March 21st a terrific bombardment opened out from the German front. By mid-day the guns were slowly moving towards Arras at the rate of two miles an hour. Arras was being heavily shelled, troops were marching out of the town and civilians stood at thier house and shop doors wondering what was going to happen next. Some civilians were already beginning to move out as they expected the enemy to capture the city any hour. Later in the day we found that we were being moved to Doullens by way of the Arras-Doullens Road which was the "Routes Nationale" of France. It was very wide, lined with trees for many miles and paved in the centre with granite setts. It was uncomfortable sitting on a gun limber, being bumped over the setts with the noise of the caterpillars in our ears. There was a high level railway parallel with the road. Enemy long range shells were frequently dropping near both road and railway. Staff cars and motorcycle despatch riders continually passed our gun column at high speeds. Captain Dawes and Lieutenant Duncan of the Army Service Corps were in charge of the guns and caterpillars. They were getting quite a few messages from headquarters.

On March 22nd, our guns were turned around on the road. We were to trek back to Arras, but it was difficult because of the crowded traffic of all kinds. The French "official persuaders" were telling the civilians that they had to leave their homes. Cattle, horses and pigs were mixed up with everyone as they fled. A retreat was one of the worst parts of war. It showed how the innocent could be suddenly plunged into its vortex, with the probability of imminent death and destruction.

The Canadians had held Vimy, but south of Arras our line had been pushed back. Our men were eventually complimented for getting out guns into position so quickly. Every man was asked to do his best. After we had been pushing the Hun back for so many months, he was having his turn pushing us back. Things were quiet for a few days, but things were held in readiness for an enemy surprise attack. The German push against the British Fifth Army had exhausted itself in the Amiens region. All ranks were expecting Heiny to break out somewhere else.

The Germans used tanks, gas, liquid fire and aeroplane bombing as well as their artillery on March 21st. Their "Big Bertha" guns fired on Paris at a range of over sixty miles away. General Byng's 3rd Army stood the shock of the attack steadily, but General Gough's 5th Army was broken up early in the attack. Gouzeaucourt had fallen. It was not long beofre Bapaume, Peronne and Albert were captured. The enemy were at the gates of Amiens and Montdidier in the south. Our battery was well on the northern flank of Byng's army, so we escaped the hurried movements of the unfortunate Fifth Army. Evidently the reason why our guns were turned round on the Doullens Road was that if we had proceeded much further we might have been captured lock, stock and barrel! We were not aware of the danger at the time.

German Observation Balloon

Germans could keep an eye on the Allies with this type of balloon (1918).

On the night of March 27th there was a strange stillness over the entire Arras front. Before daybreak on March 28th the enemy started another bombardment on the Arras front. Arras was their objective. They retook the heights of Monchy-le-Preux. From this advantageous observation point they spotted our battery among others. Their gunfire was concentrated on us. On the 28th of March, we were to cease firing, limber up and pull out as fast as the men could work. The Bosche were in the village only fifteen hundred yards away.

Lieutenant Howe and Sergeant Cook were directing operations. A monster long range gun seemed to have found the range of our battery as that afternoon wore on. The holes it made were like caves. The earth and wreckage blown into the air seemed to go sky high. It was only a question of minutes before another shell would drop among us. By four p.m. our last gun, limber, and platform-carrier was hitched to a caterpillar and moved along the road away from the shambles. Mr. Gabbott and Gunner Slack were the last two to get out. Travelling backwards towards Doullens or somewhere we were mixed up in a general retreat on the part of everybody. Major Blackadder got a great ovation from Brigade Headquarters when he reported to the Colonel that he got all the guns out. General Foch was appointed Commander-in-Chief of the allied armies on the western front on March 28th. Sergeant Cook won the Military Medal and Major Blackadder won the M.C. for getting the guns out. We got as far as Wanquetin where we halted and eventually went into billets.

Then we moved back to the south of the river Scarpe, then again to Blangy, then south of Bethune. Some of the 99th Brigade guns were sent up to the Ypres sector where the Germans had broken through. They advanced to the Nieppe Forest and the chain of Flanders hills. That battle lasted from April 9th to April 20th. The enemy recaptured Messines Ridge and advanced past Bailleul, partly capturing Kemmel Hill and taking Merville, Lestrem, La Couture and Richebourg. All places we had previously occupied.

Private Robert W. Parnaby
ROYAL ARMY SERVICE CORP

I was put in "The Flying Column" from Number Two Headquarters. We were involved in anything to do with assisting the troops.

During the big German push I was approaching Albert, but we were shelled right out of there. A staff officer stopped us and asked where we were going. We said, "To Albert." "Turn around you bloody fools and get the heck out of here!" Our fellows were fleeing hell bent for leather! Albert was just a mass of ruins when I went back later on. A few days later all the machine gun instructors were brought out to help try and hold the ridge near Bapaume. We were evacuating the area, clearing out a casualty clearing station. We had to get all the stores on the trucks that we could and rig all the power sources for the hospital; all the lights. We delivered all the stores and went back up to St. Omer. The Germans were right on our heels.

We had to wear gas masks on some of our driving runs. It was difficult without any lights at night, wearing a mask. It was a problem. We travelled in a convoy, feeling our way more or less.

Corporal Craigie T. Mackie
6TH GORDON HIGHLANDERS — 51ST HIGHLAND DIV.

We had just come out of a retreat. The Germans nearly broke through the British Army on March 21st. They were on our front, advancing before we knew what hit us. It was foggy. They drove us back for five or six days from Ypres. We had intended to take a rest after this retreat, but instead, that night we were ordered into trucks. We pulled up by this canal and were told that the Germans were directly in front of us. We had to stop them. Well it was the Portuguese who were in front of us, not the Germans. We killed hundreds of them. We did not know that the Portuguese were in front of us. They kept going until they stopped at the English Channel. The Canadian Machine Gun Corp had bicycles in the vicity of the Portuguese derelicts behind the lines. The Portuguese used those bikes to aid in their escape to the channel. We didn't stop the Germans, but we slowed them down. Our British 3rd Division eventually held Mount Kemmel. That stopped them.

Private George Stannard (1899-)
NORTHAMPTON REG. — 12TH DIVISION

Some of us went out on night patrols. It was our job to kill any Germans guards as silently as possible. Using a guitar string we would sneak up behind a German, put it over his head, give it a draw and cut his throat. It has a hideous job. On one such patrol I had to get into the trench ahead of me. I ran out and went over the top. I experienced an awful feeling. A dead man's face is cold when you put your hand on it. That was terrifying for me.

We used to use the rifle grenade often in 1918. We put our rifle down, bracing it with our legs. It was at a forty-five degree angle. It could have been held like a rifle, but it meant holding it very tightly. If you didn't it would break your shoulder or your jaw. So we dug a small hole in the ground for the rifle butt and sat down bracing it. The grenade was on an eleven inch rod that fit any 303 rifle. We pulled the pin on the grenade when ready to fire it. It was mounted on the rifle barrel. We only had so many seconds after pulling the pin, to fire it.

Bombardier James F. Johnson
5TH CANADIAN MOUNTED RIFLES

One afternoon at the Strand (while on leave from active duty) I met a fellow whom I had known. He had room and boarding accomodation with relatives who resided on York Road which branched off Waterloo Road, not far from where I was staying at the Union Jack Club. He invited me to have supper with him there. I enjoyed the visit and stayed until around ten o'clock. On my way back I stopped at a tea wagon to have a cup of tea and a bun. The only other person there was a young fellow in civilian clothes.

While talking to him I noticed he had an Australian accent. When I left, he walked along and said he was going in the same direction. A few blocks on he stopped and pulled out a pack of cigarettes, took one and offered me one. While I was lighting mine he jumped me and grabbed at my throat. I wriggled around and got clear. Looking down the street I saw two Australian soldiers running towards us. I thought they were going to help me, but they were his accomplices. The three of them forced me face down on the sidewalk so I knew there was no use resisting. While in that position I slowly eased my hand into my tunic pocket, removed my money and slipped it in under my shirt. Then I removed my hand and made no resistance. Just then a woman opened up the front door of her house and shouted for the police. By that time the thugs had gone all through my pockets, getting everything except my money. They ran after hearing the lady call.

A London Bobby was there soon. The lady invited us in for a cup of tea, then the Bobby walked on with me to the Club. He took all the particulars and told me I was lucky as there had been soldiers who had lost their lives in that manner. He also told me never to walk down York Road after dark as it was a very tough district. That was one time I did not hesitate to obey an order!

Sergeant Len Davidson
7TH BATTALION — CND. ENGINEERS

We used to have chemicals for the forward water supply. We
entered a town. Doug Wilson, my Corporal, said to me, "Davy!
Listen. There's a good well over there!" Sure enough, so we built a
partition around it so nobody would fall in. We lowered a bucket in
it to sample the water. It was beautiful. We didn't bother with it
anymore, damn good water, so we stuck a sign on it, "Fit for
Human Consumption". We left that village and returned three
weeks later. A huge barricade was put up against this well we had
set up. An Imperial was standing there. I asked him, "What the hell
is the idea of the barricade?" He said, "Some God damned
Canadian Engineers came through and stuck a sign on it, "Fit for
Human Consumption". We found two dead Heinies in the bottom
of it." We had to be careful.

Sergeant David Guild
13TH BATTALION

Arras (the city) was wide open when we arrived there. The
civilians had all fled. All the stores and estaminates were open too.
Some of my platoon got into the Y.M.C.A. headquarters and got
hold of a large wooden crate full of tins of capstan cigarettes.
Another bunch got into English Divisional Headquarters and got
hams, a case of whiskey and so on. We were billeted in caves at
Arras. We were rushed up for the attack that was expected, but
there was a lull, so we were billeted in a grocery store in a square at
Arras. We found canned peas, mushrooms and so on. We had the
life o' Riley! On the corner was a brewery. The door to it was
padlocked. We blew the padlock off. The fellows were bathing in
white wine, big vats of it. On the third day there the M.P.'s came.
Of course there was a fracas. One of our guys was wounded, but he
wasn't from my platoon anyway. Things quietened down after the
M.P.'s showed up. There were many different units of British Army
there, looking for their proper battalions. They were all scattered
around. Our platoon wouldn't drink white wine; we wanted champagne.

Lieutenant Geoffrey Marani
42ND BATTALION

The last light machine gun course I took was in France in
Byng's Corp. At the training school I was told, "You're a machine
gun specialist. We want you to go down for the new anti-aircraft
sights that just came out." It had bi-pod legs. That was because the
planes were strafing a lot lower. The new sight was marvellous.

Major Walter Moorhouse
CDN. MACHINE GUN CORP

For this battle we used a new technique in our operation orders. The Air-Force had taken low level stereo-oblique photos, and from these, with the aid of a stereoscope we were able to site M.G. positions ten miles in front of our present line. Each battery in the advance was provided with two small maps, one for the Capt., and one for the S.M. These maps showed our line of advance and projected routes to M.G. positions for each objective. We had two tanks attached, carrying ammunition and cans of petrol and water, the dumps for which were projected on the maps. The attack on Aug. 8th was a success, and on its completion, a reconnaissance showed that the guns, with a perfect field of fire, were never farther than a couple of hundred yards from their projected location. The whole operation was a complete surprise and we advanced about nine miles in the first attack with few casualties.

A later feature of this attack was one of the last cavalry charges in the war. It was a ghastly failure as they were caught in the wire and mown down by M.G. fire. I saw one trooper caught by a high signal wire under the chin and landed on his back over the horse's tail. He wasn't hurt and was one of the few survivors of his troop. There was also an example of bad handling of tanks. Two German field guns, sited at the edge of Parvillers Wood, caught the tanks over open sights as they rumbled one by one over a rise, and four were put out of action before the remaining two got wise and kept below the ridge.

On August 13, when our line was consolidated more or less, Division had a fair knowledge of our new front, but little information of the French advance on our right. I hopped into my tin Lizzie and started off to find the French Div. H.Q. Their forward operations were stationed in a small farm building and to my astonishment consisted only of stout walrus moustached Commandant with a stiff left arm, a young lieutenant, one orderly room clerk with one typewriter, and a couple of runners. What a difference from the accommodation and personnel of one of our Divisions. I told my story and handed them a map marked with our positions. They had no definite report as yet, but assured me that if I would kindly wait for about half an hour, the report would arrive. In the meantime we enjoyed a cup of coffee.

Communication has always been a vital necessity in the field, but it was rather primitive in World War I. We had practiced semaphore Morse Code with flags but never had an opportunity to use these seriously. Harry Symons and I while crossing on the 'Hesperian' — used to practice on the upper deck as far apart as possible, alternately transmitting and receiving a wild serial on the lines of 'Perils of Pauline'. The game was for the sender to leave the hero or heroine in a terrible jam, and let the receiver try and wangle a way out. Wireless was of course to change all this, but walkie-talkies, transistors and the like were things of the future. There was a signal station with a 'mast' in Zillebeke Bund in the spring of /16, and I used to go at midnight to correct my watch. The air was full of constant 'jammin'. Then suddenly there was silence as the wireless station at the tip of Cornwall boomed out the hour of midnight Greenwich time. Crouching in the dugout the effect was uncanny. We had of course our buried cables and signal lines strung all over the country but these took time laying down and were subject to frequent breaks and continual supervision. Perhaps satellites will be used in future wars, if any.

It seemed they had a trained group of liaison officers and that two of these complete with motorcycles had left at dawn and would be back shortly with their disposition report. Apparently one started at each flank and carried on until he met the other. If either became casualties there was a fifty-fifty chance that the other would get back. Presently they both returned, compared their maps and I was able to get an accurate tracing of their line to hand in to 3rd Cdn. Division.

There was a further attack on Sept. 20/18 when Bourlon Wood was encircled, after which the Cdn. Corps was moved out of the line to Warlus to prepare for the crossing of the Canal du Nord and the final advance on Cambrai. We occupied hutments above the town where that was to overtake us. That was indeed our darkest hour! On the morning of Sept. 25th, after inspection, the Companies had been released to carry on their training, and I strolled back to the Orderly Room. It was a clear, bright morning when literally a bolt fell from the blue. The Hun plane was flying very high and it was pure chance that the bomb fell between the two companies as they were marching off the parade ground. Just as I entered the Orderly Room hut, the air buzzed with flying splinters which tore into the nissen huts. The bomb was a new type with an advanced rod that detonated the blast about three feet above the ground. There was little noise and hardly any shell crater, but it caused 65 casualties including 36 killed, some of the latter being so torn to pieces that we had to collect some of them in sandbags. Lt. Gallais started the grim process of identifying and recording and arranged for a show at the Y.M.C.A. in the afternoon and for a band to march the Battn. there. Corps H.Q.

was just down at the foot of the hill, so as we were to go into action to cover the crossing of Canal du Nord the next day, I went at once to report to Gen. Brutinel at Corps. He immediately phoned the advanced M.G. Depot at Divion, who sent replacements at once by lorry. We went into action on Sept. 26th and the new trained arrivals were soon absorbed into the Battalion. What a disaster! — and yet I can remember no mention of the incident except in the Casualty reports.

There followed the encirclement and fall of Cambrai, and Col. Balfour arrived with his authority to take over the command of the 3rd Battn. C.M.G. Corps just in time for the triumphal advance to Mons, on which the weather was our worst enemy.

Second Lieut. James Senter (1895-)
6TH SIGNAL CO. CEF./US. ARMY

After the United States entered the war in 1917 they asked Canada for instructors. I was born in the United States. When they found that out the Americans offered me a commission. I talked it over with my commanding officer. He said that they would discharge me from the Canadian Army and that I would be very wise to take the commission. So I took it. I was there for several months. I had the expert rifle badge. I was also an instructor at their school of rifle fire. There was a National Guard Division at Camp Donovan. That was in Fort Sill territory. I instructed quite a few of the boys of the 35th Division, but I ran into difficulties. I ran into trouble with a Colonel in my class. He was a very disruptive man. If he was in my class he was always creating turmoil. I got permission from the man at the mission. I told him, "Do we need to hold these classes with Tucker in there? All he does is disrupt the class." He said, "We'll fix that." The next time I had a class with Tucker we just nicely sat down and started, when he started to shoot his face off again. as a result we came to blows. I had struck a superior officer. I resigned my commission and returned to Canada. I reinlisted in the Canadian Army in New York City. That may seem strange, but it's true. I was sent to the Signal Training Depot in Ottawa, as they were preparing troops for Siberia. I reinlisted as a Private soldier and finished up as a Sergeant.

We didn't get over to Russia until after New Year. We landed at Vladivostok. The days were a little shorter in winter. Not a great deal. Vladivostok is about as far north as Edmonton is. The winter conditions were not bad at all at Vladivostok. Our troops in Siberia saw no action.

The idea was that we were to go west while the troops that landed at Archangel were to go south. The Russian troops in southern Russia were to go north. They were going to destroy the Communist Army. That fell through. A lot of the northern troops were deserting their forces and going to the commanding General, Admiral A.V. Kolchak, in the south.

A few of us that were to be sent to Omsk got as far as being entrained. One afternoon we were sent back again. Canadian troops in our sector were not under fire in Russia at all. I talked to some of the men from the interior where the fighting had gone on. They said the dead were piled up like cordwood. That was at Omsk and west of Omsk. We got back to Canada in June of 1919.

THE LAST ONE HUNDRED DAYS (1918)

Private Thomas Chambers
15TH BATTALION — LANCASHIRE FUSILIERS

The first time we came under fire I was naturally scared stiff, but the more the action, the less the fear. We were so busy that we woudn't notice our feelings. In the front line, Jerry used to start strafing us in the morning as well as the evening, as regular as clockwork. I remember this poor chap who had come up from the hospital to the front. He had been treated for shellshock. As soon as Jerry opened up, his nerves would let go. He used to come over, put his arms around me and start crying. Well, this tended to make me braver. That was the sensation you got if you saw anybody who was scared. It made you feel above him. We didn't feel so scared ourselves.

I remember one occasion, on the advance, when we hadn't any water, because some silly fool had given the order to empty our water bottles. We were not given a chance to refill them. To remedy this situation, we used to get a dew drop on a blade of grass and let one dew drop collect on another, until it got bigger and bigger. Then we would crouch down and put it on our tongues, but perhaps a shell would crash down, just as we had a nice big dew drop, and bang! The whole damn thing was gone. When it rained; we would put up a groundsheet. A groundsheet was a sort of utility garment we could use as a cloak or something. We used to put it over one end of the trench and weight it down with a couple of bricks, in order to shelter us from the rain. As soon as Jerry began shelling us, we would all dive under the groundsheet. It was no protection at all, but we felt secure, psychologically, by diving under it.

Tanks were pretty well organized when on the front battlefields but the life of a tank officer was very short indeed! A tank couldn't cross at a tangent, when going over a trench. It had to go straight across it, because if it went at a tangent, it would get one of the treads in the trench and topple over. Then the officer in charge of the tank, had to get out, go in front of the tank and guide it. It was suicide, absolute suicide. The inside of the tank was one colossal engine, with about eighteen inches of space all around. With a tank crew inside and no springs at all, it was definitely crowded. I have seen a crew coming out burned beyond recognition. Their faces all yellow, their hands and bodies scarred, oh it was a terrible job. The officer was a definite write off. He would be killed almost as soon as he went out to guide that tank, in full view of the Germans.

We became contemptuous of trivialities. For instance, if you dropped a piece of bread on the floor today, you would be very careful about eating it. But in the trenches if you dropped a bit of bread and someone stepped on it in the mud, you would eat it anyway. It was amazing what dirty, rubbish like stuff we ate, but we were thankful for it.

One of my earliest recollections of life in the trenches was being detailed for a listening post, accompanied by another young soldier. I was lead through our barbed wire defences to a shell hole in No Man's Land. The purpose of that mission was to listen for any unusual activities in the enemy lines, which were about one hundred yards away. All was quiet for about an hour, when suddenly, away to our left, all hell seemed to break loose. The Jocks (kilted Scottish soldiers) were on a raid to take a few prisoners for interrogation. Their blood curdling yells frightened the guts out of us as much as the enemy. We did not know what was happening, until we had hastily made our way back to our lines.

Incidentally, before all that excitement, my partner had suggested giving himself a Blighty, which meant a self-inflicted wound. He was told that by firing a bullet into a fleshy part of his leg, through a tin of bully beef (to avoid powder marks), he would be sent back to England, as a wounded soldier. This did not appeal to me. He was killed a few days later.

There were so many different types of people in the war. Some were leaders and others were not. I remember once we had a hell of a battering. This young Brigadier, without even wearing his tin hat, stood up on top of a trench and called us all rotten cowards. Of course we had not taken our objective that day. He stood up there, utterly in contempt of the enemy firing. He said, "Now, there is your objective (pointing out over No Man's Land). Fix bayonets and go ahead and take it!" We did, we took it.

I wrote the following letter home in August, 1918: "Well! We left Belgium last Wednesday travelling all night. Next day the train stopped about midday Thursday and we got out and were told to put "Battle Order" on (that is a special "light" fighting equipment a little lighter than full pack). We all began to wonder what was wrong, but were bustled into motor lorries. We went to an unknown destination. Well! After a good deal of travelling we passed through a *very* big town (Amiens) which to our great surprise was absolutely deserted by all civilians. We then learned where we were. We were on the old front line and only that morning had the Canadians pushed Fritz from outside that town. It was fairly easy going for them as the enemy had evacuated without hardly any fighting. Well! It was our turn next and we went on further in the busses until we were forced to stop owing to the enormous amount of traffic.

I shall never forget that night, August 8/18. I have never seen as many motor lorries or horse transports in all my life before, nor shall I forget the innumerable ambulances that were coming down from the line. The organization was truly wonderful. Mail lorries and ration lorries were endlessly winding their way onward. Also all our huge guns were going up. Eventually, seeing that no progress could be made in lorries we got out and made our way on foot, greeted by wounded on their way down with various expressions such as "Stick it chum, you have got him on the run" and "Hurry up or you will never catch him". Our sleeping place that night was an open field. Division after Division came up until everywhere around was one living, moving mass of human bodies. On the morning of the 9th we moved on again passing many gruesome sights until we again were forced to sleep in an open field overnight. All this ground was but the day before in German hands. Then came "The Day", Saturday, August 10/18. We were roused at three: thirty a.m. and had a hasty breakfast. The Brigade moved off at four: fifteen headed by the 15th Lancashire Fusiliers. Our Battalion opened the attack relieving the Canadians who held a village on ahead. We did not exactly know where lay Fritz but after we passed through a village, a thousand and one machine guns opened on us. We opened out in artillery formation — the signallers in Company headquarters making a total of twelve men headed by the Sergeant Major. When the machine guns opened up on us the

Sergeant Major cried out, "Keep on boys! Go on!" I ran with the others for a few yards and then dropped in the long grass. This cover protected me from observation and I lay there in God's protection. After awhile the guns ceased and I ran forward and jumped into a trench, which happily was not occupied by Germans. At this moment I was separated from my friends, the signallers and hastened forward to find them. I met George (my friend) coming down with a message and he directed me to our boys. Having found them we remained in that trench for orders. Our objective was a wood far ahead. After a lot of wandering and bandaging wounded all signallers were told to leave their stuff behind and advance on the wood. Well I am glad to say that we reached our objective and after a hard tussle took the wood. In eight hours we advanced four or five kilos, but our casualties were appaling. I thank God for his protection for it was a miracle that anyone pulled through. Our Coy had three quarters of the total killed and wounded, leaving only one quarter of a Company of tired men. But we stuck it for another day and thank God we were relieved in the early part of the morning of August 12/18.

Corporal John (Jack) Stacey
12TH CDN. FIELD AMBULANCE BRIGADE

There was quite a display of tanks at Amiens, where the Canadians made a drive of about eight miles. Our stretcher bearers were waiting at Gentelles Wood. The tanks were going into the line followed by the infantry, with so many men behind each tank. Then we followed them up. We didn't catch up to the infantry for two days. We walked all on our own. The only thing we had were our iron rations and what we could pick up.

Some fellows made wonderful stretcher bearers. They had everything going for them, but it wasn't necessary for all the men in the 12th Field Ambulance to be dressing the wounded. We would split the Ambulance Brigade into two sections, stretcher bearers and tent sections. I think they got the "tent sections" from the Boer War. Anyway the tent section was specialized. We took extra courses in splint work, bandages and tourniquets. We used tourniquets a lot, but we don't use them anymore. Then the Ambulance Brigade was divided into A., B. and C. sections. We had the main dressing station (or the 'relay') and there was a front section. It was seldom that we were all together, unless the Brigade pulled out for a rest. After a while, one section would move up and replace the other giving everyone involved a change. We had a pretty busy time of it. We never ran short of medical supplies. We sometimes ran short of rations, but when we went in the line every man carried a kit. Every infantryman carried a bandage.

I got mixed up with a German gas shell attack at Amiens. Some gas knocked me out for two or three days. I was able to neutralize it, because we used sodium solisilidge. I used to take so much of it a day. It wasn't a cure, but it neutralized it.

Private James Doak
52ND BATTALION

August 10th, 1918 — We had been marching for an hour, the road strewn with dead horses and a few dead bodies of our boys and the foe. We rounded a turn in the road, on one side of which was a bluff. Behind it the enemy had taken a heavy toll of our cavalry. Ahead of us stretched nearly a mile of level country. Here and there a bunch of scrub willows and further on an orchard are visible.

Back among the shrubs a machine gun sent a steady stream of death. Judging from the rows of dead horses we could see how heavy the toll was. A dozen or more had charged the machine gun. The sabre slashed dead of the enemy showed the success of that gallant charge. There were plenty of dead horses, but few dead riders. Then we came across the empty shell cases of the tanks. A hundred yards away we saw the object of their fire. Hanging from a broken limb of a huge apple tree was a German machine gun, the operator with his head blown clean off lies in a distorted heap on a pile of empty cartridge cases.

Across the Roy Road lay the bodies of the coloured Colonial troops of the French army. They had advanced on foot, and never flinched. They died to a man, laying with their faces upturned to the hot August sun. Here they lie, men from distant Canada and their brothers in arms from sunny Algeria.

November 9th, 1918 — Moved to Thulin on the Mons Road. The people here are overjoyed at their release. I saw a bunch of English soldiers who had escaped the enemy by crawling through the sewers.

General Sir Arthur Currie, O.C. of the Canadian Corps came over to me while I was standing on the edge of the curb. He asked me how long I had been in France, where I came from and many other questions. I answered to the best of my ability. Then I asked him about the armistice rumours. I asked, "Can you tell me anything definite?" He told me that in his opinion 24 hours would see the end of the fighting. He said, "We may possibly have to go after him once again, but it's hardly likely. I think I can safely tell you that you've followed your last barrage." Across the street our Colonel and a bunch of officers were eyeing the General and myself. A group of company and bandsmen were staring at us too. After the General had gone, they crowded around me to hear what he had to say. They asked, "Did you know him in Canada?" I jokingly answered, "Sure I knew him. He's going to give me a job on his staff." Since that time, the General has been known among the bandsmen as "Doak's pal".

Map.

Lieutenant Geoffrey Marani
42ND BATTALION

At the Amiens show there were Whippet tanks and cavalry as far as the eye could see. The Whippet tank was faster and smaller than those used on the Somme. It had a little turret and gun. They were good for moving supplies out in the open. The Whippet tanks only held one or two men and were quite small. They went just as fast as the cavalry.

We had been waiting for the blast off on the 8th of August for the Battle of Amiens. It started at four a.m. We were down under a road and got our rum ration. The whole platoon drank to my brother, because it was his birthday. "Up your kilt," they said.

We were at St. Fuscien near Boves Wood. That was straight south of Amiens. We left our billets there to go into the line for the 8th of August. It was open warfare.

Three or four days before Amiens we had to rendevous in the woods to stay out of sight. It would be hours in and around daybreak, when men, tanks, et cetera were still mobilizing. It was hard to move. The roads were narrow. We couldn't get off the roads and the traffic was very heavy. We just had to weave our way through the transport, guns, ammunition and trains. It was slow. By the time we reached the wood we were rendezvouing. There was still miles of traffic on the road. If an odd plane spotted that then they would have known something was going on. For three days it was rainy, poor visibility, so they never spotted us. We had to stay overnight to see the place because it was misty and rainy. We were just getting into a communication trench. I had my arm up and was just going to step into the trench with my batman. I was knockled as if a sledge hammer had hit me in the back. That's where the bullet came out. A certain amount of muscle was torn out.

On the boat to Canada we had four storms. I grabbed the bannister once. It felt like stitches ripping in my arm, but it didn't hurt. I pitched some indoor softball whch helped to strengthen it. When I got back to Canada one of my reasons for playing indoor baseball was to get my arm back in shape. I use to get a fair curve on it. After a year I was okay again.

Major Ian Sinclair
13TH BATTALION

Amiens was a fortunate place for us. We did not have very heavy casualties. In all our previous attacks we had always had the weather against us. It turned out to be a perfect day for an attack.

There was a thick fog in the morning. We were on the Germans before they knew there was anybody there. I received the D.S.O. for the crossing at the Canal du Nord. That was in September of 1918. It was a peculiar action. We didn't have much trouble getting assembled along our assault line. It was fairly quiet. We could never understand why. Naturally we had to formulate our plans based on airplane photographs. Maps were completely useless at times, because of the countryside being so chewed up. Sometimes we just worked by guess and by God. We went down the valley, crossing the Canal du Nord. We did not know the depth of the river, but we chanced it anyway. We did not think it would be very difficult. When the attack began we had to move along the bottom of the valley to get to the first part of the canal. To our horror we ran into a stream that did not appear on the photographs at all. We were wet up to our armpits and practically soaked up to our necks. We fought in that condition. Opposition was not as strong as initially expected. We had a fairly successful day. The village Marquion was on our left front. We had to go around a wood and attack Marquion from the one side rather than the front. We met a very stiff opposition. A British regiment assisted us in the attack in the final kick-off. We took Marquion.

My brother Angus was in the 48th Highlanders. They were in the same Brigade when we cleared off and swung around to the left to go up and attack Marquion from the south. I saw an officer leading his platoon around a wood. I was darn sure it was my brother Angus. Suddenly a shell came over and killed the officer and half a dozen of his men. I thought, "That's the end of Gus all right." It turned out afterwards to be some other officer. Gus was perfectly all right and came through the action without a scratch.

Sergeant David Guild
13TH BATTALION

On the 8th of August, 1918 they brought us down south to Amiens. We only marched at night. In the day we hid, taking every precaution in order to make a surprise attack. The tanks only moved at night. When the tanks were moving, the planes were overhead buzzing around to drown out the noise of the tanks. As I was going up the bank I found that an enemy machine gun post opposed us. It had control, skimming the top of the bank, so I lay there and told a bunch of my men to circle around. They came back and said they couldn't circle around.

Then I thought, "Well here goes nothing." I made a blind rush at the gun. Of course a hand grenade wounded me in the side. I think five or six of us got wounded there. The remainder got the gun. I remember lying there and the gang went on and left us behind. Then the Germans started sending over gas shells. I thought I'd better get out of there. My side was torn open.

I was walking in open territory. I saw a shell-hole and do you think I could steer around it? I could only go straight, so I walked right into it. I couldn't get up the other side, so I lay there. I don't know how long. Then I saw a battery of artillery coming up with horses. I waved my hand and their officer came over. He asked "How's it going Jock?" I said, "All right. I'd like a drink of water." He said, "Boy, I'm sorry. I've got orders to take my battery up to a certain point and I've got to go." I said, "That's all right. Somebody will get me." I thought I was going to die, but the officer went over to his battery. I could see him talking to someone. He came galloping back and said to me, "To heck with it Jock. I'm going back for somebody. My battery Sergeant Major is in charge now. I'm going back." In about fifteen minutes or so, he rode up and said, "There will be somebody along for you Jock in a short time. I've got to go. Good luck." Away he went. I never knew who he was. I lay there for awhile, then I saw four Heinie prisoners coming up with a stretcher. They gave me a cigarette, put me on a stretcher and carried me down.

They put me on a table. An orderly started to cut away my tunic and things. I had a couple of Mills bombs, one under each pocket. I had forgotten all about them. They had the pins straightened, ready to fall out. We used to do that so that the pins would pull out easier. I can remember the expression on the doctor's face when he saw them. He said, "Get rid of those darn things!" I was laughing even though I was down and out.

Private Thomas Fairweather (1899-)
W. YORKSHIRE REG. 49TH DIVISION

I was wounded on July 28th in the leg and the arm. I was only eighteen. Some of our German prisoners carried the wounded back, including me, down to the clearing stations. When I got wounded, my brother was in a trench mortar battalion. They were on one side of us and he saw me being carried down the line by these German prisoners. He came right over. He was talking to me and walking along with me. As a result, he got court martialed for leaving his trench mortar position behind. There was no action, even though we were in the line. The Commanding Officer was arranging his court martial when news came that my brother was killed. There was no evidence after that, so there never was a court martial. Being wounded I was sent to Le Havre and boarded the Hospital Ship, H.A.M.S. Warilda. The ship was torpedoed going over to England. About one hundred and ninety-three soldiers went down with the ship, including nurses. I was a stretcher case and managed to get out. It was quite exciting. Most of the victims were trapped below the waterline. All the stretcher cases were on the top deck. We were the only people our rescuers could get to, so they pulled us out of the lifeboats and boarded us on a naval patrol boat. We had been adrift for about ten to twelve hours in those lifeboats, just floating around, when the Royal Navy picked up all three hundred of us.

After we were hit, the patrol boats circled the area, dropping depth charges. We heard a shout and we could see the German sub coming up, oil and everything.

Corporal Craigie T. Mackie
6TH GORDON HIGHLANDERS

We passed by Mont St. Eloi quite a bit. In 1918 we were pushing the Germans back, but they fought like hell, fighting bitterly, especially when we caught up to their artillery. The fields were more open. It was a different style of fighting than what we were used to in the earlier part of the war.

Lieutenant John (Jack) Chambres
54TH BATTALION — 4TH DIVISION

After my wounding, they operated on me in France. I was there for five days, then off to London. The orderly in France, in the hospital there, asked me how I was. I said, "Oh all right." He said, "Well I better give you a bath before your operation." "Okay." I got a hospital garment on and asked, "What should I do with my clothes?" He said, "You might as well destroy them because they are full of lice." So I went over to England with this garment on.

Sergeant Len Davidson
7TH BN. — CDN. ENGINEERS

We were among the first troops in Mons. We were right at the foot of a hill, not far from the town hall. It was quite a slope down.

Probably forty-five degrees. Six Canadians came around the corner and a German machine gunner wiped them out. That was on the Morning of November 11th 1918.

Private Gordon W. Reid
50TH BATTALION

I arrived in France on September 20th, 1918. From Etaples I went up through Arras en route to join the 50th Battalion. At Vimy I was taken out with a group for target practise with a Lewis gun. I'll never forget all the dugouts and tunnels I saw in that ridge!

We fought our way up to Denain. Fritzie was vacating and we were following. On October 27th we were inspected by the Prince of Wales. Fritzie shelled us heavily two days later. On October 31st we were in the support line, dug in on a sunken road. The next day we went over the top after a barrage. We arrived in Valenciennes. Once there, we went into support until Armistice Day.

Bombardier William Shaw
15lST SIEGE BATTERY—ROYAL/GARRISON ARTILLERY

In early September we moved to Atlantic Farm, near Poperinghe. We had a position in a cornfield between Poperinghe and Dickebusch.

On September 28th the Belgian Army and the British Second Army (under General Plumer) commanded by King Albert of Belgium, attacked and soon recaptured the ridges dominating the Ypres salient. It was not long before our guns were out of range. Not all of our six guns were sent forwarad, so the men at Atlantic Farm were sent out to do salvage work, reclaiming any steel, iron or copper which could be found in the surrounding countryside. As an inducement to the batteries to do their best, a certain number of extra leave warrants to the unit salvaging the greatest weight of material, was promised. One group of men salvaged a 4.2 gun. The scouting parties had a great time looking over the old trenches and gun positions.

From Dickebusch, three or four of our guns had other positions at Hallebast Corner, Busseboom and Ouderdoum, but we were soon out of range again, waiting for the Menin Road to be repaired. It was in that section over No Man's Land between Hooge and Gheluvelt which had been so fiercely contested for over four years.

I shall never forget the feelings we had as we went through the ruined town of Ypres, in lorries, and passed the remains of the famous Cloth Hall and cathedral, and went through what was left of the Menin Gate. We went through Hooge and Sanctuary Wood, then gradually up towards Gheluvelt. It was an odd experience. We looked back and down at the Ypres salient. It made one shudder to think that a quarter of a million men were lying dead in the area around us, most of whose remains would never be identified.

On October 16th we were heavily bombarded at Moorseele. The firing lasted for about an hour and a half, when the gunners got their orders to empty guns and "cover up", which we believe was the last order of its kind that the 151st Siege Battery gunners received in the war.

After a time in Courtrai, on November 6th, our guns were moved forward to Moen. A fresh advance was expected to be made, but owing to rumours of an armistice, this did not take place. On November 10th, news was received in Courtai of an armistice taking place. The Battery started to celebrate, twelve hours ahead of the real hour! A mistake had evidently been made, as the men were not officially informed until November 11th. The 151st Battery did not take part in the general advance to the Rhine after the signing of the armistice, but stayed in Courtrai until November 23rd. We eventually moved to Halluin, a place on the Belgian-French frontier, near the famed Menin Road and the Menin-Lille Road.

Sapper Robert Dickson
5TH BN. CDN. ENGINEERS

I remember feeling very badly one time as we moved forward. There was a dead Canadian soldier lying on his face. His haversack was open. A little wooden box which had contained his valuables was there. It was addressed to a home in Canada. It was broken open. All the contents were stolen. I thought that was a pretty miserable affair.

A good deal of our job was pick and shovel work. We made corkfloat bridges at the canals. They were big bundles of cork done up with chicken wire for floats. A plank layer was on top for the bridge floor. Hand rails were added. Men could cross, but vehicles could not. We put those bridges up ahead of the infantry. We worked steadily.

For three nights we slept in a graveyard. Three others and myself were fortunate enough to get in a family vault which had shelves in them for the coffins. Those shelves served as bunks. We slept in there nice and dry, quite comfortably. We generally found cover somewhere.

Bombardier James Logan
39TH BATTERY — CANADIAN FIELD ARTILLERY

During our attack on Cambrai on the 8th and 9th of October, I talked to one of the German prisoners for a few minutes. He said to me, "You think our artillery barrage is bad. You want to be in one of your own over there. You fellows are even killing the sparrows on our side. Nothing could live through it unless you got cover."

We used to tell the infantry that we were going to fire at a certain place for five minutes and lift the barrage every fifty yards. That would be one hundred and fifty feet. After five minutes we fired for two more minutes over another fifty yards. The infantry would follow up, knowing how far we were going to lift each time. It was called a creeping barrage.

Our 18 pounders firing shrapnel were surely deadly. There was two hundred and seventy bullets in each shrapnel shell. It went out like hail when it spread.

At Amiens we were a mobile Battery. For four days we never fired a shot, because they moved us all over the front.

On the fourth day they told us to get ready to go out. The English were going to relieve us. The English came in, got up on top of the trenches and started playing football as we were preparing to leave. The Germans started knocking them over with shells, so we were called back into action. We unloaded our limbers. The guns were hub to hub, some so close that the hubs from other batteries were hitting each other. We fired for about five minutes. The Germans didn't fire another shot. It didn't take long for the English to get consolidated in the trenches after that. We were mad at the English. They thought it was so safe. The Germans would have killed them all if we hadn't been up there.

We were also at the Drocourt-Queant Canal in early September. The Engineers must have drained it, because it was dry. It was like an irrigation ditch in a valley. It was used as a roadway. The Germans were cutting through there. I was on number four gun. We started to fire a barrage in the morning. After about three shots were fired, about fifty Germans came out with their hands in the air, through this cut in the canal. I went out to take some souvenirs from them. I pointed my finger at them. Down they went, saying, "Oh Kamarade! Mercy kamarade!" I couldn't touch them, they were so excited. I did not get a darn thing off them.

It was a nice day. We were sitting out there, when a bunch of German prisoners came and sat down. A young German asked me when our dinner was served, "You fellows get white bread?" I said, "Yes." He spoke good English, saying, "Will we get fresh white bread?" "Sure." "I haven't had any white bread for four years. I had six brothers and my Dad killed in this war. I'm the last boy of the family and my Mother told me that when I got in front of the English to give myself up. This was my first time in front of the English. I didn't know you were Canadians. When you started to shell this morning I came on the dead run. There were fifty of us. " I asked, "Did you come through that split in the canal?" "Yes." "Did you see a gun on the right when you came through?" "Yes." I said, "Well that was the gun I was on." He said, "We were sure afraid somebody would shoot us when coming over. We were told to keep on going back and here we are." There was an older German fellow, a nice distinquished looking man, and he said to me, "You don't know it, but the war's over." He spoke better English than I did. I asked, "How is it that you speak such good English?" He said, "I'm an English teacher at the University of Berlin." I commented, "A University Professor and you're in the war?" He said, "They're scraping the bottom of the barrel. There's nobody left. They're taking everybody! We've lost the war. We should have quit long ago." The officers heard me talking to him. They had me go away somewhere. I wanted to talk some more, but they wouldn't let me.

German P.O.W.'s escorted by Canadians down a badly shelled support trench (1917).

By the time I went on leave I had five hundred francs saved. I didn't know if the money was any good on leave or not. I was going down the road with two pals Jess Pollard and Tom Holliday. The unit gave us three days to do down and get a boat to England. We left Valenciennes and all jumped on another truck. At the first crossing, the driver turned off. We took another truck, went a block and turned off. We had a great deal of difficulty finding a ride. Finally we noticed an airplane tendor, kind of a station wagon used to bring aviators back after they had been shot down, speeding down the road towards us. I stood in the middle of the road and held my arms out. Tom Holliday said, "You'll get killed!" "No I won't. He won't run over me." I waved my arms. He slowed down and stopped. I said, "Give us a ride!" In a thick English accent he said, "Ahh, the last time I took Canadians I got bloody hell about it!" I said, "Oh you won't get no trouble with us." Tom Holliday added, "He'll put us off." I said, "No he won't." I got on there. The driver kept complaining, so I asked him, "Say do you know where there's a good place to eat?" He said, "Yes," and he quit grumbling right away. He asked, "Why?" I took out a whole handful of francs and said, "You take us someplace where it's good to eat and I'll buy you the best supper you ever had in France." He said, "By jove I know of a dandy place." It was ten miles further than we had to go! He started talking and was a different guy altogether. We had a great supper, which I payed for. We had lots of champagne and stuff. He wanted to drive us right down to Boulogne that night. Tom said, "He'll never pass a Canadian up again!" I sure wasted some good money, but it was for a good cause.

There were twenty-two of us in our Battery. When the Americans won the war they told us that if we wanted to transfer to the American forces we'd go in with the same rank as we had had in the Canadian Army. We could also go in any branch we wanted to, like the artillery. The twenty-two of us held a meeting one night. We decided that if we joined the Americans we would be with another bunch of green fellows making a lot of mistakes like we originally did, so we stayed in the Canadian Army. The Americans had also offered us a $2,400.00 bounty whereas we only got $475.00 from the Canadian government at the end of the war.

One night I was walking in a town alone. There were three English fellows ahead of me. I overheard them saying, "Well Bill, it's over." The other fellow said, "Yes. I don't know. I don't want to go back to my old job back in England. I want something different." The other man said, "I'm the same as you. I've been thinking that I might go out to one of the colonies." The other fellow said, "I was thinking about the same thing." "Which colony

are you going to?" The man said, "I've been with the South
Africans, the Australians and the New Zealanders. They're all pretty
nice. I've been with the Canadians and out of all that bunch, I like
the Canadians better than any of them. I think that I'll go to
Canada." The three of them all decided right there that they were
going to go to Canada. I've often wished I had their names to see
how they made out.

Brigadier General John S. Stewart
C.R.A. 3RD DIVISION — C.E.F.   *(Diary Notes)*

On Thursday, August 15th, General Mary of the 42nd
Divisional Artillery (France) presented me with the Croix De
Guerre. The enemy are shelling the hills between Monchy and
Orange Hill from the north. By four p.m. we had advanced about
eight thousand yards. The 2nd Division on our right did very well. I
was up a greater portion of the night. General Lipsett's horse was
hit. By August 31st we were still cutting wire on the Drocourt
Queant Line. The 4th Division came in between the 4th Imperial
Army and the Arras-Cambrai Road. On September 2nd, at five
a.m. we attacked the Drocourt Queant Line. We did very well. Our
batteries stayed back in order to stave off any counterattack. The
Boche seems to have beaten it. They are disorganized and are being
pushed back in many places.

    I presume the Boche will try to winter in the Hindenburg Line.
We are making all preparations to use Boche guns and find the
ammunition they have left behind. I met General Loomis on the
morning of September 13th. He seems to be very nice and
agreeable. General Lipsett sent out a farewell order as he is now
going to the 4th British Division. By September 15th, the front was
getting quieter. The Hun was anxious to have outposts this side of
the Canal du Nord as he pushed some of ours back. The Americans
are doing well near St. Mihiel. I feel however that the Boche is still
full of fight and the war will last for some months yet. We are
having a tough fight with the Boche. He is coming over the Canal
du Nord daily. On the morning of September 18th we were
informed that a trench mortar of ours had shot short and killed
two, wounding seven of the 5th C.M.R.'s I ordered a Court of
Inquiry to be held at once. General Loomis is ill and remained in
bed. I hear that the Boche morale is low; he will have a hard time
making men stick it this winter is we go pounding on. On
September 27th we attacked along a big front. The 4th and 1st
Division succeeded in capturing Bourlon Wood and Rollencourt.

There were very few casualties and not too many prisoners. I hear the French and Belgians are to attack tomorrow. General Loomis seems to be very courteous and easy to work with. On September 29th the Bulgarians asked for an armistice. It has been granted and peace is to be declared between the Bulgarians and the allies. The Boche are burning Cambrai. I am of the strong opinion that the allies will carry the war into Germany and devastate that country. There will be bitter feelings between the people if this is the outcome.

By October 24th, the 3rd Army had attacked and are making progress towards Valenciennes. Our horses are thin and require a good deal of attention. The end of the war is in sight. It ought to finish by July, 1919. The Hun will fight for months to come. He has fought a very good rear guard action. Unless we can get him close to home he will not give in. On October 29th, Ludendorff resigned. The Huns are asking for an armistice. There is to be a meeting of allied leaders and statesmen in Paris. The next day Austria threw up its hands and asked for an armistice. If that is so, Germany will have to give in before another six months go by. Everyone is very excited that the prospect of peace may come soon. On October 31st, Austria and Hungary are torn by internal strife and will soon be out of the war. Prospects are bright for an early peace. No doubt exists in my mind as to the crushing of Germany. Everyone is saying that peace will be declared in a fortnight. On November 1st, the 4th Division attacked to the south of Valenciennes and made good progress. Austria-Hungary have agreed to an armistice on favourable terms.

On November 2nd, the 4th Division have taken Valenciennes and are pushing on. The 8th Canadian Infantry Brigade have crossed L'Escaut Canal. Colonel McNaughton will become a Brigadier General in a few days, taking over for General Massie at C.C.H.A. Next day I went to see the forward positions at Bruay and then took the car to Valenciennes. I had my picture taken with the mayor and the first load of food for the people. Our troops are approaching Vicq. The 38th and 39th Batteries moved acorss the L'Escaut Canal via Valenciennes to Ste. Saulte.

On November 7th, news spread that the Huns had sent four peace proposals to General Foch and everyone is pleased. The traffic is heavy on the Valenciennes-Mons Road. It is sad to see the refugees coming back, pushing thier belongings with them. The Boche are still going back. We reached Thulin, which they did not destroy to any extent. On November 9th, I took the car through Thulin to Jemappes. The Hun is believed to be behind Mons. Our procession seemed to be that of a triumphant march; the women and children and men were all pleased to see us, cheering time and again. The 8th Army Brigade was following along closely. It was a memorable sight never to be forgotten. We have captured Mabuerge; the Boche has until Monday at eleven a.m. to accept or reject the terms of the allies. God grant that Peace may come.

On November 10th we were on the outskirts of Mons. The Boche are still shelling near Jemappes. Longworth of the 36th Battery was severely wounded during the afternoon and may die. Quite a number of casualties occured which are to be regretted as the war seems to be over.

Monday, November 11th, 1918:

Thank God for the news read upon warning that hostilities cease at eleven a.m. We had a triumphant march into Mons. Lieutenant General Sir Arthur Currie, G.C.O.E., I.C.B., Commanding the Canadian Corps, made a formal entry into Mons. The 39th Battery, 10th Brigade under my command were the first to cross the Grande Place, via Nimy Boulevard. I ordered the General Salute, during which the R.C.R. band played the National Anthems of the Allies, commencing with that of Belgium. General Currie was received by the Bourgomaster of Mons and the Vice-President of the Belgian parliament and other representatives of the city. The Bourgomaster delivered an address expressing their thanks and joy at being delivered from German tyranny after four years of war. General Currie replied and presented his pennant to the city of Mons, a token that will always serve to remind the people of Mons of the arrival of Canada. He then called for three cheers for the King of the Belgians, which met with a hearty response.

I heard that the Kaiser and Crown Prince have gone to Holland. After eleven a.m. no more firing took place. Word came late at night that we are to march into Germany. I have a fine place in Mons and am glad to see the place has not been destroyed. The men *have* had a good time today. Many had several drinks of cognac.

On December 14th, I went to Nivelle where the Division has its H.Q. I saw the column march past and found that the men of the 7th Canadian Infantry Brigade and the Gunners had more or less refused to advance unless their packs were carried. The men of the 49th and the machine gun battalion seem to be the worst. The men had a mutiny at Grand Place square at times. Some agitators worked them up. The next day the men marched quietly without any fuss. The 9th Canadian Infantry Brigade marched by. They were all in fine shape. Most of the men wish to go home. They cannot content themselves to do anything even to playing games.

General Loomis and I went to Germany on December 26th and toured around Bonn and Cologne. We stayed at the Palace of the Princess of Schaumberg Lippe. I received this telegram, dated November 14th, 1918 from Edmonton, Alberta: "Alberta proud of Distinction won by her brave troops. We are eagerly looking forward to day when you will all be home again."

Restoration at Ypres (1919).

ARMISTICE DAY
(NOVEMBER 11TH, 1918) & HOME

Corporal John (Jack) Stacey
12TH CDN. FIELD AMBULANCE BRIGADE

We were at Anzin, near Valenciennes on Armistice Day. A
muster parade was called and everyone came out. This declaration
was read at eleven o'clock in the morning. All the boys said, "Let's
go to Valenciennes." It was quite an industrial city and famous
apparently among the French, for it's breweries. When we got there,
Fritzie had opened up all the beer tanks and you can imagine the
fun we had! I had a good friend in the 78th Battalion (Winnipeg
Battalion) who was a sniper until he got a slight wound, so he was
put in the kitchen. He turned out to be a hell of a good cook. We
were always in and around together with the 12th Brigade, so we
kept in touch all the way through the war. He said to me, "Jack if
ever we're alive when this thing ends I'll meet you at the
cookhouse." So I looked him up that morning, went down and had
a good steak dinner that day. He was cooking for the officer's mess,
so maybe an officer didn't get his meal that day.

When I was demobilized and back in civilian life, the sodium
solisilidge treatment I had had started to bother me. I couldn't even
follow my trade. The medical profession had nothing for gas except
neutralizers which were taken orally. In time it was known to rot
one's intestines out, so I stayed away from the treatment. I give no
credit to the medical profession at all. I didn't even report to
hospital in England although I was going through a terrific stage of
stomach convalescence at the time. I finally took a treatment of
nichotrine. That was how I recovered. I didn't live like anyone else.
It took about two to three years. Sometimes I couldn't even keep
water on my stomach, but I knew if I had been put in the hospital I
would have died within ten years like a lot of the others ended up.
The constant medical treatment is what did it. I went for physical
culture.

Private James Doak
52ND BATTALION

November 11th, 1918— Only those who were privileged to be
in close touch with French and Belgian troops and civilians can
fully realize the intense hatred these people have for the Germans.

On the morning of November 11th, our Battalion was billeted
in Wasmuel, eight kilometres from Mons. The civil population were
wild with joy. Down a side street we noticed an unusually noisy
mob. Their cries seemed filled with anger. Out of curiosity we
wandered down that way and saw a sight which would be beyond

the wildest dreams of even the most bloodthirsty moving picture
scenario writer. The victim was a woman; a resident who was also a
war widow. For the past year she had been living in Mons with a
German officer. She was suspected of giving information, which led
to the arrest and imprisonment of several civilians. She had been
immune to harm before, because in the event of any injury done to
her, the whole village would have suffered. But she was among
them now. Her powerful German protector could protect her no
more.

Someone jostled against her as she walked along. In an instant
she was the target for all manner of abuse. Women tore at her hair
and clothes. Men and boys threw sod and stones until the poor
wretch begged for mercy. There is no doubt in my mind that she
would have been torn to pieces, but some more of our soldiers came
along. Forcing their way through the mob they formed a guard
around the woman, taking her to a guardroom for shelter. She had
a little boy who sobbed bitterly. He, at least had done no wrong,
but suffered along with his mother.

Certain German engineer officers were sent into Mons to show
the location of all hidden mines. They were continually kept under
a strong guard. The treatment of Canadian dead was entirely
different. Each dead Canadian was covered with flowers where he
lay, until huge mounds of flowers were formed on the streets. At
the cemeteries, flowers were piled so high that all signs of graves
were obliterated.

The victorious Canadians marching to support lines (1918).

A soldier goes back to his homeland and loved ones he recalls to mind the promise made by his townspeople who stayed behind to "carry on". We believed that to a certain extent the promises for jobs were made to be kept. Returning unscathed and given a grand welcome at the station, for a few days we enjoyed the glad handclasps of friends. But we must work in order to live, so we started looking for jobs.

We go to an old employer and find that our place has been filled quite efficiently by a bright young man, who during the years of the war has worked his way up and become familiar with changing conditions. Therefore, the employer, though expressing great regret at not having an opening, sees no reason or excuse to let his present man go. He tells the ex-soldier how glad he is to see him back safe and sound. He explains the belief that he will have no trouble in finding an equally good job as good as the one he had before the war.

Meeting with the same answers everywhere he wonders if he has been wrong all the time. Other returned men share the same story. In his wanderings around the city he hears much of the heros who died, but no mention of the men who lived. He eventually becomes bitter and disillusioned. He knows that he has seen comrades fall beside him and he was taking the same chances as they were, yet the dead are heros. Monuments are erected to their memory. They are publically acclaimed, while he tramps the streets searching in vain for a job that will keep body and soul together. The living are almost outcasts. Those who have passed beyond are free of all misery and hardship. The returned soldier must carry on.

THE CANADIANS

(Written by James A. Doak while in the "Half Way" dugouts on the China Wall, in supports for the front lone at Hooge— May, 1916):

> We'll leave our dirty dugouts
> And we'll buckle up our straps,
> We'll take our "rusty" rifles
> And all our other "traps".
> We'll bid good-bye to bully beef,
> And hard tack biscuits too/
> Maconochies and marmalade
> And the bull cook's famous stew.
> We've helped our Uncle Johnny
> Call the German bluff
> We're going back to Canada
> When the Kaiser's said, "Enough"

We've sweltered in the sunshine
We've shivered in the rain
It takes the brawn and sinew
To stand the awful strain
We've stood upon the firing step
With rifles in our hands
And kept the wily German
From crossing "no man's land"
We've suffered from the shrapnel
And other hellish stuff,
But we're going back to Canada
When the Kaiser says, "Enough"

We've stood knee deep in water
Until our legs were numb
Waiting for the morning
That never seemed to come
We've watched the glorious sunrise
in the heaven's dome
And thanked God that our dear ones
Were safe and well back home
But we've only done our duty
Though it's been rather rough
And we're going back to Canada
When the Kaisers says, "Enough".

We've seen our comrades falling
Neath German shot and shell
We think of them as brothers
Who've done their duty well
They died as British heros
Our freedom to maintain
And to keep the name of Britain
And the old flag free from stains
The strife will soon be over
We've called the German's bluff
We're going back to Canada
When the Kaiser says, "Enough".

(Originally published in The Toronto Star, 1916).

Lieutenant Albert E. Winn
ROYAL FIELD ARTILLERY

We were very excited on Armistic Day. We did the Highland
Fling. Of course many of us got down to the cafes for our vin
blanc, vin rouge and cognac. There was a lot of crime amongst the
troops after the armistice, because everybody thought we would go
straight home, but we did not. It was a shock to our own regiment!

Private Thomas Chambers
I5TH BATTALION — LANCASHIRE FUSILIERS

On November ll, 1918, I was in hospital. We broke out of the
convalescent camp and went down to Boulogne. We went absolutely
wild! Someone must have anticipated the armistice, because there
was plenty to drink. We all managed to get drunk! It was a good
feeling to know that we were in safe beds that night.

It took us a long time to get home after the war. We were not
demobilized until twelve months later. From Dinant, Belgium, we
were sent up to Germany for the remainder of our service; mind
you we had a damn good holiday there.

The Salvation Army were really wonderful to us. They
operated canteens for us and were nearer to the front lines than any
other group when in time of need. They were the best, no doubt
about it.

Private Leonard Wood
2ND EAST LANCASHIRE REGIMENT

We did plenty of marching after the armistice. It was extremely
tiresome. The idea of marching and more marching, without
knowing our destination, tended to get us down. The officers didn't
tell us anything; they just passed the word back to us: keep on
marching! My feet had been bleeding, red and raw. I even had the
sole off one shoe.

Private Thomas Fairweather
WEST YORKSHIRE REGIMENT — 49TH DIVISION

I left the hospital in England on Armistice Day. I was paid and
sent on indefinite leave. A note was sent from Army Headquarters
saying that I would be discharged on February 23, 1919. It was
really nice seeing everyone lashing about, everything turned upside

down. We started changing all the road signs. People were gathering in the market squares, giving the policemen something to drink. Everyone was drinking. It was really something to see; all the wounded getting out of hospitals.

Private Alexander Wilson
4TH CANADIAN MOUNTED RIFLES

I don't know how long I was at this convalescent camp. One morning I got up and I couldn't hear a single shot. There was no noise at all. I asked someone, "What's the matter? I don't hear any gunfire out there!" "Oh," the fellow answered, "the war's over." I just wandered around there like a lost sheep until they moved me back to my own battalion.

Private Harold (Pat) Wyld
CANADIAN FORESTRY CORP

We were in Valenciennes when the armistice was declared. There was not a soul in the place. The only thing we could do to celebrate was to shoot off flares down the street and dodge them as they went bouncing along.

Before we left Valenciennes, the French people started coming back into the city. One woman saw a dud shell lying on her back porch. She asked us if we would move it. We said, "No, We won't touch it." We didn't want to take a chance falling on that rubble and dropping it, so we waited until the demolition squad came along. She got mad and cussed at us in French, calling us everything she could think of: the biggest cowards on earth, but it didn't fizz on us.

We almost went to Germany with the Army of Occupation, but I got sick and camoflauged a heart condition, so they sent me back to England.

The word out at that time was "Get home! Get home!" It was terrible when we crossed the English Channel in cattle boats going up to the North Sea. I thought the boat was going to break in half. All the crew were sick, let alone the men. I threw everything I owned, my kitbag, souvenirs, everything overboard. I felt so sick, I just about wanted to jump in with my stuff. That was the only time I was ever seasick. I spent a few months there, before going back to Canada in September, 1919.

We were in Rhyl, Wales during that big riot. They kept calling men out on drafts to go home; then they would cancel them. They kept doing that until everyone was fed up. A riot resulted which really demolished the place. All the canteens were raided and beer stolen. All the quartermaster's stores were raided and they wrecked the Y.M.C.A. huts, but they never touched the Salvation Army. Not even a glass or window was broken in a Salvation Army hut.

Then they started using ammunition. I think eight people were shot. One young fellow was sitting down, writing a letter home on his knee. He had his back up against the wall. A bullet came through the wall and went right through his head. The Military Police couldn't do much.

We had a nice trip coming back to Canada. I got off the train in Ottawa to look up a chap who owed me five pounds. He payed me and my taxi fare both ways. When I got back to the station our troop train was just pulling out. A freight train got between me and the troop train, so I missed it. I took the train out west as a civilian. As a result, I got to Calgary two days ahead of the troop train.

Bombardier William Shaw
151ST SIEGE BATTERY ROYAL GARRISON ARTILLERY

By May, 1919, the 151st was reduced to a small unit with Major Blackadder still in command. We moved to St. Omer, France after visiting such places as Brussels, Antwerp and Bruges, all in Belgium. Our job there was mainly salvage work, picking up guns and things that had been abandoned.

Corporal James Rourke
1ST FIELD COMPANY — CANADIAN ENGINEERS

We drilled all the time before coming home. They discharged us before we entrained for Winnipeg. There was a strike on in Winnipeg at the time. We felt like getting out of the city. It was hard getting jobs. You had to hunt your own job. Wages were smaller then. There were no special privileges because we had been in the army. If another guy got there first, he got the job.

Private Ernest C. Robins
LORD STRATHCONA'S HORSE — 8TH BATTALION

I was in London, England on Armistic Day. I tried to get back to Seaford, where I was stationed for three straight days, but I couldn't. I could not even get near the trains for the crowds. I volunteered to go back to Germany.

They sent me back to the 8th Battalion, which was stationed at Bonn. We went in and out of there three times a week. We stayed right near the Hohenzollern Bridge, which was the quickest route to Cologne. I was on guard and munition dump duty at Cassel. When I guarded this ammunition dump, we had over two million rounds of ammo to look after, that Jerry had piled up.

We all loved to go and see the Dumbells when we could. Ross Hamilton, who came from Pugwash, Nova Scotia along with two others from Hamilton, were among them. They put their shows on all over. They were wonderful. When they were dressed up like women you couldn't tell the difference. They walked and talked exactly the same. They used to play a lot in the huge canteen at Gouy Servins, near Vimy. The stage was in the back of the canteen. The shows were a couple of hours long. They were great shows. We roared with laughter all the time!

Sapper Robert Dickson
8TH BN. — CDN. ENGINEERS

We realized the war was almost over and weren't at all anxious to get killed before it finished. We were just outside Mons when we got news of the armistice. We didn't do anything in our unit that morning. We weren't called up to the line at all. We were in billets. Nothing happened. We stayed there for ten days, then we marched up to the Rhine with the Army of Occupation in Germany.

Before arriving at the Rhine we stopped in a small hamlet to stay overnight. Eight or ten of us were billeted in a house that had a small bar in it. Some of our boys entered the bar and bought a few drinks. One of them said, "Why should we be paying for these drinks? We're in Germany now. We're going to have free drinks." They got behind the bar, smashed some of the bottles and helped themselves to as much booze as they wanted. I thought it was a pretty lousy performance. No great credit to the Canadian Army. There were all kinds in the army.

When we crossed the Rhine River at Bonn, Germany, General Arthur Currie was there to take the salute as we went over the bridge. Currie wasn't popular, but I don't think a General must be necessarily popular in order to be a good General.

After the war I became a court reporter. I worked in the Supreme Court of Ontario for many years. In 1928, Sir Arthur Currie, who was the Commander in Chief of the Canadian Corps brought a libel action against the owner and editor of the Port Hope newspaper, which had published a very scandalous article about him. It claimed that on the last day of the war Currie had sent men up to the Canadian front, so that for his own personal glorification he could say that the Canadians were farther ahead than anybody else. He sued for libel. I reported the trial of the libel action, which took two weeks to try. Currie got a judgement against the newspaper, but for a comparatively trifling five hundred dollars.

Private Harold Wilson (1899-1978)
28TH N.W. BATTALION

On November 11, 1918 we passed through the outskirts of Mons in daylight. We were about four to five miles east of Mons. We didn't know anything about the armistice, until about ten-thirty a.m. We captured a German dispatch rider on horseback, who had their dispatches explaining the armistice.

At eleven a.m. we got into this little village. As we approached it, German machine guns opened up and we got into a ditch. I was in "B" Company. Another Company came up a parallel road. The roads converged. I think it was a Corporal Price, who didn't get down and walked across the road. He was the last Canadian killed in action in World War One.

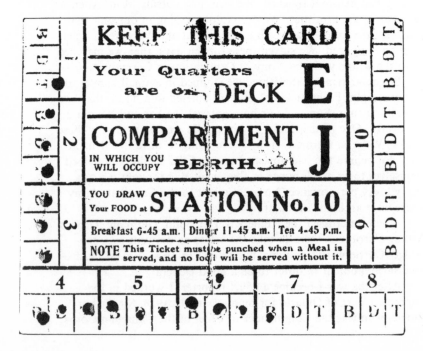

Private G. Reid's ration card for the R.M.S. Aquitania (1919).

Lieutenant John (Jack) Chambres
54TH BN

We had to go to a camp near Rhyl. It was the worst place I've
ever been in my life. We were starting to send the boys home. It
was all a mixup of different people from various battalions. It was
hard to get along with one another. There was a Major in charge of
the camp. The men on the parade ground were complaining one
day, "When's the next boat? When are we going home?" The Major
asked me, "Do you think you can do anything with them?" I said,
"Yes. I'll take them for a route march." I went and told the men,
"How about going for a little walk? You've got nothing to do all
day. All right. Right turn! Quick march! Follow me!" Away we
went. That's how we treated them.

The war was over, but there were strikes and we couldn't
always get to the boats because they weren't always running. We
eventually got them all home.

Private William (Bill) Hemmings
CANADIAN MACHINE GUN CORP

Two hundred and fifty of us in our battalion were told we were
to go on this Victory March in London. Our uniforms were
threadbare. We had been wearing them for months and months.
They rushed us to Bramshott for new uniforms. We went up there
looking like a bunch of recruits! In London, Sir Arthur Currie took
the salute at Marble Arch, then they turned us loose in London.
There were lots of sandwiches to eat. I'm not sure about the beer. I
didn't drink that much. Then we went back to Bramshott. We were
without any money that day in London. They told us we sould stay
until midnight. We had nothing to spend as we had just rushed over
from Belgium.

Sergeant Len Davidson
CANADIAN ENGINEERS — 7TH BATTALION

We had a parade in the square at Mons on November 11th.

After November 11th, King Albert of Belgium came to give us
the freedom of the city of Mons. In fact, I've got a little aluminum
medal they gave us as, "the victorious Canadian Third Division".

Then we went in this little estaminet and stood at the window.
Of course we had been invited. All the Belgians were there. One
little fellow kept yelling, "Vive la var!(King) Vive la King!) He let

out a few more yells. Somebody told him to shut up and almost caused a fight. The estaminet owner said to me, "You're in the Engineers. Got any crowbars, picks and shovels?" I said, "Yeah, why?" He said, "During the German occupation I hid all my liquor in the basement and sealed it up. Nobody could get it. Will you help me out?" I got hold of a few other fellows and said to them, "Got a fatigue job for you guys." When I told Doug, he was very excited, so we took the crowbars and dug the cement up. Needless to say, we got well paid for it. Oh boy! What a night we had there!

On the way home they put us on a forced march. My Corporal from Montreal was there. When General Currie drove by on his rounds, somebody threw a Mills bomb at his car and blew the tire off it, because the guy was angry. We had been marching about thirty kilometres a day. We had been taking a rest when Currie passed, as we were very tired. The brass blamed the incident on this Corporal from Montreal. He disappeared somehwere.That was why the 3rd Division didn't go into the Army of Occupation. That's my opinion. The Major told us, "Hey! Come on! Get these men up on their feet!" "No way," I said. The men stayed there and wouldn't move. We eventually ended up in Bramshott again.

We were in Bramshott in mid February. They were going to send us up to Rhyl, but then they had a riot up there and they didn't want to enlarge upon it, so they started the demobilization program in Bramshott. They lined us up in alphabetical order.

We returned to Canada in March, 1919 on the ships, Baltic and the Olympic.

I went back to the police force.

Bombardier James Logan
39TH BATTERY — CDN. FIELD ARTILLERY

I was on leave in London on November 10th. The next day I was in Southridge's store buying a raincoat in Sunderland, England. I didn't think the war would be over for awhile. It was wet at that time of year. I just got the coat and payed for it when the sirens started to blow. The store girl pushed me out the door, saying, "Get out! The war's over!" When I got outside everybody was celebrating. Girls were coming along with scissors and knives, cutting the buttons and badges off of soldiers. I kept my badges in my pocket for safekeeping. Some men had lost every button they had. The girls were half drunk, carrying around champagne bottles. They got hold of the soldiers, threw them in the air and passed them from one crowd to another. Oh they just went crazy there!

They celebrated for a whole week. I got tired of it and went and stayed with some people. I told them, "There's more danger down there than there was in the war. Some fellow's apt to get killed down there."

Talk about Scotch clannish, the Canadians were worse. One day we visited a town near the hospital. When we came back, the nurses snowballed us. It was during a snowstorm. The girls came out of their offices and started throwing snowballs. We hit, when we threw them back. We drove them right back in the offices. Their boss said to them, "You ought to know better than start snowballing Canadians! They know how to throw them. They practise a lot. They're crack shots with those snowballs!" We kept them in there for about ten minutes before we let them out. Their boss got quite a kick out of it, telling the girls, "I don't think you'll bother with snowballs from now on."

Then I went down to Epsom,. then to Witley and to Rhyl, Wales. I got to Rhyl,two days after the big riot, where an officer was killed. If somebody let a yell out there, the officers were so scared their knees would knock together. They were scared to death of the men. Rhyl was a good camp.

A Victory Parade was celebrated near Robinson St., Oakville, Ontario (November 11, 1918).

When we went home in 1919, there were two of us seated in the train together that were artillerymen. We stopped in Montreal. Two officers asked us if we were in the artillery. We told them we were in it. They said, "We'd like you to enlist for another three years. If you enlist we'll guarantee you Lieutenant's commissions. Right off the bat. No joking about that." I asked, "What's the idea?" He said, "We need instructors. You fellows have been through the war and we're short of instructors." That was the first mistake I ever made. I should have taken them up on it. I told them, "No. I've had all the army I want and I want to get out of it." The other fellows with me felt the same. I would have had a nice pension coming.

Naturally, there was great rejoicing, but many of the fellows who had seen much fighting, and had been in uniform for four years just still could not believe that it was all over. The only disappointed soldier I saw was my step-brother Ralph. He had just become of age and just joined my unit to go on the next draft to France. I felt real sorry for him as he was so anxious to see action. He had been in the army for two years, but was held in England until he came of age. From this time on, soldiers in general were becoming restless. The war was over, they had done their bit, and now they were anxious to return to Canada.

Corporal James F. Johnson
5TH CDN. MOUNTED RIFLES

Early in 1919 I made my last move. All the Canadians who were not in hospitals were sent to a large camp near Rhyl, Wales, which was used as a dispersal area for sailing to Canada. (All troops were assigned to areas according to the Province in which they enlisted. For instance, our camp was the one where all Nova Scotians and Newfoundlanders were assembled.) This camp was not to be desired, especially in winter months. The huts were cold, the rations were small and bad, the weather was rainy and cold. All in all, it was a dismal outlook. One consolation was that we were on our way home and surely we would be sailing soon. However, that was not to be. The time dragged on. Sailings were cancelled. Many had throat infections and we all had to gargle some unpleasant concoction every morning before breakfast.

I, being a Corporal, was in charge of a hut. The most unpleasant duty I had was to serve out the meals to each soldier. No one was getting enough and conditions got worse and worse. Most of the men in my hut were Newfoundlanders, around sixty in number. So finally in desperation I called them together before dinner and told them that I was going to serve out a good helping as far as it would go, and that there would be several, including myself, without any. That meant the hungry ones would have to parade to the Orderly officer and place a complaint. The men were very fair about it all and said, "We don't want to get you into trouble as you might lose your rank." I told them to heck with the rank, the war is over and I want to get back to Canada. Well, the results were that about sixteen had no dinner. I paraded them down to the cook house and asked to see the Orderly Officer. The cooks got busy and scraped up enough food and fed us. The orderly Officer told me I would probably hear from the Colonel about this, although he was really quite nice about it.

Sure enough, around three o'clock I was called to the Colonel's office. He asked me several questions and I told my story. He then said, "You have had quite a lot of service in France. Would you have done this there?" I said, "Of course not Sir, but we are not in action and the war is over. Furthermore, these are the worse conditions I have ever seen in the British Isles." He added, "You know, I could have you demoted, but I don't want you to do it again, and I will personally look into the whole situation." I think he must have, as the food situation did improve to some extent. Not so in the rest of the camp as things got worse. Around the last of February things came to a climax, which should go down as the blackest page in the history of the Canadian Expeditionary Force.

One night, around eleven o'clock, a riot broke out, starting in the Montreal depot, from where it spread to the other sections of Camp. Hundreds went on a wild rampage looting everything in sight including Tin Town, beer canteens, quartermaster stores. Everything was left in a shambles. Rifles and ammunition were secured by the rioters; girls working in canteens lay down on the floor to escape bullets which passed through the building. This spectacle lasted all night and continued the following day. Our depot number 6 was situated at the extreme end of the camp. So far, we had not observed anything, but could hear the noise. We knew from the start what was going on.

Around noon, our Colonel called a parade. He told us that we were going to protect our depot so he gave orders to roll out all the beer barrels and told us, "What you don't drink, pour out so the rioters will not get it." N.C.O.'s were issued rifles and ammunition, and ordered not to shoot unless absolutely necessary; if so, shoot low at the legs. Soon afterward, we saw the mob coming down the main road. They stopped at our main gate and started to come in.

Just in front of me was one of our officers. He walked to meet them with a revolver in his hand. A big burly fellow was leading them. The officer told them to turn about. He also told them there were armed men to stop them. The crowd just jeered and called the officer names, and started coming. The officer said, "I'm not fooling," and shot the big fellow on the knee. I guess it surely hurt, as he hopped around and made an awful fuss. When the rest of the mob saw that we were armed and meant business they clunked back through the gate and I think most of them were apprehended by the authorities. Of course, by this time many who began to realize the serious nature of the whole event had left the ranks and returned to their respective quarters. One man from our unit, a Corporal, was killed that day and had nothing to do with the rioting. We had a military funeral for him later. Here was a man who had come through the war, and on the eve of his homecoming, was killed by his own comrades. I never found out just how many casualties there were, but there were several.

The next morning General Turner, V.C., was flown into Camp from London. He went from depot to depot and addressed the troops. His address to us was short and to the point. He said, "I want to commend your Colonel and other ranks for the action you took in quelling this riot. If by any chance there are any here that took part in this contemptuous demonstration, you are a disgrace to the uniform you wear." Some said he wouldn't dare say that in the Montreal depot, but he did!

After the riot everything went back to normal. Conditions generally were improving. Sailing lists appeared on the order boards and finally I saw my name, around the middle of March, appear on the long list. This time it was not cancelled. About March 27th, my homeward bound group, which were comprised of soldiers of every province, from the Maritimes to B.C., boarded a train to Liverpool where we boarded the *S.S. Northland*, bond for Halifax, Nova Scotia.

During the time aboard until we sailed, a newsboy's brass band played on the floating docks. After each selection, the men aboard would toss a few coins ashore. The band stayed until our ship moved out from the docks. The last sound we heard from the British Isles was the band's final rendition of "God Be With You Till We Meet Again." Soon after, we passed almost directly under the muzzles of the giant 15 inch naval guns of the Queen Elizabeth battleship. She was lying at anchor just offshore. For the time being her job was completed, and what a job she and her crew had done.

The next day our pilot left the boat just off the south coast of Ireland. Our trip across the Atlantic was uneventful, taking nine or ten days. The Northland was not a bad boat, however the troop ships were always packed to capacity, and everywhere you went was crowded.

I believe it was April 11th that we sailed into Halifax harbour. There was a large crowd on the pier to greet us. We walked along the gang planks right after we docked, stepping on Canadian soil after nearly four very eventful years. Those of us who had enlisted in Nova Scotia were marched down to the armouries to receive our discharges. We thought to ourselves, "I suppose there will be a lot more waiting and red tape," but that was not the case. Inside of an hour I had my money due and my discharge.

I walked out on the street still in uniform, but I was really a civilian again. All of our other papers had been attended to in Rhyl before we left England. After coming out of the armouries, I stopped on the street corner looking my discharge paper over. Two girls came walking along and one of them said, "I bet you have a letter from your sweetheart as you look so pleased." I showed them the discharge and said, "This is the best sweetheart letter I ever had in my life."

Armistice Day in Toronto, at King Street — November 11, 1918.

They both shook hands with me and said, "Welcome home, soldier, and thank you for all you have done." After saying, "So long, girls," with my kit bag over my shoulder, I made my way down to the railway station. While walking down there, I passed through some of the ruins resulting from the Halifax explosion which took place on December 7, 1917. The scene reminded me of the great devastation I had seen in France.

Soon I was aboard a train headed for Truro, the place where I had enlisted. While sitting on the train, I could hardly realize that from now on I was on my own. For the past four and a half years, practically every hour of my life had been planned for me. While it was a grand and glorious occasion, I felt kind of alone with some concern toward the future. I was now over twenty-six years old. What was I to do, etc.? Well I knew one thing, and that was that I had reason to thank God that I had been spared and privileged to come home. Many fine fellows, who had been great pals of mine, would never return. Many more were crippled and maimed as the result of war. I was still in uniform, but this was my last day in the army.

BUCKINGHAM PALACE.

The Queen and I wish you God-speed, and a safe return to your homes and dear ones.

A grateful Mother Country is proud of your splendid services characterized by unsurpassed devotion and courage.

George R.I.

A "reward" for going to war for King and Country — care of Private Gordon W. Reid.

Here is a brief summary of the price of victory:

Cost of World War:
Germanic $110,000,000,000
Allies $200,000,000,000

Total $310,000,000,000

Lives lost for all belligerents:

Germany   5,000,000
Allies   6,422,738

Total   11,422,732

Total casualties:

Germanic   15,050,000
Allies   18,437,684

Total   33,481,684

These figures are reckoned as very conservative. Furthermore, millions throughout the world starved owing to War. Millions of tons of material and foodstuffs were sunk to the bottom of the sea, never to be recovered. Many, many cities and towns throughout France were reduced to a pile of rubble. One wonders if it really was a victory to any nation.

Glossary

A.L.G. — Alternate Landing "G"
B.E.F. — British Expeditionary Force
Bde. — Brigade
Bn. — Battalion
Cdn. — Canadian
C.E.F. Canadian Expeditionary Force
Coy. — Company
C.R.A. — Commander Royal Artillery
C.R.E. — Commander Royal Engineers
D.A.Q.M.G. — Deputy Adjutant Quartermaster General
Div. H.Q. — Divisional Headquarters
Engr. — Engineer
F.O.O. — Forward Observation Officer
Gen. — General
M.C. — Military Cross
M.O. — Medical Officer
M.G. — Machine Gun
M.G.O. — Machine Gun Officer
O.P. — Observation Post
R.C.R. — Royal Canadian Rifles (infantry)
R.S. — Regimental Sergeant Major
S.M. — Sergeant Major
T.M. — Trench Mortar
Uhlans — German Cavalry
V.A.D. — Voluntary Aid Detachment
German soldiers known by Allies as
    Heinie, Jerry, Hun, Boche
    Fritz or Fritzie

Index